The Writing System

A step-by-step guide for
business and technical writers

Daniel O. Graham and Judith H. Graham, Ph.D.

Preview Press — Fairfax, Virginia

ISBN 0-9644495-7-9

Printed in the United States of America

Cover design by Laurie Graham.
Cover photo credits to C. Mayhew and R. Simmon (NASA/GSFC). This stunning photograph of Earth shows the beautiful juxtaposition of natural and manmade light.

Other Books by the Grahams

The Writing System Workbook. Fairfax: Preview Press, 1994.

The Gatekeepers. New York: Baen Books, 1995. (Winner of the 1996 Compton Crook Award)

The Politics of Meaning. Fairfax: Preview Press, 1995.

Entering Tenebrea, with Roxann Dawson. New York: Pocket Books, 2001.

Tenebrea's Hope, with Roxann Dawson. New York: Pocket Books, 2001.

Tenebrea Rising, with Roxann Dawson. New York: Pocket Books, 2002.

Preface

The writing system taught in this book serves as a best practice in large international corporations and government agencies. By using the system's techniques, you organize your thoughts better and get to the point quickly. You write clear, concise, better quality documents in less time. Professionals for whom English is a second language especially benefit from the system's thorough step-by-step approach.

We encourage every professional to learn this writing system and practice its techniques. Today, much corporate product is written communication. Increased writing speed cuts cost. Improved document quality increases client satisfaction. Therefore, professionals who use the writing system increase profits.

The Writing System authors, Daniel and Judith Graham, Ph.D., teach writing seminars and provide writing consulting throughout North America and Europe.

Acknowledgments

We thank the engineers, scientists, and business professionals who, during our writing seminars, give us valuable feedback and help us refine our writing techniques. This book is yours.

The Writing System

A step-by-step guide for business and technical writers

The Writing System teaches you a system of proven techniques to help you write business and technical documents faster and better.

Designed as specific how-to instruction, this book takes you through the writing system: 3 phases, 13 steps, and 51 techniques. Writing techniques feature tips, warnings, error traps, examples, references, brief discussions, and exercises. We put the answers to the exercises in Appendix A, with a Quick Reference in Appendix E.

Additional appendices show you how to apply the writing system to other writing challenges:

Letters, Memos, and Email	Appendix B
English as a Second Language	Appendix C
Long Documents	Appendix D

We wrote this guide for practical, task-oriented engineers, scientists, and business professionals. If you've mastered your discipline, you can master these simple techniques. Think of this book as your user manual for written communication with built-in tutorial. Use *The Writing System* three ways:

1. Learn the writing system by doing the exercises — about 72 hours' work.

2. Consult the steps as you write your documents.

3. Refer to the techniques to solve writing problems.

Relax. Set your own pace. Now, enjoy taking the mystery out of good writing.

Table of Contents

Table of Contents

Writing System Overview

The writing system helps you make best use of your skills by dividing your writing activity into three phases. Each phase uses a different skill set. To write faster and better, you must finish each phase in order.

During the pre-writing phase, you use analytical skills. You determine purpose and solve content and organization problems. You decide *what topics and subtopics must I write about? how much detail is necessary? how shall I organize the material?*

During the writing phase, you use composing skills, the same skills you use when speaking. Some of us are glib; some are the strong silent type. However, all of us — when we know what we want to say — can find the words.

During the post-writing phase, we use editing skills: all of them mechanical. We make mechanical decisions to ensure that our sentences have one meaning. We make mechanical decisions to cut unnecessary words. We follow the mechanical standards of grammar and punctuation.

Within each phase you must complete certain steps. For each step, we provide proven techniques and tips.

Ideally, you can write a document with one pass through the writing system. Sometimes, longer documents or collaborative writing projects do not conform neatly to a single, never-look-back pass, because you embrace new ideas or discover gaps while writing and editing the document. The writing system helps here as well. Many techniques in the system act as error traps to catch problems and expose gaps early. Each error trap points directly back to a former step and suggests a remedy.

Discussion

Many writers unfortunately mix analysis and editing with composing. They analyze the first point to make, they compose that point, then they edit as they compose. Paragraph by paragraph, they mix analysis, composing, and editing, plodding through the document.

Writers that shift skill sets waste time. Learn to increase writing speed by 20 to 40 percent: finish analysis before composing, and delay all editing until you finish the draft.

The writing system manages a complex set of tasks within skill sets, liberating you from the false and frustrating logic of beginning your writing on the first page and ending on the last. For example, many writers compose the introduction *before* the rest of the document. Using the writing system, you compose the introduction only *after* you compose the body and conclusion.

Writers who plod through the document shifting skill sets quickly get overwhelmed. In effect, they are trying to simultaneously use all 51 techniques applied to complex subject matter. Such writers need a system to manage the tasks.

The Writing System

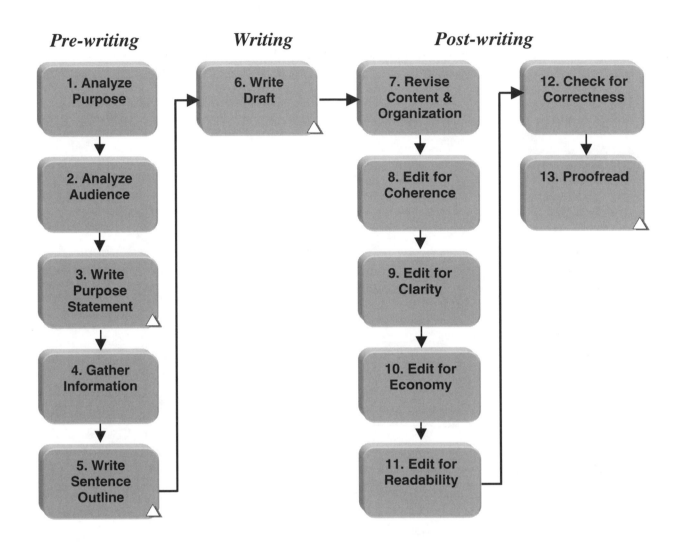

Pre-writing

1. Analyze Purpose
2. Analyze Audience
3. Write Purpose Statement
4. Gather Information
5. Write Sentence Outline

Writing

6. Write Draft

Post-writing

7. Revise Content & Organization
8. Edit for Coherence
9. Edit for Clarity
10. Edit for Economy
11. Edit for Readability
12. Check for Correctness
13. Proofread

Discussion

Budget your writing time: pre-writing phase — 25 percent, writing phase — 25 percent, and post-writing phase — 50 percent.

Use the writing system to help coordinate writing projects. Key milestones (indicated by △) for any writing project include four products: purpose statement, sentence outline, draft, and final proof.

By following the writing system, you get four tangible benefits:

1. **You increase writing speed**. Writers waste much time when they do not know what to do next, or lack clear techniques to solve writing problems.

2. **You manage time**. You know how much time to budget to each writing phase, even to each writing step, and you can monitor your progress to meet deadlines.

3. **You improve coordination**. You resolve controversy early and efficiently. A team of diverse writers on a team can achieve one voice for their document.

4. **You improve the quality of your documents**. The pre-writing steps ensure that you present the information the audience needs. The post-writing steps ensure quality in content, style, and grammar.

Pre-writing Phase

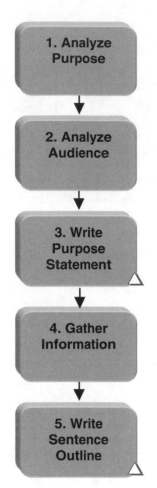

The pre-writing phase includes all the preparation needed before you write your draft. Use your analytical skills as you follow these five steps:

Discussion

During the pre-writing phase, you use your analytical skills. As in other endeavors, you must finish your analysis before execution. For example, a wise builder does not attempt to build a house without a blueprint. Similarly, a wise writer does not write the draft without a sentence outline.

Analyze on paper. A wordprocessor is a poor analytical tool.

In most projects, a strong beginning ensures smooth execution and a satisfactory result: the same holds true for writing. Do not neglect pre-writing. Skipping pre-writing invariably slows you down and causes problems in content, organization, and style.

Step 1. Analyze Purpose

1. Analyze Purpose

Begin your writing task by analyzing purpose using these two techniques:

1.1 Identify your purposes for writing.

1.2 Determine audiences' purposes for reading.

Discussion

An audience can be an individual reader or group of readers with similar needs.

Business and technical writing differs from other forms of writing, because your audience always *does something* with the information.

Some documents lack purpose for one of these three reasons:

1. The message is not worthwhile.
2. The message may be worthwhile, but doesn't need to be written.
3. The message may be worthwhile, but the author fails to tell the audience why.

Don't waste time writing documents that lack purpose. For example, don't hide behind impersonal memos to avoid confrontations. You may unwittingly document a conflict that might be better forgotten. Also, don't write anything you would not want read back to you in court.

Technique 1.1   *Identify your purposes for writing.*

Tips   Answer "what does the document do for you or your organization?"

Consider the possibility that you have more than one purpose for writing. If you have more than one purpose for writing, you most likely have more than one audience.

Warning   Do not confuse the topic with your purpose for writing about it. *My purpose is to explain the functions of the new billing system* just discloses the topic. Instead, focus on what you achieve by explaining the topic: *I want the client to approve our set of functions, and I want the technical staff to develop a detailed design with the approved set of functions.*

Don't be altruistic when identifying your purpose: *I want to inform the client of a new upgrade* is altruistic. Instead, identify what outcome you want from the document: *I want the client to buy the new hardware upgrade from me.*

Example

Typical documents	Writer's typical purposes for writing
Request for proposal	Acquire qualified bids
Proposal	Get profitable work
Requirements document Functional description Detailed design	Get agreement of user requirements; scope work; record baseline
User manual	Answer users' detailed questions without them calling me
Trip report	Account for time; report findings; summarize experience
Meeting minutes	Record statements; track progress and pending actions

See also   Purpose statement.

Discussion

As you analyze your purpose for writing, consider these three advantages of written communication:

1. accuracy — provide many details with precision
2. economy — reach many with the same message
3. record — create an audit trail or record for future audiences

---

Exercise: Evaluate these scenarios and identify your purposes for writing. (Answer A-1)

1. You must write a required monthly status report to your client, the City of Boston, who hired your company to clean the water in Boston Harbor.
    Your purpose for writing:

2. After receiving many phone queries, you decide to write a memo to your plant employees describing procedures for getting their monthly parking sticker from their shift supervisor.
    Your purpose for writing:

3. As office manager, you write a staff study to your immediate supervisor, recommending leasing rather than buying a copy machine.
    Your purpose for writing:

4. You organized the annual holiday party. You write a thank-you note to the hotel manager who helped you host a particularly successful party.
    Your purpose for writing:

5. As the lead editor for a large documentation effort, you write a style guide for the many contributing authors.
    Your purpose for writing:

6. As project manager you must write an annual job review for each employee assigned to your project.
    Your purpose for writing:

Technique 1.2   *Determine audiences' purposes for reading.*

Tip 1   Answer "what does the audience do with the information in the document?"

Consider the possibility that you have more than one audience, where each does something different with the information in the document.

Warning   Do not answer, "The audience reads the document to understand . . ."
Instead, determine what the audience *does* when he or she understands the information.

Avoid vague descriptions of the audience's purpose.
Vague: This brochure helps the student understand the enrollment process.
Specific: This brochure tells the student how to enroll for classes.

Example   Detailed designs often have multiple audiences, each with a different purpose.

Audience	Technical staff	Client management
What audience does with the info	Build the system	Approve the design before committing to build system

See also   Front and back matter.

Discussion

If you don't know what the audiences do with the information in your document, don't guess: find out.

Your supervisor is not necessarily an audience. Often, supervisors provide quality control for written communication, but do not use the information.

When you analyze purpose, you may discover that you have a multiple audience. You need to partition the document to meet their different needs. However, before you can partition the document, you must identify and partition your audiences.

Common multiple audience combinations include
   Staff study — Manager decides course of action; expert staff validates feasibility and provides feedback to management.
   Functional description — Client users ensure the document addresses their requirements; client staff experts validate your approach; client managers approve or reject; your management records a baseline; your technical staff prepares the detailed design.
   Detailed design — Managers approve or reject design; technical staff builds system.

Audience combinations also occur when you have large complex tasks: Team A configures the hardware; Team B builds the graphic interface; Team C converts the databases; Team D develops training.

You can even have a multiple audience when *only one person* reads your document, but *for two distinct purposes*. For example, you may write a decision paper for your boss, and your boss also acts as her own staff expert. You still partition the document: write the core document for your boss reading as a manager and an appendix that she reads as an expert.

Your document succeeds when it satisfies both writer's and audiences' purposes.

Exercise: For each scenario, determine what the audience does with the information in the document. If you have more than one audience, consider each audience in terms of *what each does with the information.* (Answer A-1)

1. As project manager you must write an annual job review for each employee assigned to your project.
    What audience does with the information:

2. You must write a required monthly status report to your client, the City of Boston, who hired your company to clean the water in Boston Harbor.
    What audience does with the information:

3. After receiving many phone queries, you decide to write a memo to your plant employees describing procedures for getting their monthly parking sticker from their shift supervisor.
    What audience does with the information:

4. As office manager, you write a staff study to your immediate supervisor, recommending leasing rather than buying a copy machine.
    What audience does with the information:

5. You organized the annual holiday party. You write a thank-you note to the hotel manager who helped you host a particularly successful party.
    What audience does with the information:

6. As the lead editor for a large documentation effort, you write a style guide for the many contributing authors and your staff of copy editors and proofreaders.
    What audience does with the information:

Tip 2   Identify audiences based on what they do with the information in the document: expert, manager, operator, and general audiences.

Warning   Do not be misled by job titles, education, or background. Consider only how the audience uses your document. For example, your audience might be computer experts, but they use your document to decide which computer to purchase. Because your audience reads to make a decision, you write to the manager, not the expert.

Example   Your new boss, who happens to be a Ph.D. in computer science, asks you to write a memo describing how he can access the company's electronic files through his workstation. Despite the job title and advanced degree, you write to the operator audience, because your Ph.D. boss wants to perform a task — not form an opinion or make a decision.

See also   Multiple audience.

Discussion

As a professional you deal with four kinds of audiences: expert, manager, operator, or general. We identify audiences by how they use information.

Experts use information to master subject matter and make recommendations. They want to replicate your reasoning, so lead them through your data, methods, findings, and conclusions.

Managers use information to make decisions and plans. Don't force them to work through your reasoning. They want your recommendations or results first, then the discussion. Rarely do they want to see data and methods.

Operators use information to perform a task. They want to know the expected result, then get clear, practical instructions how to achieve the result. Limit discussion to the result and the instructions. Avoid theory — don't tell how you built the machine.

General audiences read just to stay informed. Typically they do not use the information to make recommendations, plans, decisions, or follow instructions. Put your conclusions, if any, before discussion and limit discussion to practical information. Rarely do they want to see data and methods.

Subject matter does not determine audience. Consider three examples of disputing bills. You treat the IRS as an expert audience, because it renders its *expert* opinion to resolve your tax bill dispute. You treat your health insurance company as a manager audience, because it simply decides whether your medical bill meets its narrow interpretation of coverage defined in its inscrutable contract. You treat your VISA™ Card company as an operator audience, because credit card bill disputes are pretty automatic. Writing a general interest story about your bill dispute is probably a waste of time.

Structure the body of your document according to your audience's needs:

1. **expert** — data, methods, findings, conclusions
2. **manager** — recommendations, discussion
3. **operator** — expected result, instructions with discussion
4. **general** — conclusions (if any), discussion

Audiences have different — *often incompatible* — needs for information, so you must partition your document according to audience. For example, you may write a decision paper to a manager, organized with your recommendation first. You add an appendix for the staff expert, organized with the conclusion at the end.

Exercise: Identify the audience(s) and their purposes for reading in each scenario. Based on how the audience uses the information, decide if the audience is expert, manager, operator, or general. Thereby, decide how to begin the body of your document. (Answer A-2)

1. You write a safety manual for your employees who install and maintain high voltage air conditioning equipment.

2. You must write a detailed design for building software to automatically switch and bill calls among cellular phone networks. The contract states that the client must approve the detailed design.

3. You send a letter with your resume to a company that just advertised your dream job.

4. The boss, Dr. Ann Smith, asks you to research the history of glass manufacturing as it applies to the healthcare industry so she can include some details in a paper she presents next month at the American Medical Association convention.

5. You must write the section of a proposal called *Technical Approach for Building the Wilson Bridge*, in which you must prove to the Federal Highway Safety Board that building an eight-lane drawbridge to span the Potomac River is technically sound, although the drawbridge serves the busiest stretch of interstate highway in the United States.

6. You send an email to all company employees announcing that the company henceforth gives each employee the option of either free parking worth $100 or a mass transit subsidy worth $100.

7. You work at Universal Laboratories for Occupationally Safe Environments. You conclude a three-year study on the effect of breathing printer's ink and paper dust at large newspaper printing plants. The American Lung Foundation, which commissioned the study, requests that you provide a report to the unions and Congress, and publish your findings on the Internet.

8. You are working on an advanced degree in International Finance. Your term paper topic is Economic and Cultural Challenges for the European Union. (Instead of writing your paper to the professor, imagine an audience that might use the information, such as Central Banks.)

Final Exercise: List and contrast the writer's and the audiences' purposes associated with this writing task. (Answer A-4)

Scenario: You are a software engineer. Your company, BAP Software, has a long-term contract to fix software problems and change software to enhance Telefona, Inc.'s many computer systems.

Telefona uses its budget authority to enforce a strict policy for managing software changes. The four-step process for approving an enhancement follows:

1. Either BAP or Telefona identifies a requirement with a change request memo.

2. Telefona authorizes a few man-hours for BAP to write a design that must include a cost estimate for the change.

3. Telefona reviews and approves the design for function, technical merit, and cost, before allocating budget to pay for the change.

4. Telefona issues a work order for the change.

The design for the typical enhancement is four pages long. Typically, the software engineer who writes the design also gets the work order to write the software change.

In this case, Telefona identifies a requirement to combine customers' wire phone and cellular phone bills into one invoice. At present, the customer gets two bills: cellular and wire. You have the task of writing a design for a module that adds itemized cellular calls to the customer's monthly wire phone bill. Most likely, you later use the design to write the code.

Three parties review the design. The appropriate Telefona users review the design for function and impact on their operations. The Telefona systems administrator assesses the feasibility and impact of the code change on the rest of the system. Then the Telefona comptroller approves the expenditure and releases funds with a work order.

What is your purpose for writing?

Who are your *four* audiences, and what is each audience's purpose for reading? What do you learn about organizing your document?

Audience				
What audience does with the info				

Step 2. Analyze Audience

1. Analyze Purpose

2. Analyze Audience

After analyzing purposes associated with your writing task, use four techniques to analyze your audience:

2.1 Determine what the audience needs to know.

2.2 Determine if the audience has a high or low level of knowledge.

2.3 Determine if the audience believes you or requires proof.

2.4 Plan how to accommodate each audience.

Discussion

The most common failing in business and technical writing is a poor sense of audience. Writers, especially subject-matter experts, too often dive straight into writing about what they know. They document their knowledge for themselves.

Throughout this book we use the word audience to mean *type of reader*. An audience can be a group of people who have in common the same reason for reading, the same need for information, the same level of knowledge, and the same inclination to believe you.

The great problem in trying to write to a multiple audience is that you attempt to simultaneously satisfy readers who do not share a reason for reading. These readers need different information; they likely do not share the same level of knowledge; and they may not share an inclination to believe you.

During this analysis of audience, you develop a chart that leads you from the audience's purpose for reading through what the audience needs to know, to the audience's level of knowledge, and finally the audience's inclination to believe you. If you have a multiple audience, develop a chart to analyze each.

Technique 2.1   *Determine what the audience needs to know.*

Tips   Based on what the audience does with the information, determine what each audience needs to know.

Warning   Do not assume that what the *audience needs to know* about a subject is what *you need to know* about the same subject. For example, on the subject of building a web site, your client, a retailer, may need to know the features, benefits, and costs associated with a web site, while you, the technician, need to know details about internet servers and how to code in different software languages.

Example   Detailed designs often have multiple audiences, each doing something different and therefore having different needs for information.

Audience	Technical staff	Client management
What audience does with the info	Build the system	Approve the design before committing to build system
What audience needs to know	Technical details about processes, data conversion, user interfaces, and outputs	How design addresses requirements

See also   Analyze purpose.

Discussion

As soon as you list what the audience needs to know, you know if you need to research, or if you have the information the audience needs in your head or at your fingertips. In either case, use this valuable insight to help budget your research time for any writing task.

Remember, experts read to evaluate your argument or comment on your recommendation. Fellow experts, professors, auditors, and lawyers are more concerned with the methods you used to get your answer than the answer itself. Managers read to make decisions, approve decisions, make plans, and give direction. Operators read to follow a set of instructions. They are more interested in the answer than your process.

Limit your document to what the audience needs to know. Otherwise, you fall into the old trap where the manager asks the engineer what time it is, and the engineer tells the manager how to build a clock.

Exercise: For the following two scenarios, fill in the chart to determine what the audience does with the information, and what the audience needs to know. (Answer A-5)

Scenario 1: You are the inventor of an infrared sensor and missile guidance algorithm that industry can use to improve robotics for civilian commerce. You founded your small corporation to prove your technology, and now you need to raise capital to put it into manufacturing. You prepare a briefing to pitch your promising technology to Venture Capital, Inc., who can raise the capital you need.

Audience	Venture Capital
What audience does with the info	
What audience needs to know	

Scenario 2: You are a cost accountant for Tri-Skalion Transport. Management asked you to write a decision paper to help them determine if they can profit by dropping the collision rider from their insurance coverage. You research Tri-Skalion's history of claims as compared to the industry averages. You estimate the costs of self-insuring, not insuring, or purchasing insurance. You anticipate that management will share your findings with Tri-Skalion's insurance underwriters, who can add their expert opinion.

Audience	Tri-Skalion management	Insurance underwriters
What audience does with the info		
What audience needs to know		

Technique 2.2   Determine if the audience has a high or low level of knowledge.

Tips   Assess the audience's level of knowledge based solely on what the audience needs to know.

Warning   Do not assess the audience's knowledge about *your* area of expertise, or about what *you* need to know about the subject. For example, you write a brief fact sheet for your co-workers about how to use the interoffice email system. They need simple step-by-step instructions. Most likely, they don't need to know the software and hardware configuration that makes your interoffice email possible, whereas you do.

Example   Detailed designs often have multiple audiences, each doing something different and therefore having different needs for information. Fortunately, each audience has a high level of knowledge about the information they need to know.

Audience	Technical staff	Client management
What audience does with the info	Build the system	Approve the design before committing to build system
What audience needs to know	Technical details about processes, data conversion, user interfaces, and outputs	How design addresses requirements
Audience's level of knowledge	High	High

See also   Purpose statement.

Discussion

You most often find yourself writing to an audience that has a high level of knowledge about the subject matter they need to know, which means you can be more concise. You can use acronyms and jargon.

To communicate to a low-knowledge audience, use four techniques:
1. Define terms.
2. Give examples.
3. Provide analogies.
4. Draw pictures.

Therefore, the low-knowledge audience always gets the longer document, often two to three times longer than the same document written to a high-knowledge audience. Use this valuable insight to help you budget your time for any writing task.

Note that we do not compromise. We do not write for middle-knowledge audiences, because we can't give half-definitions, half-examples, half-analogies, and half-pictures.

If your supervisor tells you that your document is "too short," you probably wrote to a high-knowledge audience and your supervisor wants you to address a low-knowledge audience. Expand with definitions, examples, analogies, and pictures — *never fluff*.

Exercise: For the following ten scenarios, determine whether the audience has a high or low level of knowledge. In other words, does the audience need you to define terms, give examples, provide analogies, or draw pictures? (Answer A-5)

1. A financial manager reads your staff study to decide whether the company ought to lease or buy a Cray Computer.

2. A financial manager reads your technical report about the capabilities of a Cray Computer.

3. The client plant manager reads your business analysis document to comment on your recommendations for streamlining workflow.

4. Employees read instructions telling them how to submit requests to get reimbursed for tuition as part of the company's continuing education program.

5. The project manager requests a weekly status report of your work: tasks completed, tasks on going, and tasks begun. At present, you struggle with a complex systems integration problem.

6. Venture Capital, Inc., listens to your briefing about the commercial possibilities of your new invention, an infrared sensor plus missile guidance algorithm, as it applies to robotics. You explain the capital required, the potential gains, the schedule of payback, and the risks of failure.

7. Management reads your report that makes the case that the cost of self-insuring against collision is higher than the cost of paying insurance premiums plus deductibles.

8. Programmers read your detailed design telling them the data formats, processes, and outputs required in the client's new automated billing system.

9. Client managers read Appendix A to your detailed design, in which you show that each of their requirements, first addressed through the general design, is now in the detailed design.

10. Bill Gates reads your instructions on how to assemble a tricycle.

Technique 2.3   Determine if the audience believes you or requires proof.

Tips   Assess the audience's inclination to believe you.

Warning   Do not assume that you must prove everything. Most of us hire experts, and we believe what they tell us. For example, when your dental hygienist suggests that you need to floss your teeth more often, believe it. Only a masochist demands proof. When in doubt, assume the audience believes you.

Example   Detailed designs often have multiple audiences, each doing something different and therefore having different needs for information. Fortunately, each audience has a high level of knowledge and believes you for the information they need to know.

Audience	Technical staff	Client management
What audience does with the info	Build the system	Approve the design before committing to build system
What audience needs to know	Technical details about processes, data conversion, user interfaces, and outputs	How design addresses requirements
Audience's level of knowledge	High	High
Audience believes you or wants proof	Believe	Believe

See also   Multiple audience; purpose statement.

Discussion

Other points being equal, the audience who demands proof always gets a longer document. Use this valuable insight to help you budget your time for any writing task.

Sometimes the proof is beyond the ability of the audience. What do people do when they desire proof, yet they do not understand the underlying complex technical subject? They get a second opinion from another expert they trust. Often you help the manager more by directing your proofs to the manager's staff expert instead of confusing the manager with an erudite technical argument.

For example, you send a proposal to the manager who makes a buying decision. She can handle the features, benefits, risks, and costs. She may want proof, but she relies on her expert staff to validate your technical approach. Therefore, write the proposal in two parts: one for the manager and one for her staff. The proof the manager requires is not in the manager's part of the proposal, but in the staff expert's part.

Some managers are also subject-matter experts. Essentially, they act as their own expert staff. Nevertheless, partition the document for two audiences: the manager who decides, and the expert who validates. Write your proof to the expert audience.

Exercise: For the following ten scenarios, determine if the audience believes you as you tell them what they need to know, or if they want you to prove your points. (Answer A-6)

1. You are a certified public accountant. Your manager reads your staff study to decide whether the company ought to lease or buy a Cray Computer.

2. You are a summer intern with three college credits in computer science. A financial manager reads your technical report about the capabilities of a Cray Computer.

3. BAP Industries brought you back from retirement to study ways to make your old factory more efficient. The plant manager reads your business analysis document to comment on your recommendations on how to streamline workflow.

4. You are the administrative assistant who processes requests for reimbursements. Employees read your instructions telling them how to submit requests to get reimbursed for tuition as part of the company's continuing education program.

5. You are a programmer. The project manager requests a weekly status report of your work: tasks completed, tasks on going, and tasks begun. At present, you struggle with a complex systems integration problem.

6. You are a 48-year-old Ph.D. in quantum physics. Venture Capital, Inc., listens to your briefing about the commercial possibilities of your new invention, an infrared sensor with a missile guidance algorithm, as it applies to robotics. You explain the capital required, the potential gains, the schedule of payback, and the risks of failure.

7. You just got a promotion from supervisor of vehicle maintenance to head of the purchasing department. Management reads your report that makes the case that the cost of self-insuring against collision is higher than the cost of paying insurance premiums plus deductibles.

8. You wrote the general design that the client approved. Now, programmers read your detailed design describing the data formats, processes, and outputs required in the client's new automated billing system.

9. You wrote the general design that the client approved. Now, client managers read Appendix A to your detailed design in which you show how the detailed design addresses each requirement and function identified in the general design.

10. You sell tricycles. Bill Gates reads your instructions on how to assemble a tricycle.

Technique 2.4   Plan how to accommodate each audience.

Tips   After you analyze and partition your audiences, plan how to accommodate each one by partitioning subject matter. Use one or more of these three ways to partition subject matter:
1. Write separate documents.
2. Break your core document into sections, each section serving a different audience.
3. Write the core document to one audience, and use front or back matter to accommodate other audiences.

Warning   Do not obsess about who gets the core document. Partitioning is the key. For example, you might write the core document for the manager with an appendix for the expert staff. Also, you might write the core document to the expert staff with an executive summary for the manager. Either way, partitioning ensures that audiences focus on the information they need.

Example   A complex detailed design may have sections for different development teams as well as front and back matter:

Executive summary — for the manager
Section 1 Data conversion — for the data management team
Section 2 Processes — for the main code team
Section 3 Graphic user interfaces — for the GUI team specialists
Appendix A Requirements indexed to detailed design — for contract officer
Appendix B Data dictionaries — for the data specialists on the data management team
Glossary — for the managers or clients who delve into the main sections

See also   Purpose statement; coherence devices.

Discussion

A core document has an introduction, body, and conclusion. When you break the document into sections, each section also gets an introduction, body, and conclusion. An example of a sectioned document is a proposal, where the sections may include corporate capabilities, understanding the client needs, technical approach, management section, and cost section.

Front matter includes executive summaries, abstracts, and letters or memos of transmittal. Back matter includes appendices, attachments, exhibits, notes, glossaries, and indexes. Three typical documents with front and back matter strategies include

Decision paper — core document for manager, appendix for the expert staff
After-action report — executive summary for manager, core document for operators
Test plan — transmittal letter for supervisor, core document for testers

You can combine the three strategies when you partition your document. For example, often a document with sections also has front and back matter.

Use front and back matter to help other audiences use your document. For example, if the main audience is technically expert, include jargon and theory in their section, but add an executive summary and glossary for less technical audiences. If your main audience has only a general knowledge of the subject, keep technical details in an appendix. Use titles, subheads, and other devices to help other audiences skim past sections that lack relevance to them.

Exercise: Plan how to accommodate this multiple audience. (Answer A-6)

Scenario: You work for Salubrious Pharmaceuticals, and your research team just recently finished tests on your latest creation, Wonder Pill, a new over-the-counter dietary supplement that helps the user stop smoking, lose weight, grow hair, brighten teeth, and build resistance to the common cold.

The research team leader assigns you, the junior member, the responsibility for all documentation regarding Wonder Pill. The team has already written the internal laboratory report on Wonder Pill that includes all the research data for chemical compounds, tests, methods of production, and quality assurance.

The team leader tells you that the documents must include

1. an application to the Food and Drug Administration (FDA) that includes a report of your tests on Wonder Pill, plus proposed Wonder Pill labeling for FDA approval

2. a press release to be included in a letter to Salubrious Pharmaceutical shareholders

Fill in the chart to analyze purpose and audience.

Audience	FDA	Public (label)	Press	Stockholders
What audience does with info				
What audience needs to know				
Audience's level of knowledge				
Audience believes you or wants proof				

Plan how to document Wonder Pill:

1. Determine which audiences get the core document and whether you partition the document into sections.

2. Determine which audience gets front or back matter, and plan the kind of front or back matter to use.

Final exercise: Analyze purpose and audience in this scenario, and plan how to accommodate each audience by partitioning the subject matter. (Answer A-7)

Scenario: Sesquatch Shoes, Inc. hired your information systems company to build a new system to streamline distribution and reduce inventory. Retail stores place and track their orders by accessing their store account on your secure web page.

Your new system tracks orders, adjusts shoe production in near-real time, and automates order fulfillment. The new system essentially overhauls the entire way Sesquatch distributes product. You got the job of writing the manuals for the new system. Sesquatch management specifically wants your manuals to address seven topics:

1. how the new process works, explained to *managers* from line supervisors up

2. how *marketing* receives orders and directs the quantity of each shoe style manufactured

3. how *floor workers* barcode shoe boxes

4. how *packers* sort bar-coded shoe boxes and put them on pallets according to retail store, region, and truck

5. how *engineers* maintain the machinery, stock spare parts, and order special parts

6. how *floor operators* use the new order fulfillment machinery safely

7.   how *retail stores* order shoes online, then receive confirmation and shipping dates

In addition, Sesquatch wants you to write the manuals in such a way that persons familiar with the factory and the distribution process don't have to read the manuals cover to cover.

Use your techniques to analyze purpose and audience, then partition the subject matter. How do you accommodate this multiple audience: separate documents, sections, front and back matter?

Step 3. Write Purpose Statement

2. Analyze Audience

3. Write Purpose Statement

After analyzing your purpose for writing and your audience's purpose for reading, you can determine the document's purpose. Use two techniques to write a purpose statement. Then use your purpose statement to focus yourself, reviewers, and audience.

3.1 Write a five-part purpose statement.

3.2 Ensure that the five parts work together.

3.3 Use the purpose statement to focus yourself and others.

Discussion

Your purpose statement becomes the first sentence in the introduction, and thereby manages the expectations of the audience before they get into the document's content. Use your purpose statement to set the tone, identify the target audience, and limit the document to what the target audience needs to know. Most importantly, the purpose statement makes your document relevant by telling the target audience what they do with the information.

With a well-crafted purpose statement, you focus yourself, because you limit your research and writing to what the audience needs to know.

The purpose statement improves the coordination of documents. If your audience rejects your purpose statement, they will reject the document. By crafting your purpose statement during pre-writing, you can use your purpose statement to discover and settle controversies *before* you spend time and energy writing and editing the document. You can show your purpose statement to colleagues, supervisors — even to the intended audience — to get pre-approval of the document's premise.

The purpose statement is also an excellent technique for introducing briefings.

Technique 3.1   Write a five-part purpose statement.

Tips   Determine the five parts of the purpose statement:

1. **Actor** is a noun naming the document, section, or piece of front and back matter.
2. **Action** is a verb telling what the document does.
3. **Audience** is the document's or section's primary audience.
4. **Topic** is what the audience needs to know.
5. **Outcome** is what the audience does with the information.

If you have a multiple audience document, write a purpose statement for each section and each piece of front and back matter.

Warning   Do not omit parts, except in rare circumstances. For example, you can omit the document name when implied from context, such as magazine articles. You might omit audience in a letter with a salutation.

Example   You write a short guide telling new hires how to use voice mail.

Audience	New hires
What audience does with information	Use voice mail
What audience needs to know	How to

guide	explains	new hires	how to	use voice mail
Actor	**Action**	**Audience**	**Topic**	**Outcome**

Purpose statement: *This guide explains to new hires how to use their voice mail.*

See also   Analyze purpose and audience; introduction.

Discussion

You already identified audience, outcome, and topic when you analyzed purpose and audience. Having planned your strategy, you also know the actor. The audience wants to know these essential facts about the document before reading further:

Actor   Identify your document by its content. Although the paper may have *Memorandum* printed in the heading, your document content might be a staff study, trip report, meeting minutes, proposal, or some other recognized format. Be as precise as possible.

Action   Tell what the document does, *not* what the author does. You may want to *recommend a course of action*, but the document merely *describes the course of action* so the manager can decide. Put your recommendation in the body of the document. The verb you choose for the action sets the tone. For example, a memo that *notifies* is more authoritative than a memo that *informs.*

Audience   Write to the primary audience, the one that actually uses the information in the topic to achieve the outcome.

Topic   Pull the topic directly from your analysis of audience: what the audience needs to know.

Outcome   Pull outcome directly from your analysis of purpose: what the audience does with the information.

Exercise: Write a purpose statement after analyzing purpose and audience. (Answer A-8)

Scenario 1: The building maintenance manager called you, the office manager, to say they are scheduled to put sealant on the parking lot next week. Weather permitting, they plan to seal half the lot (the east side) on Monday, and the other half (the west side) on Thursday. The sealant dries in two days. They plan to paint lines on Saturday.

Therefore, only half the parking lot would be available Monday through Friday. The entire lot would be closed on Saturday and reopen the next Monday morning. The building manager asked you to inform your employees and ask for their cooperation. He also said that your lease gave the landlord the option of passing any towing fees to the company. He would contact the other fourteen tenants. Throughout the next week, parking space allocations would not apply and all parking would be first-come-first-served.

You have 320 employees in the building and you decide it would be most economical and accurate to give each employee a memo.

Scenario 2: You are building an interactive web site for your client, Universal Bank. Your client asks you to submit a change proposal to expand the scope of your work to add a function whereby commercial clients can access their accounts to view account history as well as transfer funds.

Your staff believes they can add the commercial account functions for less than $80,000 for code and $8,000 for additional hardware, but the proposed new work extends the delivery of the web site by 60 days. You want the additional work. Write a purpose statement for the change proposal.

Scenario 3: You handle customer complaints for a national chain of bagel stores. You receive an angry letter from John Lee, a customer who complains that you discontinued his favorite sandwich — the goat cheese and caper spread on a jalapeño bagel. The *gc&c on jb* sandwich lost money nationwide, representing less than $1/10^{th}$ of one percent of total sandwich sales; so you discontinued it from the menu with deep regret. However, you added a promising new sandwich: a baba ghanoush and humus spread on a bed of alfalfa sprouts on a sesame seed bagel — *the Babahuma*. As customer complaint handler, you can give away coupons for free bagel sandwiches to placate dissatisfied customers.

Technique 3.2   Ensure that the five parts work together.

Tips   Ensure that the actor fits the topic and outcome.

Ensure that the action makes sense for the topic.

Rearrange the five parts to change emphasis, if desired.

Omit actor if self-evident, audience if it simply repeats salutation, and outcome if the document is truly for information only.

Use two sentences if necessary; topics and outcomes can be complex.

Warning   Avoid vague topics and outcomes.

Example

Poor: This letter recommends to management the costs and benefits of testing so management can decide whether to invest in further testing. (The verb *recommends* does not work with the object *costs and benefits*.)

Good: This letter describes the costs and benefits of testing so management can decide whether to invest in further testing. (We let the reference to *management* in outcome serve as the audience.)

Stiff: This advertisement explains to working parents how the new job-share concepts proposed in many progressive companies can help parents spend more time at home.

Better: Are you a working parent (audience) who wants to spend more time at home (outcome)? Let us describe (action) the new job-share concepts proposed by many progressive companies, and learn how. (actor is self-evident — advertisement)

Long: This memo describes to employees the new health care coverage, rights and benefits, preventive medicine programs, co-payment policies, and procedures for submitting claims, so employees can take advantage of our quality health care program, and they and their families can live healthier lives.

Better: This memo describes to employees the new health care coverage, rights and benefits, preventive medicine programs, co-payment policies, and procedures for submitting claims. Use this information to take advantage of our quality health care program, so you and your family can live healthier lives.

See also   Analyze purpose and audience; coherence.

Discussion

Omit the audience, if self-evident, in a document with limited distribution. Sometimes, the outcome implies the audience. Otherwise, always state the audience.

Be flexible. Advertisers often rearrange the five parts. They engage us by identifying the audience or the outcome first. Advertisers instinctively know that audience and outcome are the most important parts of the purpose statement.

For emphasis, assume the outcome you seek — *the assumptive close.* For example, *This letter details the costs of outsourcing our payroll, so management can decide to keep payroll in house.* The assumptive close is much stronger than *This letter recommends . . .*

You might discover that a purpose statement has multiple actions with multiple topics and multiple outcomes. If so, consider the possibility that the author had a multiple audience problem and failed to partition the subject matter according to audience.

If a supervisor or client issues you a purpose statement, examine all the parts to ensure that the parts work together and are specific enough.

Exercise: Evaluate these ten purpose statements. Are all five parts included? Do the five parts clearly and logically state the document's purpose? (Answer A-9)

1. This magazine article (actor) explains (action) to the public (audience) the advantages of recycling paper (topic) so residents know how to cooperate in the county's recycling program (outcome).

2. This user guide tells new employees about procedures for using the office email system.

3. This proposal explains our technical approach for the client users, and it presents our concept for the management plan, schedule, and costs for the financial department, and it justifies our bid in terms of time and materials, so you have the necessary information to evaluate our qualifications to successfully complete your project.

4. I thought I'd like to write down some thoughts and concerns for you in regard to the TDMS as we approach trials. We need to be constantly aware of several things, monitor their progress, and/or verify the fix.

5. This letter is a follow-up to our phone conversation today regarding the above captioned.

6. Please find attached to this email the cost data you requested for your proposal effort.

7. Are you over 65, in good health, and looking for a way to reduce the high cost of health insurance? Call our toll-free number and get answers today.

8. A representative from Image Tech, Inc. will give a lecture in the boardroom next Tuesday at 3:00 p.m.

9. This is in reference to your application, NDA #40235, submitted January 20, 1999.

10. This letter will orient you, officers of the higher echelons, in the principles of command, combat procedure, and administration which obtain in this Army, and will guide you in the conduct of your several commands. (Patton's General Order, Third Army — March 6, 1944)

Technique 3.3   *Use the purpose statement to focus yourself and others.*

Tips   Focus yourself on what the audience needs to know, before you gather information, outline your thoughts, and write the draft.

Focus your reviewers by telling them about your intended audience.

Coordinate your team members by making sure everybody understands each other's purpose statement. Thus, you avoid duplicate effort and identify holes.

Eliminate controversy before you write by getting supervisors and even clients to approve your purpose statement.

Use the purpose statement to steer your message to the right audience, despite organization protocols for routing communication.

Warning   Do not worry now about the exact wording of your purpose statement. Concentrate on getting agreement with your team, supervisor, and client. Edit later.

Example   You show the boss your draft purpose statement: *This memo informs employees about the company's 401K plan so you can decide whether to participate.*

Your boss alters your purpose statement: *This memo explains step by step how to enroll yourself in the company's 401K plan so you can take advantage of this benefit.*

You just saved hours of writing a document that your boss didn't want.

See also Analyze purpose and audience; introduction.

Discussion

The purpose statement forces you to get to the point. Limit research and writing efforts to telling the audience what they need to know to accomplish their purpose.

By stating the audience, you help the audience, reviewer, and yourself. Unless told differently, audiences and reviewers assume the document was written just for them. If they are not the intended audience, they get frustrated and criticize you. Reviewers tell you how to change the document to better serve the reviewer. Avoid criticism and misdirected reviews by including the audience in your purpose statement.

Protocol often determines to whom you must address a letter, even if the addressee is not the intended audience. Therefore, use a purpose statement to get your message directed to the right audience: *Dear Colonel Halftrack: This message informs your driver where to park your jeep at tomorrow's ceremony. Courtesy copy to PFC Bath, driver.*

If you omit what the audience does with the information — the outcome — your document becomes just another For-Your-Information (FYI) document. Most professionals ignore FYI documents. Therefore, the outcome is key to writing persuasively. When you tell audiences the outcome, they know what details they need to look for; therefore, they can find them in one reading.

The purpose statement becomes a contract between you and your audience. With the purpose statement, you define the criteria to determine the document's success.

Use the purpose statement to settle controversies before you write. The purpose statement forces people to make firm decisions about the document. Consequently, the purpose statement uncovers fuzzy thinking and vague requirements. Despite difficulty, press for concrete and specific guidance. Managers need to review their staff's purpose statements to catch fatal flaws early and ensure that writing assignment instructions are clear. If your client approves your purpose statement, you can be sure the client will accept the finished document.

Exercise: You have a bad experience with an office temp, so you give your assistant these hurried instructions: "ACME Temps says they guarantee satisfaction. Tell them how dissatisfied I am and that I do not expect to be billed for this disaster." Your assistant prepares the following letter for your signature. Unfortunately, the letter fails to get to the point. You realize that you needed to give your assistant better guidance. Help your assistant write a purpose statement as a means of focusing the writer and audience. (Answer A-11)

BAP Industries
555 Maple Ave. NW, Farburbs, VA 22045

September 27, 2000

Kay Kemnick
ACME Temps
123 Main Street, Gothom, MD 20002
Re: Employment of Temp (Ida Smith)

Dear Kay Kemnick:

As project manager of the Mars Explorer Bouncer, I had a critical design document due to NASA on September 19. I contacted ACME Temp during the month of August seeking someone knowledgeable about both basic graphics software and Word 7.0. ACME Temp sent temporary assistant Ida Smith who was, in fact, a fine match for our project.

Ida was well aware that September 19th was the deadline for our project. September 19th also happened to be the same day she planned to go out of town on vacation. To ensure that the deadline would be met, and to accommodate Ida's schedule, we agreed to special working conditions for the weekend of September 15th and 16th. For this weekend only, she was provided with a building pass, my home phone number, and instructions to contact me if she had any problems. Therefore, she could complete her work and leave for vacation as planned.

On Monday, I received a note from Ida, by means of courier, explaining that she had not completed the project as agreed, because she had left town early for her vacation. By failing to contact me earlier, and by subsequently leaving town, she left me with an unfinished project and no time to properly train someone to take her place.

Ida was our first contact with ACME Temps for a major project, and we did not have a good experience. Please follow up on this situation as soon as possible.

Sincerely,

B. Guire — Project Manager

Final exercise: Analyze purpose and audience, then write a purpose statement for the system design. (Answer A-11)

Scenario: Your team won the contract to build a computerized "Fulfillment and Invoicing" system for Pinnacle Trail, Ltd., a fast-growing catalogue sales company specializing in hiking and camping equipment. In your technical approach, you proposed acquiring a UNIX-based software package, then customizing it to meet Pinnacle's special needs.

The next deliverable for the contract is a detailed system design from which your technical staff writes code to modify the UNIX-based package. The Pinnacle Information Systems (IS) manager, who represents the Pinnacle users, must approve your detailed system design. The Pinnacle VP of sales and marketing, nervous about "all this hi-tech stuff," also wants to see the system design so he can understand what's going to happen to his slow but effective low-tech procedures.

1. Fill in the chart as you analyze your three audiences.

Audience	Technical staff (programmers)	Client Information Systems manager	VP sales
What audience does with the info			
What audience needs to know			
Audience's level of knowledge			
Audience believes you or wants proof			

2. Plan your strategy for partitioning the subject matter by audience. Who gets the core document? Do you use separate documents, sections, or front and back matter for the others?

3. Write purpose statements for each of the three audiences.

Actor	Action	Audience	Object	Outcome

Actor	Action	Audience	Object	Outcome

Actor	Action	Audience	Object	Outcome

Step 4. Gather Information

3. Write Purpose Statement

4. Gather Information

Having focused your document with a purpose statement, gather information using two techniques:

> **4.1 Use your purpose statement to help you gather ideas and facts.**

> **4.2 Ask who, what, where, when, why, and how to get the details.**

Discussion

Recall your analysis of audience and what the audience needs to know. When you answer that question, you also determine if you need to do research. Sometimes gathering information is simply gathering your thoughts. If you have conducted extensive laboratory research, do not simply provide the audience your notes. Instead, gather the information the audience needs from your notes, and *then* write your report.

Often the author needs to know more than the audience needs to know. For example, your audience needs to know the best price for a GQ Laser/9000 high-speed laser printer. You spend six hours researching price quotes from five suppliers and two mail order companies. The audience doesn't want you to recount all your research — just the best price.

Most technical experts become technical experts because they like research. Consequently, they often dive into the research before defining the purpose of the document. Later they determine if the research is relevant to the document, and sometimes they include the fruits of their research whether relevant or not. Irrelevant facts distract the audience.

Unfocused research wastes both the writer's and the audience's time.

Technique 4.1   Use your purpose statement to help you gather ideas and facts.

Tips   Use your purpose statement to focus gathering ideas and facts. In particular, limit your inquiry to what the audience needs to know.

Warning   Do not expand your research into nice-to-know details.

Do not try to organize ideas yet — you sort and order ideas later.

Do not write in paragraphs yet — you write the draft paragraphs later.

Example   Consider gathering information to support the following purpose statement: *This manual* (actor) *describes* (action) *to new owners of the Fastcut Lawnmower* (audience) *proper maintenance and safe operation of your new lawnmower* (object) *so you can get more out of your machine* (outcome).

1. Actor — *manual* — suggests a how-to document. Gather information on procedures.

2. Action — *describes* — suggests that we need not *explain* the mechanics or attempt to motivate the new owner. Gather specific details that describe the lawnmower.

3. Audience — *new owners* — indicates an operator who has no interest in the theory of small four-cycle engines. Gather only practical information.

4. Object — *maintenance and operation of the new machine* — limits the discussion. You need not discuss the history of lawn mowers.

5. Outcome — *can get more* — suggests details must be complete and anticipate audiences' needs as they try to operate and maintain their machine.

See also   Analyze audience; purpose statement.

Discussion

Expect to gather more information than you use in your draft. Later when you organize your points, you select the useful information and discard the superfluous.

Meetings are really forms of gathering information. If you write meeting minutes, craft a purpose statement before attending the meeting. Meeting minutes vary in purpose. Ask your supervisor or the group to approve your purpose statement. Then let your purpose statement focus your information gathering at the meeting. Otherwise, you become an inefficient stenographer, taking down every word that you must later synthesize onto paper. You soon discover that taking and recording meeting minutes is much easier when you focus your efforts with a purpose statement. The same logic applies to trip reports.

Exercise: Describe how the following purpose statements focus information gathering. (Answer A-12)

Scenario 1: You are a real estate manager and you must write two letters that describe the same empty office space to different audiences for different purposes. You have a purpose statement for each letter that you use to help gather information.

1. *This bid request specifies to ACME Carpet Co. the dimensions of eight vacant offices at 123 Maple Avenue, so your carpet company can bid on installing wall-to-wall carpeting.*

2. *This brochure outlines for prospective renters the features and benefits of our vacant offices at 123 Maple Avenue, so prospective renters can decide whether to schedule an appointment to view the office space.*

Scenario 2: Your boss asks you to take the minutes of the next Change Management meeting in which the client, your company's engineers, and the project management team meet to discuss proposed changes to the baseline system due to be delivered next year.

Before the meeting, you get your boss to approve the following purpose statement: *These minutes describe the status of each proposed change to help members of the Change Management committee track proposed changes through the process of technical approval, budget approval, scheduling, execution, and final testing.*

Technique 4.2   Ask who, what, where, when, why, and how to get the details.

Tips   Ask *who, what, where, when, why,* and *how* from the audience's point of view.

Write down all questions that come to mind. Expect some redundancy.

Gather information to respond to your questions.

Warning   Don't waste time answering questions that your purpose statement shows are irrelevant.

Don't expect to use all the detailed information you gather.

Example   The following purpose statement may generate these questions:

This letter describes for prospective renters the vacant offices at 123 Maple Avenue, so renters may appreciate the many fine features and benefits that come with the office space.

- *Who* are the prospective renters and *who* are we?
- *What* features and benefits interest renters?
- *Where* is 123 Maple Ave? *Where* can the prospect contact us?
- *When* does the offer expire? *When* can renters move in?
- *Why* must renters act now?
- *How* can a prospective renter take advantage of this offer?

See also   Analyze audience; purpose statement.

Discussion

Who, what, where, when, why, and *how* questions help you gather information that audiences need, not just what you want to tell them. These questions help you think of details that you might otherwise neglect.

Most information you gather are simply data, facts, and opinions. Later, during sentence outlining, you stand back from the detailed information as you determine what points you need to make.

Faced with unfamiliar subject matter, writers typically assemble their detailed information before determining their points. When writing about a familiar subject, writers may leap ahead to the points they want to make. Be flexible. The logic can work both ways: *Here's my detailed information, so what's my point?* Or, *Here's my point; therefore, what detailed information do I need?* The key is to recognize the difference between a detail and a point.

Exercise: Ask *who, what, where, when, why*, and *how* questions to generate details for documents with these purpose statements. (Answer A-12)

1. This report describes the repairs and tests we conducted on your PDQ Laserprinter to stop the intermittent errors you reported, so you know what we cover by warranty and what service you must pay for.

2. This guide provides you, the new owner of a Megawheel plastic tricycle, simple step-by-step assembly instructions, so you can quickly put your little tyke on his Megawheel trike.

3. This letter notifies LD Cellular Phone Co. billing office about $12,456.56 of unauthorized calls charged to our account, so you can change our phone access code, investigate the fraudulent calls, and remove the charges from our account.

4. Are you over 65, in good health, and looking for a way to reduce the high cost of health insurance? Call our toll-free number and get answers today.

5. This memo describes to employees the new health care coverage, rights and benefits, preventive medicine programs, co-payment policies, and procedures for submitting claims. With this information you and your family can take advantage of our quality health care program and live healthier lives.

Final exercise: Use your purpose statement and the questions *who, what, where, when, why,* and *how* to focus information gathering. (Answer A-13)

Scenario: You are in charge of recruiting new employees — mostly entry level — to staff your rapidly growing company: a chain of franchise pet stores, *Pet Arama.* You need to hire 50 floor clerks, 20 cashiers, and 2 assistant managers in the next 90 days. You want to attract applicants through your company website. Following is your analysis and purpose statement.

Audience	Prospective employees
What audience does with the info	Decides whether to apply for job
What audience needs to know	Our business, hiring practices, compensation, job opportunities, and how to apply
Audience's level of knowledge	High
Audience believes you or wants proof	Believe

We welcome prospective employees (audience) to our site (actor). Here you can learn about *Pet Arama* (topic), and determine if you want a future with us (outcome). Plus you can follow five simple steps (more topic) to apply online (more outcome).

1. How does your analysis and the purpose statement focus your information gathering?

2. Give an example of data you don't need to gather.

3.   Ask *who, what, where, when, why,* and *how* to determine what information you gather for your audience.

Step 5. Write Sentence Outline

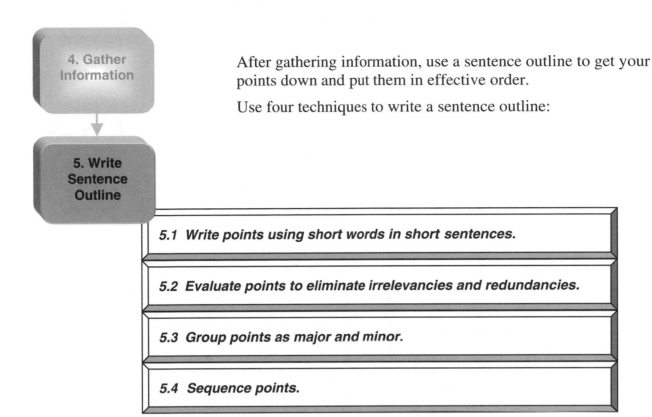

4. Gather Information

5. Write Sentence Outline

After gathering information, use a sentence outline to get your points down and put them in effective order.

Use four techniques to write a sentence outline:

5.1 Write points using short words in short sentences.

5.2 Evaluate points to eliminate irrelevancies and redundancies.

5.3 Group points as major and minor.

5.4 Sequence points.

Discussion

Most people skip outlining altogether, or they arrange a couple key phrases or words — a topic outline. Unfortunately, most high schools teach outlining incorrectly, violating two key principles. Consequently, students quickly abandon the practice as too burdensome. Apply two key principles to keep outlining useful:

1. Outline just major and minor points. Do not outline facts.
2. Outline only the *body* of your document. The *introduction* and *conclusion* of a business or technical document follow formats and therefore don't need outlining.

Properly used sentence outlines save much time and effort for both the author and audience.

A sentence outline helps you write your draft. You can show your sentence outline to your team, supervisor, or client to get feedback. Together you find omissions, irrelevancies, redundancies, and out-of-sequence points before you invest further effort writing and editing a draft. The points in your outline become the key sentences for your draft — in fact the first sentences of your paragraphs. Having thought through your points, you can *quickly* add supporting details when writing the draft. Furthermore, your sentence outline can serve as a summary of your document. If you must write an executive summary, your outline includes all your key points in sequence.

Sentence outlining makes your document easier to read. Your points appear at the beginning of paragraphs. People skim documents by reading the first sentence of each paragraph. Also, your points are easy to remember, because they are short sentences.

Technique 5.1   Write points using short words in short sentences.

Tips   Write each point as a short sentence, three to ten words.
              Use one- and two-syllable words that clearly state each point.
              Make each point an assertion or generality.
              Use gathered information as the source for your points.

Warning   Do not outline details or facts.
              Do not evaluate your points yet. Do not edit your points.

Example   Purpose statement: *This memo announces to employees changes in the cafeteria's hours and services. Please cooperate by adjusting your lunch breaks accordingly.*
              You think of 12 potential points to make in your memo:

1. At present we have 216 union-member employees.
2. The changes allow us to keep costs down and increase service during peak demand.
3. The vending machines outside the locker rooms are available all the time.
4. We expanded the cafeteria's dining area.
5. All employees have access to the cafeteria.
6. Some employees bring lunch and eat outside instead.
7. We shortened the cafeteria's hours.
8. At present the cafeteria is understaffed.
9. The cafeteria was too crowded during the peak lunch hour.
10. We plan to increase the cafeteria staff.
11. We regret any inconvenience caused by the shortened hours.
12. We augmented service two ways to handle increased volume.

See also Gather information; storyboards.

Discussion

Learn the difference between facts and points. Facts stand on their own. Points made as assertions can be argued. Points made as generalities introduce a set of specific facts. Often, facts and generalities look alike. For example, *The new rocket has four independently throttled engines.* Depending on your context, this statement may stand on its own as a fact, or you may use the statement to introduce more specific facts about the rocket engines.

A sentence outline forces you to make your point. Compare the difference between these methods of organization:

Stream of consciousness: When we first learned of your accelerated launch schedule, we naturally gave the matter serious consideration.
Topic outline: Schedule
Sentence outline assertion: Our team can meet your accelerated launch date.
Sentence outline generality: An accelerated launch depends on three factors.

Write points with short words in three-to-ten word sentences. Long words and sentences tend to obscure or lose the point. Also, long sentences tend to express more than one point. Some writers put points on 3x5 cards; others use stick-on notes. Use anything you can sort later. Concentrate on getting your ideas down as simply as possible. Relax. Don't worry about tone, relevancy, redundancy, or order. Don't worry about supporting your point with facts. Many writers call this aspect of writing *brainstorming*.

Your recommendation is always a point that belongs in the body.

Exercise: Using gathered information as your source, write points for a sentence outline. Use short words in short sentences. (Answer A-14)

Scenario: Susan Walters recently ran a successful pilot program for job sharing for BAP Industries. Management asks her to write an article for the company magazine. Susan writes a purpose statement and gathers information. Help Susan begin her sentence outline by writing short points based on each group of information below. These points later become part of Susan's sentence outline.

Purpose statement: This article describes how the BAP Northeast Region recently implemented a successful pilot program for job sharing. Other regional managers can use job sharing to attract and keep qualified employees.

Information gathered:

1. Who applied for job sharing? Twenty BAP employees and ten non-employees applied for the job sharing pilot program. Applicants varied from a part-time attorney to a full-time senior manager. Most applicants were administration and human resource department professionals with a range of experience. Point: *Many competent applicants with a wide range of experience applied.*

2. What are the advantages and disadvantages of job sharing? The corporation retains good employees who know the job and the organization. Job sharing entails little extra cost. Job sharing increases employee morale. Management can lose control. Customers can become confused. Job sharers can be incompatible. Point:

3. Where does job sharing occur? The percentage of U.S. companies that job share by region: West — 8 percent; Mid-west — 13 percent; South — 6 percent; Northeast — 7 percent; Great Lakes — 16 percent. Point:

4. When do job sharers work? Each partner works 20 hours a week and earns ½ company benefits. Each partner works a 2½-day schedule. Partners work 2 hours together mid-week to ensure continuity. Point:

5. Why did applicants want to job share? Some wanted time to pursue personal interests like education. Some working parents wanted more family time. Point:

6. How did job sharers communicate the new working arrangement to others? They published internal memos and email introducing the change. They sent a letter to vendors and clients. They reminded contacts of the job sharing arrangement when using voice, email, telephone, or written communication. Point:

Technique 5.2 Evaluate points to eliminate irrelevancies and redundancies.

Tip 1   Use your purpose statement to eliminate obvious irrelevancies. If a point does not support your purpose statement, the point is probably irrelevant to the body of the document.

Set aside any supporting facts that you mistakenly included as a point.

Find the right place for your points. The point may be valid, but not for the body of the document. Assign the point to another document, section, introduction, conclusion, or front or back matter.

Warning   Do not expect to get your points down exactly right the first time. Writing points gives you a chance to evaluate them. Expect to throw some away and combine others.

Error Trap If too many points don't support your purpose statement, consider the possibility that your purpose statement is flawed.

Example   Purpose statement: *This memo announces to employees changes in the cafeteria's hours and services. Please cooperate by adjusting your lunch breaks accordingly.*

Your points follow, not grouped or ordered yet, with some deleted as irrelevant.

1. ~~At present we have 216 union-member employees.~~ simple fact
2. The changes allow us to keep costs down and increase service during peak demand.
3. ~~The vending machines outside the locker rooms are available all the time.~~ irrelevant
4. We expanded the cafeteria's dining area.
5. ~~All employees have access to the cafeteria.~~ irrelevant to body but suitable for introduction
6. ~~Some employees bring lunch and eat outside instead.~~ irrelevant
7. We shortened the cafeteria's hours.
8. At present the cafeteria is understaffed.
9. The cafeteria was too crowded during the peak lunch hour.
10. We plan to increase the cafeteria staff.
11. We regret any inconvenience caused by the shortened hours.
12. We augmented service two ways to handle increased volume.

See also   Purpose statement.

Discussion

Your sentence outline makes points that you and others can evaluate. Proposals tend to have more assertions; detailed designs and user manuals tend to have more generalities. Your recommendation is always a relevant point that you make in the body of the document.

If you have a cluster of points that don't support your purpose statement, you may have another audience that you overlooked during analysis.

Sometimes, the point does not support the purpose statement, but you want to make the point anyway. If so, make any off-topic points in the introduction or the conclusion, but not in the body. Limit the body to relevant points — what the audience needs to know.

Exercise: You are the company systems expert. You must write a fact sheet to convince two senior managers, the VPs of Accounting and Marketing, to invest in a data security system. You gather information, then write your points.

Evaluate your following points against your purpose statement. Eliminate irrelevancies. If a point is irrelevant to the document's purpose, but nevertheless, you want to make the point, you can set the point aside for the introduction, conclusion, or front and back matter. (Answer A-14)

Purpose statement: This fact sheet highlights for senior managers the *costs and benefits* of our proposed automated data security system so you can decide whether to invest in data protection.

Points:

1. Ninety percent of Fortune 500 companies use data security systems.

2. Our professionals keep a lot of valuable information on our computers.

3. We rely on computers and data now more than ever to be profitable.

4. Losing data can severely reduce profits.

5. The proposed system uses three optical drives tied to our local area network.

6. The next-best alternative uses old technology, a 16-BPI tape drive.

7. The three optical drives, ten cartridges, optic fiber cables, and software cost $6,490.

8. Causes for data loss range from employee error to natural disaster.

9. Industry surveys provide statistics on industry-wide information loss.

10. The proposed system limits data loss to a worst case 24 hours.

11. Last year, lost data cost us more than 3,500 direct labor hours at $40 per labor-hour.

12. Our costs for losing data exceeded industry averages.

13. We generate almost 800 megabytes of critical data per month.

14. Eighty percent of the monthly data overwrites old records; however, 20 percent is new.

15. Expect our proposed data security system to reduce data losses by 99 percent.

16. Lost data results in misplaced or late orders, hence angry customers.

17. Our proposed data security includes state-of-the-art protection against computer viruses.

18. Perpetrators of computer viruses are seldom found or prosecuted.

19. Our data security system can rebuild our entire online database in less than a day.

20. We require data security to protect our company's profitability.

21. The Systems Steering Committee recommends investing in this data protection system.

Tip 2   Eliminate redundancies and unnecessary repetition. If two points say basically the same thing, delete one.

Warning   Do not discount repeated thoughts too quickly. The fact that a point is repeated probably means the point is important. If you have a multiple audience, you may need to make the point for both audiences.

Example   Purpose statement: *This memo announces to employees changes in the cafeteria's hours and services. Please cooperate by adjusting your lunch breaks accordingly.*

Your points follow — not grouped or ordered yet — with some deleted as redundant.

1. We expanded the cafeteria's dining area.
2. The changes allow us to keep costs down and increase service during peak demand.
3. We shortened the cafeteria's hours.
4. ~~At present the cafeteria is understaffed.~~ redundant to point 6
5. ~~The cafeteria was too crowded during the peak lunch hour.~~ redundant to point 8
6. We plan to increase the cafeteria staff.
7. We regret any inconvenience caused by the shortened hours.
8. We augmented service two ways to handle increased volume.

See also   Purpose statement.

Discussion

The technique of eliminating redundant points solves most problems associated with topic outlines.

Documents written from topic outlines tend to be one- to two-thirds longer than necessary. Topic outlines tend to be filled with redundancies. A topic outline tells you only vaguely what you're going to write about, not the point you want to make about the topic.

For example, consider this topic outline for a short change proposal: *costs* and *schedule*. First, you dump information about *costs*: past, budget, actual, and projections. Then you provide a similarly exhaustive treatment for *schedule*. Finally you come to the point: *We can reduce the cost of this change by ten percent if you allow us to extend the deliverable date one week.* You support your point by reiterating the key facts already detailed above.

When deciding if a point is redundant, ask yourself, *do the two points use essentially the same supporting details?*

Exercise: We continue with the exercise from page 43. You have eliminated the irrelevancies. Now evaluate the remaining points to eliminate redundancies. (Answer A-15)

Purpose statement: This fact sheet highlights for senior managers the *costs and benefits* of our proposed automated data security system so you can decide whether to invest in the new system.

Points:

1. Our professionals keep a lot of valuable information on our computers.

2. We rely on computers and data now more than ever to be profitable.

3. Losing data can severely reduce profits.

4. The proposed system uses three optical drives tied to our local area network.

5. The three optical drives, ten cartridges, optic fiber cables, and software cost $6,490.

6. Industry surveys provide statistics on industry-wide information loss.

7. The proposed system limits data loss to a worst case 24 hours.

8. Last year, lost data cost our company more than 3,500 labor hours at $40 per labor-hour.

9. Our costs for losing data exceeded industry averages.

10. Expect our proposed data security system to reduce data losses by 99 percent.

11. Lost data results in misplaced or late orders, hence angry customers.

12. Our proposed data security includes state-of-the-art protection against computer viruses.

13. Our data security system can rebuild our entire online database in less than a day.

14. We require data security to protect our company's profitability.

15. The Systems Steering Committee recommends investing in this data protection system.

Technique 5.3   Group points as major and minor.

Tips   Group minor points below major points.

Find and correct omissions in your outline. If minor points lack a major point, consider three alternatives:
1. Add a major point.
2. Delete the minor points as irrelevant.
3. Change the minor points into major points.

Warning   Do not outline details and facts.

Do not over-complicate your outline. If you can build your outline as a series of major points without minor points, so much the better. Flatter organization is better.

Example   Purpose statement: *This memo announces to employees changes in the cafeteria's hours and services. Please plan your lunch breaks accordingly.*

Points, grouped but not ordered yet, follow:

1. We augmented service two ways to handle increased volume.
2.   We expanded the cafeteria's dining area.
3.   We plan to increase the cafeteria staff.
4. We shortened the cafeteria's hours.
5. We regret any inconvenience caused by the shortened hours.
6. The changes allow us to keep costs down and increase service during peak demand.

See also   Storyboards.

Discussion

Keep your points at a high level. When we learned to outline, the teacher told us to begin with the Roman Numeral I, then work to minor points AB, then to progressively finer points: 1. a. (1) (a) iii, until we delve into various bullets. As soon as you go below the AB level, you usually are outlining supporting details — mere facts. If you try to outline details below the AB level you suffer two consequences:

1. You lose your train of thought, and incidentally, so does your audience.

2. You quickly abandon outlining as not worth the effort.

Be flexible. When you group your points, you may discover gaps in your outline. Add points to fill the gaps.

Do not write a stream-of-consciousness draft instead of a sentence outline. A stream-of-consciousness draft often reads like a story — how events or thoughts occurred to the author. Irrelevant and out-of-sequence thoughts result.

Exercise: Identify major points and group minor points below them. (Answer A-15)

Scenario: Your New Jersey company plans to build a can manufacturing plant somewhere in the Southeast. Management is especially concerned to find a good business environment, a well-established transportation network, and a good living environment for the New Jersey transplants. You must write a staff study to the company board of directors recommending building the plant in Tuscaloosa, Alabama. Below is your purpose statement and your points already filtered for irrelevancy and redundancy. Now identify major points and group them with minor points.

Purpose statement: This staff study details for the board of directors *the business climate, the transportation network, and the living environment* for building a can manufacturing plant in Tuscaloosa, Alabama. The board must decide where to locate the new plant.

1. The Black Warrior River-Tombigbee Waterway offers easy access to the Port of Mobile.

2. At present, Tuscaloosa's business climate meets or exceeds our needs.

3. Tuscaloosa provides many big-city amenities.

4. Tuscaloosa has no big-city costs.

5. The University of Alabama offers many cultural opportunities.

6. The Tuscaloosa Airport requires connections through Atlanta.

7. The local area costs are low for our business.

8. Personal income, property, and sales taxes are low.

9. Recent layoffs in local chemical, rubber, paper, and iron factories make an abundance of cheap, skilled labor.

10. Tuscaloosa has many recreational facilities: lakes and parks.

11. Tuscaloosa has mild winters and hot summers.

12. Alabama offered us a five-year tax holiday to move to Alabama.

13. Local public schools are rated below the national average, but improving.

14. Tuscaloosa's transportation is geared for manufacturing companies like ours.

15. Tuscaloosa serves as a minor hub for both highway and rail traffic.

16. Tuscaloosa presents a major change in living environment for our New Jersey transplants.

17. The search committee recommends building the new factory near Tuscaloosa, Alabama.

Technique 5.4   Sequence points.

Tip 1   Sequence the points for your specific audience.

Use the topic — *what the audience needs to know* — in your purpose statement as a clue how to sequence.

Warning   Do not write your draft until the sequence of points works. Otherwise, after writing the draft, you waste much time trying to edit logical sequence into the document.

Example   Purpose statement: *This memo announces to employees changes in the cafeteria's hours and services. Please plan your lunch breaks accordingly.*

Your sequenced points follow:

1. We shortened the cafeteria's hours.
2. We augmented service two ways to handle increased volume.
3. We expanded the cafeteria's dining area.
4. We plan to increase the cafeteria staff.
5. The changes allow us to keep costs down and increase service during peak demand.
6. We regret any inconvenience caused by the shortened hours.

See also   Analyze purpose and audience; multiple audience; purpose statement.

Discussion

Recall your four types of audience: expert, manager, operator, and general audience.

In the cafeteria example above, note that the results come first, appropriate for the manager audience who uses information to plan. Note the results appear in the same order they occurred in the purpose statement: cafeteria hours and services.

At some point, sequencing can be a matter of opinion about emphasis. Show your outline to your supervisor or colleagues before you write the draft. You can easily rearrange the sequence in the outline. Rearranging the draft is much harder.

Exercise: We continue with the exercise from page 47 — to write a staff study about building a can manufacturing plant in Tuscaloosa, Alabama. You have your points grouped in major and minor points below. Now sequence them for your audience: members of the board of directors. (Answer A-16)

Purpose statement: This staff study details for the board of directors *the business climate, the transportation network, and the living environment* for building a can manufacturing plant in Tuscaloosa, Alabama. The board must decide where to locate the new plant.

14. Tuscaloosa's transportation is geared for manufacturing companies like ours.

    1. The Black Warrior River-Tombigbee Waterway offers easy access to the Port of Mobile.

    6. The Tuscaloosa Airport requires connections through Atlanta.

    15. Tuscaloosa serves as a minor hub for both highway and rail traffic.

2. At present, Tuscaloosa's business climate meets or exceeds our needs.

    7. The local area costs are low for our business.

    9. Recent layoffs in local chemical, rubber, paper, and iron factories make an abundance of cheap, skilled labor.

    12. Alabama offered us a five-year tax holiday to move to Alabama.

16. Tuscaloosa presents a major change in living environment for our New Jersey transplants.

    3. Tuscaloosa provides many big-city amenities.

    4. Tuscaloosa has no big-city costs.

    5. The University of Alabama offers many cultural opportunities.

    8. Personal income, property, and sales taxes are low.

    10. Tuscaloosa has many recreational facilities: lakes and parks.

    11. Tuscaloosa has mild winters and hot summers.

    13. Local public schools are rated below the national average, but improving.

17. The search committee recommends building the new factory near Tuscaloosa, Alabama.

Tip 2   Use natural patterns to help you sequence.

Consider the *topic* of the purpose statement for clues on how to organize shorter documents and which natural pattern applies.

Warning   Do not present information chronologically unless you have a good reason. Avoid telling a story — explaining the situation as it happened to you — instead of ordering the information to best serve the audience. Chronological presentations sound like our grade-school essays: *How I spent my summer vacation.*

Example   Natural patterns for presenting points and details include these:

Topical	(Attribute 1, attribute 2 . . . like a list)
Ordinal	(Step 1, step 2 . . . like a cook book)
Priority	(Greatest to least, or least to greatest)
Functional	(How things work . . . like describing a computer)
Spatial	(Top down, or bottom up . . . like describing a house)
Examples	(Generalization illustrated with supporting details)
Cause-Effect	(Also problem-cause-solution or effect-cause)
Compare	(Also contrast or compare-contrast)
Chronological	(First this, then that . . . like a protocol)

See also   Purpose statement; content and organization tests.

Discussion

Audiences and writers are accustomed to certain natural patterns to present information. These patterns reflect the ways our minds work; they are practically second nature to us.

You can combine natural patterns, one within another. For example, your status report's standard format might use an overall topical pattern: actions completed, actions ongoing, actions planned. You might combine a priority pattern within each topic: urgent, important, postponed.

Do not confuse the logical steps of your work with the logical pattern for the document. For example: You may conduct a five-day safety inspection of a chemical plant where you track the manufacturing process. Do not write your report using a chronological sequence: *On day one, I inspected . . . .* Instead, report your findings organized by some other natural pattern: priority, plant function, topic, or spatial.

Exercise: For each purpose statement below, identify the natural patterns you can use to order points. You may combine one natural pattern within another. (Answer A-17)

1. This test plan provides for each software module the scenario, data, and expected result so the quality assurance team can verify that the system operates correctly.

2. This policy outlines the rules employees must obey when using the company gymnasium.

3. This guide provides you, the new owner of a Megawheel plastic tricycle, simple step-by-step assembly instructions, so you can quickly put your little tyke on his Megawheel trike.

4. This letter notifies your company of the safety violations and systemic deficiencies found during your annual factory inspection. To avoid a substantial rate increase in your insurance premium, you must correct the violations within 30 days and provide a plan to address the systemic violation.

5. This memo describes to employees the new health care coverage, rights and benefits, preventive medicine programs, co-payment policies, and procedures for submitting claims. With this information you and your family can take advantage of our quality health care program and live healthier lives.

6. This change proposal outlines the equipment and direct labor costs to add an alternate power generator for your business. As soon as you authorize the purchase, we can schedule the installation.

7. This memorandum outlines our three main reasons for purchasing the Dulles land parcel early, so the chief financial officer can inform the board of directors.

Tip 3   Use standard formats to sequence points and details.

Warning   Do not invent new formats.

                Do not skip any of the analytical steps; rather, use formats as aids to analysis.

                Do not rely totally on document templates. Templates, like checklists, are good tools to manage repetitive tasks, but they do not work well as outlines for complex documents. Templates that prescribe specific details often cause repetition or have many headings followed by the abbreviation *n/a* for *not applicable*.

Example   These business documents often use standard formats:

Proposal	Executive summary, technical approach, management plan, and cost proposal, unless otherwise dictated by the request for proposal
Business Plan	Strategy, organization, product, marketing, physical plant, personnel, finance, accounting controls; appendices for proforma income statements, balance sheet, cashflow
Agenda	Old business, new business
Resume	Functional or chronological or combined
Staff Study	Problem, solution, discussion, facts

See also   Multiple audience; purpose statement; organization test.

Discussion

Use standard formats when possible. Sometimes, many professionals worked through the pre-writing phase analysis for your writing situation before you, saving you time and effort. They already figured out how to partition the document into sections according to the audiences. They determined the broad topics that each audience needs to know and sequenced to those topics. Note that formats do not predetermine the points or the supporting data.

Although formats are the fruits of others' successful analysis, a format is no substitute for doing your own analysis of purpose and audience.

Standard formats help your audience, because they know what to expect and how to use the document.

Different organizations sometimes have their own standard formats for similar documents. For example, the classic Army staff study format — problem, facts, alternatives, solution, discussion — differs slightly from most business staff study formats — problem, solution, discussion, facts.

When formats are too detailed, they can do more harm than good, because they not only tell the author how to write, but also how to think.

Distinguish between formats, templates, and boilerplate.

Consider these three definitions from the *American Heritage Dictionary*:

Format A *plan* for the organization and *arrangement* of a specified production, the material form or *layout* of a publication

Template A pattern or gauge such as a thin metal plate with a cut pattern, used as a guide in making something *accurately,* as in woodworking

Boilerplate Journalistic materials, such as syndicated features, available in *plate or mat form*

Use a **format** as a recognizable *plan* or *arrangement* for the document. Use formats for writing situations that are similar but not identical. With a format, someone else has already done the analysis up to, but not including, the sentence outline.

Use a **template** to ensure *accuracy*. Applied to documents, templates are excellent tools for acquiring and organizing data. With a template, someone else has already done all the analysis, including the outline. You are not expected to provide ideas. All you do is fill in data. A fill-in-the-blank form is essentially a set of questions — inverted points. Templates work well for shorter, repetitive tasks such as scheduled reports.

Use **boilerplate** when text is already preset — *plate or mat form* — thereby taken as a whole and not revised. With boilerplate, someone else has already done all the analysis, including the outline, then written the supporting details and proofread the text. You use the text verbatim, refraining from using your judgment. For example, the Security and Exchange Commission requires as a matter of regulatory law that investment offerings include verbatim disclosures — boilerplate.

Within a format, you can have boilerplate and templated material. For example, a stock offering may use a format: concept, history of returns, and risks. The offering may use a template to show the history of returns, and the offering includes legal boilerplate.

Distinguish between the work system and the writing system.

Consider this definition from the *American Heritage Dictionary*:

System A *method, procedure*. Systematic: characterized by, based upon, or constituting a system; or a step-by-step procedure, characterized by purposeful regularity.

Any work that requires documentation employs two systems. You have a system — *a method or procedure* — for accomplishing the work, and you have the writing system. Unfortunately, people often confuse their work system with the writing system, often because many documents bear the name of the underlying work.

Work System	Documentation Name
Design a system	Detailed design
Plan a business	Business plan
Audit a business	Audit
Review a drug	Review

Although work systems differ significantly, the writing system remains the same for all documents. For example, an insurance investigator uses a system — perhaps a checklist — to inspect a factory. The checklist helps the investigator gather complete and accurate information. The inspector doesn't hand the underwriter the filled-in checklist; instead, the inspector uses the writing system to write a report. Work systems and the writing system often intersect during the analytical steps of the writing system, especially in the gathering information step.

Final exercise: This exercise is based on real events at one of the nation's top ten banks. Read the scenario and follow the instructions to write a sentence outline. (Answer A-18)

Today is October 20.

Universe Bank hired your company to implement a $3 million upgrade to the Universe Bank credit card transaction and billing system — VISA™ Card. You are the project manager.

Your contract states that you deploy a working system next February 20; then you have 45 days to make modifications to achieve all proposed capabilities.

When completed, the new system increases throughput from 17,500 to over 200,000 transactions per hour. The greater throughput reduces transaction costs, which saves Universe Bank up to $120,000 each month. Also, with the new system, the bank can exploit new markets and increase the size of its credit card business by a multiple of 15.

Excited about the immediate potential savings and impressed with your progress, senior bank management asks you by means of internal memo to accelerate deployment of the system no later than November 20, to "take advantage of the heavy Holiday sales volume."

Your senior engineer tells you that the project is on schedule for the February delivery, but in its present condition, the system still has some minor interface problems that can slow down or crash the system. The new system is a complex integration of commercial-off-the-shelf packages with an Orion database and your company's proprietary user interface. You have only two engineers who have experience on a project this complex. Your technical staff cannot accelerate delivery unless they take short cuts on bench-testing the software. Even then, they expect that the new BankCard system needs the 45-day shakedown specified in the contract to work out unanticipated problems.

You think the Holiday season is the worst possible time to install, then "debug" a new, therefore, unstable BankCard system. In fact, you contracted for the original deployment date because of the low retail sales in February. Your engineer estimates that the new system might crash often enough to be off line as much as four hours per day. Also, the unstable system may operate much slower than expected. You estimate that Universe Bank might suffer $1.3 million or more in lost revenue. In addition the bank may lose customers. The bank's retail merchants live or die on their Holiday retail trade. The bank's reputation may also suffer. You know that your own company's reputation will suffer also if the acceleration fails.

Your direct bank point-of-contact is the bank's Information Systems (IS) manager, who agrees with your objections to accelerating system deployment.

You decide to write a letter to state your position about the proposed acceleration.

1. Fill in the chart as you analyze purposes and audiences. Consider the needs of the IS manager and senior bank management.

Audience	Universe Bank's IS manager	Universe Bank's senior management
What audience does with the info		
What audience needs to know		
Audience's level of knowledge		
Audience believes you or wants proof		

2. Plan how to partition the subject matter to accommodate each audience. Consider separate documents, sections, and front and back matter.

3. Write purpose statements for each audience.

| Actor | Action | Audience | Topic | Outcome |

| Actor | Action | Audience | Topic | Outcome |

4. Write a sentence outline for the senior bank management audience. Write points, eliminate irrelevancies and redundancies, check for omissions, then put points in effective order.

Writing Phase

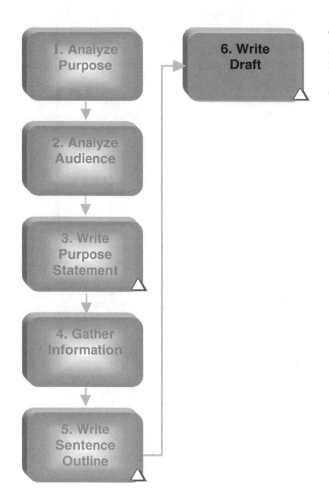

1. Analyze Purpose

2. Analyze Audience

3. Write Purpose Statement

4. Gather Information

5. Write Sentence Outline

6. Write Draft

The writing phase relies on your composing skills as you develop your sentence outline into paragraphs. You use your gathered information as supporting detail.

Discussion

Most writers fall into one of three categories:

- *Sprinters* write the draft disregarding word choice, grammar, punctuation, or mechanics, and they do not stop to analyze content.

- *Plodders* think of a point, write the corresponding paragraph, then edit the paragraph. Plodders combine analytical, composition, and editing skills as they move from paragraph to paragraph.

- *Bleeders* analyze, write, and edit each sentence, making sure they have a Pulitzer Prize-winning sentence before moving on to the next.

Plodders and bleeders waste time and energy shuffling between skill sets. And after finishing the draft, even the bleeder must revise, edit, check for correctness, then proofread.

If you're a plodder or a bleeder, resolve to become a sprinter. You can increase your writing speed by as much as 50 percent.

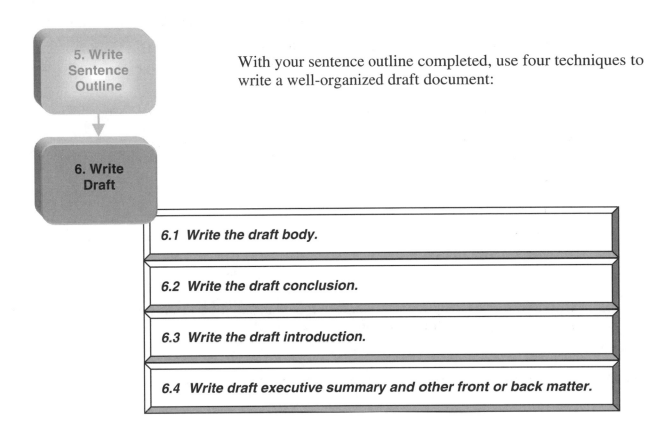

With your sentence outline completed, use four techniques to write a well-organized draft document:

5. Write Sentence Outline

6. Write Draft

6.1 Write the draft body.

6.2 Write the draft conclusion.

6.3 Write the draft introduction.

6.4 Write draft executive summary and other front or back matter.

Discussion

Having finished analysis, you are ready to write your draft. You can write your draft quickly, because you have a good sense of purpose and audience. You have your plan to accommodate multiple audiences, which makes your writing project a set of manageable tasks. You have pertinent information and a complete sentence outline of relevant and supported points.

Transcribe your purpose statement and sentence outline into your wordprocessor. Then write your draft as if you were speaking extemporaneously to the points in your sentence outline. You write the body first, then the conclusion, then the introduction.

Your sentence outline increases your writing speed two ways:

1. With your thoughts organized in an outline, you can compose with almost the same ease as giving a briefing, using talking points on a viewgraph.

2. With an outline, you can return from breaks and begin efficiently with the next point in your outline. Without an outline, you must re-read your draft to your stopping point before you can resume. Most writers cannot resist editing as they re-read their draft.

Most wordprocessors have tools to check spelling and grammar, often with an optional setting to make corrections while you type. *Do not use these tools while you type your draft. Also, disable annoying autocorrect settings.* These tools distract you by pestering you to correct insignificant or non-existing problems, when you need to concentrate on writing your thoughts. Use tools to check grammar and spelling later, when you edit for correctness.

Technique 6.1   Write the draft body.

Tips   Practice these seven tips to sprint through your draft:

1. Put yourself in a good environment — quiet, well lit, and physically comfortable.

2. Get information down in the first words that come to mind. Use short words and short sentences. Disregard word choice, grammar, punctuation, and mechanics.

3. Write the details to support each point in your sentence outline. You can cut details later when you have the whole picture.

4. Use personal shorthand to get information down as quickly as possible. Use brackets to mark [questionable words or facts]. Come back and fill in later.

5. Write the body first, then the conclusion, and the introduction last.

6. Take short ten-minute breaks every hour.

7. Select your tools to make the job easier. Use a keyboard or paper, whichever works best for you. Disable any wordprocessor tools that distract.

Warning   Don't permit interruptions — you lose thoughts and time. Don't use your dictionary or thesaurus. Don't edit before you finish the draft.

See also   Analyze audience; purpose statement; gather information; sentence outline.

Discussion

Many writers complain of writer's block — staring at the screen or paper. Writers who skip analysis of purpose and audience, skip writing a purpose statement, or skip the sentence outline often suffer writer's block. In fact, their problem is really *analyst's block*. Recognize these five sources of writer's block and apply the corresponding remedies.

1. *Lack of well-defined purpose.* You find yourself asking, "Why am I writing this?" You need to re-analyze purpose.

2. *Poor knowledge of audience.* You find yourself trying to write to multiple audiences at once, an impossible task. You need to analyze audience, write a purpose statement, then organize your content for your primary audience.

3. *Lack of information; nothing to say.* You don't have a sentence outline made of points. If you lack enough information for a sentence outline, you need to gather information, and if you can't determine what information to gather, you must backtrack to purpose statement.

4. *Lack of confidence.* You don't know why you're writing, or to whom, or how they use the document, their level of sophistication, or their need for proof. Therefore, you don't know what to say. Go back to analyzing purpose, and work through the purpose statement to a sentence outline.

5. *Fatigue.* You're pleased with your efforts so far, but you're too tired to pick up a pencil. Take a break.

If you suffer writer's block, STOP writing. Do not waste time trying to write through writer's block. If you attempt brute force, you'll write the wrong message to the wrong audience for the wrong reasons. If you are tired, rest. Otherwise, identify the analytical problem. Go backward through the analytical techniques to solve the problem. Then come forward to resume the writing phase.

To help reduce blocks caused by writer's fatigue, use the writing process to allocate time. If you try to cram a four-day writing project into two days, you get tired, and quality suffers.

Example In the following draft, the writer sprinted through the memo using the purpose statement and sentence outline from the example on page 48.

Note that the draft has spelling and mechanical errors. The author is not sure if the figure 20 percent is correct, but rather than stop, the author puts the figure in brackets. The style needs some work. Also note that the subject line comes from key words in the purpose statement.

Memorandum

TO: BAP, Inc. Plant #2 Employees
FR: Mr. Smith, Plant Manager
Subject: Changes in the cafeteria hours and services

This memo announces to all employees changes in the cafeteria hours and services. Please plan your lunch breaks accordingly.

(Write the rest of the introduction last.)

We shortened the cafeteria's hours to 12:00 p.m. — 2:00 p.m. In the past, fewer than five percent of all patrons used the cafeteria after 2:00 p.m.

We augmented service two ways to handle increased volume. Our more eficient facility and staff can easily feed twice as many people in less time. You can spend more time enjoying your meal and less time in line.

Frist, we expanded the cafeteria's dining area. We added 2,200 square feet of indoor dining plus a patio with seating for 50 patrons. Using the savings of shorter hours, we added a salad bar, pizza by the slice, and a grill to our exisitng food offerings. We also added a self-service drink station.

Second, we plan to increase the cafeteria staff. We will augment our food preparation and serving staff, but we plan to keep the cleaning staff the same size. Therfore, we still ask all patrons to bus their own trays.

The changes allow us to keep costs down and increase service during peak demand. The alternative is to raise prices by as much as [20 percent check figure]. In our survey, cost cutting measures were strongly preferred to pirce increases.

We regret any inconvenience caused by the shortened hours. Our goal is to provide you execellent value for your food dollar. We are pleased to announce that our food prices will remain the same for the next year.

(Write the conclusion next.)

Technique 6.2   *Write the draft conclusion.*

Tip   In the draft conclusion, tell the audience *what happens next.*

Warning   Do not end business and technical papers with the summary of findings.

            Do not simply stop and thereby leave the audience guessing *what happens next.*

Example   Business documents conclude with *what happens next:*

Memo	Please call if you have any questions.
Sales letter	I'll call you in a week to answer any questions you may have.
Proposal letter	We look forward to working with you.
General design	When approved by the client, this general design provides the basis for the detailed specifications.
User manual	By using your *My Account* software, you can start saving money today.

See also   Analyze audience; purpose statement; gather information; sentence outline.

Discussion

Make your conclusion as specific as possible. The expression, *Your help in any way . . .* begs to be ignored. Instead write, *Please correct my account and send me an accurate W-2 form before January 30.*

You do not outline the conclusion, because the conclusion follows the simple format: *what happens next.*

In academic writing, the paper often ends with a summary of key findings. However, in business and technical documents, any summary of key findings goes in the executive summary. In business and technical documents the conclusion is simply *what happens next.*

Your conclusion — *what happens next* — usually mirrors the purpose statement, specifically the outcome or what the audience does with the information. For example, compare the purpose statement and conclusion below:

     Purpose statement: This message informs you of my itinerary so we can schedule a meeting.
     Conclusion: Please inform me by return email the time and place of the meeting.

Exercise: Match the following purpose statements with corresponding conclusions. (Answer A-19)

1. This memo announces to all employees changes in the cafeteria hours and services. Please plan your lunch breaks accordingly.

   a. If you qualify, we will contact you directly to arrange an interview.

2. This letter alerts Universal Bank management of the serious business risks of accelerating deployment of the Visa system, so management can decide when to rollout the new system.

   b. Upon completing the database, be sure to send the new record and field layouts to the testing team.

3. This staff study details for the board of directors *the business climate, the transportation network, and the living environment* for building a can manufacturing plant in Tuscaloosa, Alabama. The board must decide where to locate the new plant.

   c. We look forward to serving you.

4. Attention animal lovers! We welcome prospective employees to our web site. Learn about *Pet Arama*, and determine if you want a future with us. Plus you can follow five simple steps to apply online.

   d. To learn more about the legal or employee benefits of job sharing, please contact Human Resources at the BAP Northeast Office in Tyson's Corner, Virginia.

5. This guide provides you, the new owner of a Megawheel plastic tricycle, simple step-by-step assembly instructions, so you can quickly put your little tyke on his Megawheel trike.

   e. The site-selection committee looks forward to your decision.

6. This section describes the data inputs and conversion algorithms to the operators who build the new taxpayers database.

   f. If you decide to accelerate the rollout of the system to November, we must renegotiate our contract with you immediately. Otherwise, we shall proceed with the original schedule.

7. This article describes for BAP's regional managers how the BAP Northeast Region recently implemented a successful pilot program for job sharing. Managers can see if job sharing can help your region attract and keep qualified employees.

   g. Now, you and your child can enjoy hours of fun, but remember to ride safely, and always wear a helmet.

Technique 6.3   *Write the draft introduction.*

Tip 1   Include two parts in your introduction: purpose statement and the organization of your document.

Feature your purpose statement at the beginning of your introduction.

Briefly state the organization of your document. If your purpose statement adequately states the organization, don't repeat it.

Warning   Do not provide background before you introduce the document's purpose and organization.

Example   This pamphlet (actor) tells (action) students (audience) how to (outcome) apply for a First Thrift auto loan (topic). You learn about eligibility, insurance requirements, rates, and responsibilities (organization of the document).

This proposal letter provides ACME Printers the features, benefits, and costs of our automated production management tool, Poly-Job, so you can decide whether to invest in this resource-saving tool. (The phrase *features, benefits, and costs* adequately states the organization,)

See also   Purpose statement; sentence outline; letters, memos, and email.

Discussion

All documents need an introduction, even if just one sentence. *Remember, the introduction primarily introduces the document itself, not the underlying subject, references, or author.*

Always write the introduction last. People who write the introduction first tend to use the introduction to collect their thoughts. Consequently, the introduction gets cluttered with information that the audience doesn't need to know or information that reappears in the body.

Recall your purpose statement. You used it to focus yourself; now use it to focus your audience. By placing the purpose statement as the first sentence of your introduction, readers know immediately if they need to read the document, because they learn these five key facts about the document:

1. what kind of document they have
2. what the document does
3. if they are in the target audience
4. what the topic is
5. what they can do with the information

In addition, the purpose statement sets your document's tone.

Next, the audience needs to know the organization of the document. Your audience can concentrate on either content or organization of the content, but not both at the same time. Disclose the organization first, then follow with content.

When telling your audience how you organized your document, mention the natural patterns and any standard business format that you used. *This fact sheet (standard business format) compares (natural pattern) cost and benefit . . . .*

In shorter documents, the topic portion of the purpose statement often states the organization of the document. For example, if the topic is *the benefits and costs of building the system,* you organize your document by discussing *benefits*, then *costs*.

Exercise: Critique the following introductions. Identify any essential elements missing. (Answer A-20)

1. An inspection of Buck Fever Labs was conducted in Bristol, Virginia. During the inspection, violations of the Clear Air Act Sec 520(f) were discovered. In addition to the violations, other questionable practices and safety deficiencies are noted.

2. This guide describes how you install the new operating system Doorframe 2001. Anyone can follow these simple instructions. You need a CD-ROM drive.

3. Small business owners — Medical Savings Accounts (MSA) may be the answer to your health insurance needs. In this short brochure we summarize
   - how MSAs work
   - the economics of MSAs
   - the legal issues of MSAs
   - where to find more information about MSAs

4. The SEPO air filter is used to maintain air purity in many "clean rooms" involved in the manufacture of computer chips. The Occupational Insurers Association (OIA) believes the same filtration system can improve the health of office workers, and they want to see if the SEPO system can be cost effective in conventional office buildings. Therefore, Busard Engineering was tasked to predict the mean failure rate of the SEPO air filter used for office building air conditioning systems. In the course of the tests, wc gathered field data from commercial sites in 50 cities located throughout the continental United States.

5. This user guide describes the five simple steps to change your greeting on your voicemail.

6. This proposal describes how we can launch Collector's, Inc. into e-commerce. If you engage us to build your e-commerce site, you can begin reaching a worldwide market within 90 days. In section one, we detail our experience and qualifications. In section two, we explain the e-commerce business process for your kind of business. In section three, we explain our technical solution. Section four is our management and quality assurance plan. Section five describes our follow-on support. We provide the cost proposal under separate cover.

7. Reference is made to your complaint letter you sent August 25. The defect you cite, "The LED on the clock face is stuck at 12:00" is easily remedied. When we package our clocks, we put a clear plastic tape over the face with black ink characters: 12:00. In that manner, prospective customers can see what the clock face looks like even when the clock is in the box on the store shelf.

8. This guide provides you, the new owner of a Megawheel plastic tricycle, simple step-by-step assembly instructions, so you can quickly put your little tyke on his Megawheel trike.

Tip 2   To help your audience, add any or all of these five parts of an introduction:

1. **Background** — discuss the underlying work, significance of the topic, or the situation addressed in the body.

2. **Audience** — provide further details or make assumptions about the target audience such as *In this manual we assume the user has a working knowledge of cost accounting and is familiar with Windows 98.*

3. **Sources and research methods** — mention how you acquired your information for your professional article or research document; cite references.

4. **Key terms** — define key terms that the audience must know to continue; however, do not put a glossary in the introduction.

5. **Limitations of the document** — describe the limitations that the audience needs to know such as *We researched only Fortune 100 companies to focus our research on large employers.* You are more persuasive when you state the limitation and overcome it, rather than end your argument with the limitation.

Warning   Do not begin your introduction with background. Without a purpose statement, background is irrelevant.

Do not confuse an introduction with a summary of your document. Summaries go in the executive summary or abstract.

Do not put your recommendation in the introduction. Your recommendation belongs in the body.

Do not begin correspondence with *This letter is in reference to . . . .*

Example   See the introduction to this book (page 1).

See also   Analyze audience; purpose statement; sentence outline.

Discussion

If your audience has a high level of knowledge and does not require proof, you can often limit your introduction to just the purpose statement and organization. Many shorter documents or sections of documents need just one-sentence introductions.

The introduction is a useful place to make a point that is irrelevant to the body, but which you want to make anyway. For example, in a sales letter you make this irrelevant but charming point in the introduction: *I thoroughly enjoyed meeting you and visiting your delightful city. Omaha is lovely!*

When writing background-through-limitations, you may use any order, although typically background comes immediately after organization. Also, do not necessarily treat each part as a separate paragraph.

Templated introductions can mislead. Often templates have headings such as *Purpose* and *Scope*, but purpose and scope of *what?* Purpose of document equates to our purpose statement. Purpose of work equates to background. Scope of the document equates to organization or possibly limitations. Scope of work equates to background.

Exercise: This introduction lacks one of the seven parts. Identify the six parts it has and the one missing. (Answer A-20)

Introduction to the Executive Support Manual

This manual has been designed specifically for Executive Support Personnel in the Product Support area of BAP, Inc. This manual assumes that the reader has a working knowledge of the AutoGraphics and Slide Presentation system in the VAX environment, or at least has access to appropriate manuals or knowledgeable persons on these subjects. Furthermore, it is most helpful if the Executive Support person has experience with Oracle software and at least a cursory knowledge of generic graphics. If not, consult the manuals available in the Product Services library.

Each month, company executives view a set of charts, or slides, which have more current information than those of the previous month. Basically, the new data comes in and is checked, then slides are generated, based on the updated data, and are checked. Next, the slides are indexed and organized into specific groups. Then the entire package is released for executive viewing. There are many other small steps involved, and the sheer volume of slides keeps the Executive Support person busy.

The next page displays the optimum flowchart layout of the monthly cycle. Each step has a corresponding chapter. Follow the cycle each month and refer to the appropriate chapter as you work through this manual.

In the text, anything you type is framed by double quotes (" . . . "). Do not type the quotes, merely type everything in between them. Syntax is important. The set of characters <<ENTER>> stands for Enter key above the Right Shift key on your keyboard. FDBA stands for Functional Database Administrator.

1. Purpose statement:

2. Organization of document:

3. Background and significance of topic:

4. Description of target audience:

5. Information sources and research methods:

6. Definitions of key terms:

7. Limitations of the document:

Are any parts out of order?

Technique 6.4   Write draft executive summary and other front and back matter.

Tip 1   Include four parts in an executive summary in this order:

1. purpose statement
2. recommendation
3. key findings
4. what happens next

Warning   Do not confuse the executive summary with the introduction. Executive summaries do not include background. Introductions do not include a summary of the key findings.

Example   Short executive summary:

This amended business plan describes the alternative of building a new fulfillment warehouse for the Board of Directors' consideration. The planning committee recommends building a new warehouse as part of the factory. Further, they suggest building a pair of loading docks: one facing north, the other south. Demolishing the old warehouse and adding the new one next to our factory extends the completion date 100 days and adds $2.32 million in costs. The committee calculates payback from smoother operations in less than three years. The Board of Directors must approve the amended business plan.

See also   Purpose statement; sentence outline; introductions.

Discussion

Not all documents need an executive summary. As front matter, the executive summary comes before the introduction. An executive summary serves managers by highlighting recommendations, key points, and next steps while ignoring most technical details.

Mostly likely, you've already written the parts of the executive summary. Often, the executive summary's purpose statement is the same as the introduction's purpose statement. Likewise, you've already written a recommendation in the core document. Your key findings come directly from your sentence outline, and *what happens next* is the conclusion that you've written.

Executive summaries are short — ½ to 1 page. Usually, the purpose statement, recommendation, and *what happens next* are each one sentence long. The number of key findings varies. Simply transcribe these sentences into your executive summary. Select the "best of" key findings from your outline, those findings that concern the executive. Resist adding comments or background. Managers who want more information about a key finding can look in the core document.

Large proposals usually have a section titled executive summary, much longer than the one-page format we describe. In a proposal, the executive summary section does much more than summarize. Instead, the section acts like the closing argument, reminding the prospective buyer *why* they need to hire *you*.

Example Recall the scenario with the Visa Card system acceleration at Universe Bank on page 54. If you need to write an executive summary, you need only assemble the following parts that you have already written.

Purpose statement:
The letter alerts Universal Bank management of the serious business risks of accelerating deployment of the Visa system, so management can decide when to deploy the new system.

Recommendation:
We recommend you stay with the original schedule to avoid business risks.

Key findings from your sentence outline:
The business risks outweigh the potential gains.
Acceleration may cause a loss of $1.3 million in revenue.
You might lose customers if we accelerate deployment.
You might hurt your reputation.
To accelerate, we must modify the contract and increase our fees.

What happens next:
If you decide to accelerate deploying the system to November, we must renegotiate our contract with you immediately. Otherwise, we shall proceed with the original schedule.

Having assembled the parts, you simply transcribe them into the following paragraphs:

Executive Summary

The letter alerts Universal Bank management of the serious business risks of accelerating deployment of the Visa system, so management can decide when to deploy the new system.

We recommend you stay with the original schedule to avoid technical and business risks. The business risks outweigh the potential gains. Acceleration may cause a loss of $1.3 million in revenue. You might lose customers if we accelerate deployment. You might hurt your reputation. To accelerate we must modify the contract and increase our fees.

If you decide to accelerate the rollout of the system to November, we must renegotiate our contract with you immediately. Otherwise, we shall proceed with the original schedule.

Tip 2   Include five parts in an informative abstract in this order:

1. topic — what did we study?
2. significance of the topic — why did we study it?
3. sources and methods — how did we study it?
4. key findings — what did we learn?
5. conclusion — what can we conclude?

Warning   Do not confuse the abstract with the introduction or executive summary.

Do not write a digest (short version of your document) and call it an abstract.

Example   Short abstract:

This paper answers criticisms against the 18-ton payload single-stage-to-orbit (SSTO) launch vehicle in contrast to the 163-ton payload National Launch Vehicle supported by NASA planners. Likewise this paper discusses space policy priorities and examines the immediate and long-term economic payback of both launch vehicle designs.

See also   Introductions.

Discussion

Not all documents need an abstract or executive summary, but may have one or both, plus the introduction. You write each part — introduction, executive summary, and abstract — as if the others did not exist.

An abstract serves experts who want an overview of key technical points: purpose, methods, and findings. Experts often use abstracts when researching. Many abstracts get put into databases that allow a key-word search. Typically, abstracts use jargon and assume knowledge of advanced concepts, whereas executive summaries use plain language.

Recently, some professional journals, particularly medical journals, have started changing the order of the abstract, moving the conclusion to the front. If you are writing an article for a journal be sure to study the journal's format. Their format takes precedence over our technique.

Exercise: Which of the following two passages is an abstract, and which is an executive summary? How can you tell? (Answer A-21)

Quazel Prion in Armadillidium*

This paper examines the reaction of the Quazel prion (QP) on crustaceans of the species armadillidium. QP strengthens cytoplasm, theoretically making cells more resistant to disease and aging. At the Yuseat Laboratory, half the armadillidium were injected with QP. Subgroups were later exposed to various parasites, yeast, bacteria, and viruses. The QP-treated armadillidium showed significant resistance compared to the untreated control group. However, the treated armadillidium eventually suffered rapid morbidity when the QP-affected cytoplasm crystallized. The experiment shows that although QP prevents disease, QP cannot prevent aging. Therefore, QP must remained a controlled substance until science can provide a corresponding enzyme to control effect of Quazel hardening.

Extending Life with Quazel Proteins

This report describes the Yuseat Laboratory findings of a self-replicating protein, Quazel, to strengthen cell membranes and slow aging, so Jod management can decide whether to extend the research effort. We recommend that Jod purchase the rights to manufacture Quazel, then invest in Yuseat's research to find the corresponding enzyme necessary to market Quazel. Lab results proved that Quazel makes organisms resistant to most disease. Quazel protein also appears to correct certain genetic defects. Quazel-treated pill bugs were more vigorous than the control group. However, as protein finished replicating, cell membranes became brittle and the pill bugs died more quickly than the control group. The body does not have an enzyme to manage the Quazel protein. Yuseat Laboratory proposes a series of studies to find the enzyme in nature. After finding the enzyme, they may be able to replicate it. Yuseat Laboratory will send a research proposal under separate cover.

*Adapted from the science fiction novel *Tenebrea's Hope*. Roxann Dawson and Daniel Graham: Pocket Books, New York, 2001.

Post-writing Phase

The post-writing phase includes all the work you do after writing the draft. Be systematic. Use your editing skills to evaluate and revise content and organization. Then edit for coherence, clarity, economy, and readability. Finally, check for correctness and proofread.

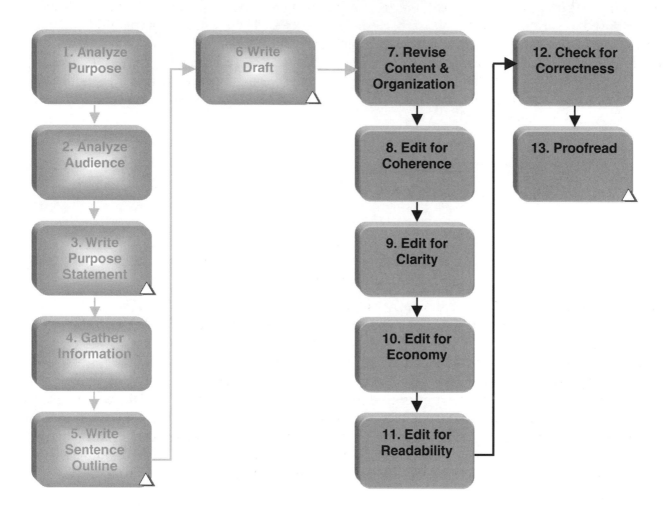

Discussion
You are the best person to revise and edit your draft. Who else is as qualified to evaluate content and organization?
When you edit your document, do not try to apply all the techniques as you make one pass. Instead, make many editing passes at your document, focusing on one or two techniques per pass.

Step 7. Revise Content and Organization

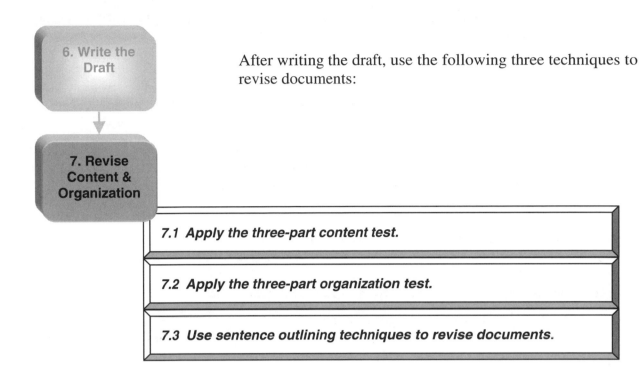

After writing the draft, use the following three techniques to revise documents:

7.1 Apply the three-part content test.

7.2 Apply the three-part organization test.

7.3 Use sentence outlining techniques to revise documents.

Discussion

Revision means re-seeing. Take a break after writing the draft to refresh and distance yourself from your writing. Work with a double-spaced paper copy of the draft so you have plenty of room to annotate. Recall the purpose statement and put yourself in the audience's place:

> What questions does the audience need answered?

> What organization suits the audience's needs?

The content and organization tests serve as major error traps. Note that with each part of each test, we recommend corrective action. When you ask others to review your draft, ask them to use the content and organization tests so you get precise feedback.

Revise your draft *before* you edit for style. Editing a document that has content and organization problems wastes time and effort.

Technique 7.1   Apply the three-part content test.

Tips   Apply the content test by answering three questions:

1. *Is the topic focused?* Does the document reveal its topic within the first two sentences? If not, use a purpose statement in the beginning to focus the topic for your audience.

2. *So what?* For each point in the document, ask "so what?" Does the audience care? If not, cut the irrelevant material or adjust the purpose statement to show the relevance.

3. *Adequately supported?* For each point that passes the "so what?" part of the test, do you provide adequate detail to support the point? Are your details clear? If not, you must gather more information or cut the unsupported points.

Warning   Do not prove every point if the audience is inclined to believe you.

Example   The poor version fails all three parts of the content test.

Poor: The building manager called to say that our parking garage has leaks. Therefore, he contracted a paving company to fix the leaks next Monday. Therefore, make other plans to park.

Good: This memo informs you that you can't park in our garage Monday. Please make other arrangements. Remove your vehicle from the garage by 8:00 p.m. Sunday. After needed maintenance, the garage re-opens 6:00 a.m. Tuesday.

See also   Analyze audience; purpose statement; gather information.

Discussion

You can effectively run the content test with one quick read of the document.

The pre-writing steps ensure that you pass the content test. The purpose statement forces you to state your topic at the beginning. Likewise, a sentence outline forces you to test your points against your purpose statement for relevance, thereby ensuring that you answer the *so what* question. Analysis of audience tells you how much supporting detail you need, including definitions of terms, examples, analogies, and pictures. The low-knowledge audience or the audience requiring proof needs more supporting detail than the high-knowledge audience or the audience inclined to believe.

The content test catches logical fallacies in your argument. To catch lies, you must add a fourth question: *Are the supporting details true?* The definition of *The Big Lie* — in George Orwell's famous book *1984* — is a statement that answers the *so what* question by offering compelling points, and seems to tell *how supported* by offering vivid details, except that those details are false. Orwell urges us to read critically to catch logical fallacies and lies, for which we need to know the facts.

In the absence of hard facts, the critical audience asks a fifth question: *Says who?* Here, we get into the realm of trust, respect, and authority. When you write as an expert to an audience inclined to believe, you expect the audience to accept your points with less supporting detail. Instead they rely on the strength of your word — *Who says? You say,* and often your word is proof enough.

Exercise: Apply the content test to this letter. Evaluate this letter as if you were the audience, a bank employee in customer service. Suggest ways to improve content. (Answer A-22)

1. Is the topic focused? Do the key words in the first two sentences make the topic clear? If not, suggest a purpose statement.

2. So what? Delete irrelevant points and details that fail the *so what?* part of the test.

3. Adequately supported? Suggest supporting details where a point needs more proof.

BAP Industries, Inc.
1 Liberty Plaza, McLean, VA 22036
(703) 555-1234

April 4, 2001

Washington National Bank
Customer Service
P. O. Box 12345
Washington, DC 20005

Dear Customer Service:

We have been doing business with your bank for more than ten years and this incident is our first cause for complaint that we have had in that time. We have substantial demand deposit, money market, sweep, and payroll accounts at the McLean branch.

We were shocked and dismayed to see a charge on our statement that we did not authorize. Enclosed please find a copy of our recent VISA bill. The transaction that I have circled is the transaction we are disputing. The date of the transaction was March 5th and the date it was posted was March 8th. The company was Greenspan & Co. in El Paso, Texas. I have never heard of this company before. The amount charged was $520.97.

I queried our accounts payable department. They have no idea where this bill has come from. We did not place an order with Greenspan & Co. We have a purchase order system and I would have known if I had approved any request involving Greenspan & Co. I didn't. It is possible that our number was mistakenly used or punched into Greenspan's computer. I personally know how easy it is to transpose numbers.

Your help in any way would be very appreciated in this matter.

Sincerely,

Dennis Smith
Accounts Payable Department
enc: VISA bill

Technique 7.2   Apply the three-part organization test.

Tips   Ensure that your message organizes the content in a way that helps the audience understand and respond. Apply the organization test by answering three questions:

1. Does the document read like a data dump? Does the document wander randomly from idea to idea? If so, you probably skipped sentence outlining and relied on stream-of-consciousness writing.

2. Does the document read like a story? Does the document present events, research, or ideas as they occurred to you? If so, you probably need to re-order your points in a way useful to the audience.

3. Is the document filled with *I, me, mine?* If so, you may be venting. You wrote your draft from *your* point of view — how the circumstances affect *you*, rather than how the circumstances affect the audience.

If your document fails one of these organization tests, go back to sentence outlining. You can take the pieces of your document that passed the content test and re-sort them as major and supporting points.

Warning   Do not go forward in the writing system until you identify and correct organization problems. Go back to analytical tools in the pre-writing phase to solve organization problems.

Example   Poor: I just received your notice of overpayment and a refund check. I wrote in April asking you to apply the money to my next bill. Obviously you didn't. I didn't want a refund. I can be reached at my business number if you have questions.

Good: Please apply this returned refund check to my next bill as I requested in my April letter.

See also   Sentence outline.

Discussion

You can effectively run the organization test with one quick read of the document.

Using a sentence outline practically guarantees that you pass the organization test.

Conversely, if you fail the organization test, you must use your sentence outlining techniques to revise the document.

Exercise: Joan Walters asks you to critique her letter. Apply the organization test by answering these three questions:

1. Does the document read like a data dump?
2. Does the document read like a story?
3. Is the document filled with *I*, *me*, and *mine*?

Give Joan specific advice how to improve her letter. (Answer A-22)

Joan Walters
123 Main Street, NE
Bethesda, MD 20010

February 1, 2001

Mr. Traver Stark
Vice President Government Sales
Aero Space, Inc.
1414 Vermont Ave.
Washington, DC 20016

Re: Internal Job Availability Notice B-22, Marketing Analyst/Proposal Specialist

Dear Mr. Stark:

I currently fill the position of an Administrative Assistant for the Government Business Development (GBD) Department at Acro Space. It is my desire to seek a position that would allow me to fully utilize my communication and organizational skills.

I was very excited to learn that a position has opened in the Marketing Department for Foreign Sales. This position appears to be perfectly tailored to my career goals at this time. It would afford me the opportunity to apply my knowledge of proposal preparation, and at the same time exercise my ability to coordinate projects and follow them through to completion.

As my resume indicates, my qualifications show that I am well experienced in this field. I have five years' experience in proposal preparation. In addition, my exposure to foreign languages, my desire to travel, and my experience in U.S. Government sales have prepared me for my next career move.

I look forward to meeting you to discuss my potential for securing this position.

Sincerely,

Joan Walters
enc: resume

Technique 7.3 Use sentence outlining techniques to revise documents.

Tips Use these six sentence outlining techniques to revise a document:

1. Pull major and minor points from the paragraphs: Write each point as a short sentence.
2. Analyze purpose and audience.
3. Write a purpose statement.
4. Add points you think are missing.
5. Compare points against your purpose statement to eliminate irrelevancies and redundancies.
6. Group, then sequence points the way the audience wants to see the information.

Warning Do not waste time trying to edit a poorly organized document. You can't edit your way out of an organization problem.

Example Points are often buried in the paragraph. Even worse, the points might be missing altogether. In this paragraph about a kitchen health inspection, we mark the point in italics:

Table surfaces were dirty. Walls had a sticky film of grease. The steam kettles had a ring of putrefied brown gravy. The grease in the deep-fat fryer was at least two weeks old. The refrigerator was too full and four degrees too warm. Many food containers indicated the contents were past the expiration date. The cook's uniforms had obviously been worn several days in a row. *These deficiencies alone warrant closing your restaurant.* The tile grout on the floors was green with algae.

See also Sentence outline; content and organization tests.

Discussion

We often get a writing assignment for which we inherit a poorly organized predecessor document or sample. For example, you receive a poorly organized general design from which you must write the detailed design. As you write your detailed design, do not mimic the poor organization of the general design. Pull out, evaluate, and re-sequence points from predecessor documents.

For example, your team leader tells you to write the corporate capabilities section of a proposal and hands you a copy of the last proposal to mimic. If the last proposal fails the content or organization tests, you must revise.

An astute audience can spot recycled documents quickly, and discounts your effort.

Exercise: Use sentence outlining techniques to revise this boilerplate letter. (Answer A-22)

You get tasked to send out the annual holiday season letter to suppliers, explaining your company's policy on gift giving. As a government contractor, you and your subcontractors must obey strict federal ethics laws about receiving and giving gifts. You dredge up last year's letter and apply six sentence outlining techniques.

Defense Industries, Inc.
1 Liberty Plaza, McLean, VA 22036
(703) 555-1234

December 1, 2001

To: Our Vendors

With the approach of the Holiday Season and the close of 2001, it is appropriate that we should write you and express our appreciation for the past performance of your company. Your attention to our purchasing contractual terms and conditions in the areas of product quality, reliability, and timely response to our requests is very much appreciated by all of us at Defense Industries.

It is not at all an uncommon practice for suppliers to express their appreciation to personnel in customer organizations by remembering them with a holiday gift. We have concluded, from both an ethical and a strictly business point of view, that anything more substantial than an advertising novelty, whose value is minimal, or a card expressing appreciation would be inappropriate. We hope that you will reach this same conclusion as one of our suppliers.

Our policy with respect to gifts is not intended to imply improper behavior on the part of our suppliers or employees. We are unaware that you or any of our suppliers violate any federal ethics guidelines.

However, we want to emphasize our wish that suppliers concentrate their expenditures on our behalf entirely on improving the quality of products and services they sell us. Another alternative would be a reduction of price.

Thank you for your cooperation in this and other matters within the scope of our business relationship, and our very best wishes to you for the Holiday Season and the New Year.

Sincerely,

Bob Cratchit
Accounting Manager

Final exercise: Apply the content and organization tests. Recommend ways to improve the letter. Work quickly — you need not spend much time running the tests. (Answer A-23)

TechtopIndustries, Inc.
1 Liberty Plaza, McLean, VA 22036
(703) 555-1234

May 12, 2001

General Warranty, Ltd.
Customer Service
P. O. Box 12345
Racine, WI 40105

Dear Customer Service Department:

On February 1 of this year, we asked for reimbursement for an alternator repair to our new company car, which we purchased through a dealer who sold us your extended warranty. (See attached letter.) Now as a result of the defective alternator, the company car's battery died and had to be replaced.

When the service center replaced my alternator, they had trouble recharging the battery. They suggested I keep the old battery for a while to see if it would hold a charge over a period of time. As it turned out, two weeks after the alternator was replaced, the battery died. Cold weather did not kill the battery. The battery died as a direct result of the previous defective alternator running it down over a period of time.

Unfortunately, the battery died at a most inopportune time. The company treasurer missed a flight to New York and consequently a meeting with our creditors, who did not readily accept the "dead battery excuse."

I realize that the battery is not specifically covered under our warranty, but because it died as a direct result of the malfunctioning alternator, I think it's only fair that you replace the battery. It was only 17 months old. We shouldn't have had alternator or battery problems in the first place. Please call me if you have any problems with this.

Sincerely,

Paul Jackson
Facilities Manager

Step 8. Edit for Coherence

7. Revise Content & Organization

8. Edit for Coherence

After you check content and organization, edit for coherence. Give verbal and visual cues that help your audience:

- skim your document
- follow your discussion
- refer back to your document

Use five techniques to edit for coherence:

8.1 Repeat key words throughout your document.

8.2 Ensure each paragraph begins with the point.

8.3 Use transition words to help the audience follow the logic.

8.4 Use vertical lists and tables to present series.

8.5 Apply visual devices.

Discussion

A document with zero coherence devices looks like one large, audience-unfriendly block paragraph. Coherence devices make documents easy to use.

Coherence devices work only when your document passes both the content and organization tests. The devices reinforce your logic for the audience. If your document suffers from irrelevant content or poor organization, coherence devices accentuate those flaws.

Remember that as your subject matter increases in technical difficulty, your audience needs more help from coherence devices.

Edit for coherence before you edit for clarity or economy. If audiences can't follow your thoughts, they can't go further — even if you excel in your other editing techniques. Editing for coherence helps you discover any gaps in logic as you emphasize your logical flow. Note that you have already written two important coherence devices: the purpose statement and the introduction.

Technique 8.1   Repeat key words throughout your document.

Tips   Keep titles short, using key words. Ensure that subheads express topics with consistent key words. Let key words stand out.

Add value with headings. Generic headings and subheadings like *Introduction, Purpose*, and *Conclusion* don't tell the audience much.

Tie graphics to your text with captions that use key words. Use headers and footers to help audiences keep track of their place in the document.

Warning   Do not shift key words. If you write about a *procedure*, don't shift to *process*, then *method, approach*, and *scheme* just for variety. If you shift words, the audience expects you had a real, not a stylistic motive.

Error Trap   Shifting words often indicate fuzzy thought. Re-apply the content test: *Is the topic focused?*

Example
Poor: **Data Requirements**
Accurate *information* collection is essential for maintaining the system. Each month, we gather the pertinent *facts* from the error logs and assemble the *data*. If we find patterns in the *content,* we report our *facts* and *findings* to the Change Management Group.

Good: **System maintenance requires accurate data collection**
Accurate data collection is essential for maintaining the system. Each month, we assemble the pertinent data from the error logs. If we find patterns in the data, we report our findings to the Change Management Group.

See also   Purpose statement; content test; concrete and specific words.

Discussion

In school, teachers told us to vary word choice. To avoid repeating words, we used a thesaurus and started looking for synonyms. Our teachers were wrong: Repeating key words is a virtue. Key word repetition is powerful. Recall Martin Luther King's *I have a Dream* speech. Now imagine if he had varied his word choice: *I have a dream, I have a theory, I have a premonition, I have a concept . . . .* Impress your audience with your specific and concrete detail, not your synonyms. When you shift key words, your writing becomes inconsistent, and consequently less coherent.

Keeping words consistent is more difficult when writing in a collaborative effort, especially for abstract topics such as computer applications. Whenever subject matter is abstract, technical writers must especially help the audience by keeping key words consistent.

Repeat key words in the subject line of letters and memos, in the purpose statement, and in the first sentence of each paragraph.

Subheads need to feature key words. Write your subheads using a subject and verb like newspaper headlines: *Sales forecast improves* or *Miracle drug introduced*. Repeat the subhead's key words in the first line of your next paragraph.

Use key words in the purpose statement or organization plan for your subheads. "This memo explains the *costs and benefits of leasing . . .*" The first subhead is *Costs of Leasing*. The second is *Benefits of Leasing*.

Exercise: Improve coherence by identifying shifting words and replacing them with consistent key words in these three excerpts. (Answer A-24)

Excerpt 1 — Regulatory letter

The violations cited on the Form FDA 483 and presented to your firm at the conclusion of the inspection are not all-inclusive of deficiencies at your company. It is your responsibility to ensure that your establishment adheres to all the requirements of the Federal Food, Drug, and Cosmetic Act. The specific violations of the law noted in this letter and the Form FDA 483 may be symptomatic of serious underlying problems in your corporate manufacturing and quality systems. The regulation requires you to investigate and determine the causes of the violations identified by FDA. You must promptly initiate corrective action to comply with federal standards.

Excerpt 2 — Deliverables for a training project

Telefona outsourced to Temp Staff, Inc. the task of augmenting Telefona's customer service department. Temp Staff's personnel will work under a new job title: Telefona Billing Consultants.

The Billing Consultants training program is divided into two phases. The initial step is to define the role and scope of the Billing Consultant. This step entails identification and hiring of qualified people to our staff. We train those new members and give them the tools required to fulfill the job description of Billing Consultant, before we let the consultants assume responsibilities at the client site.

The follow-up phase implements the job functions defined in the first step. This phase is heavily dependent on what is achieved in the first step and can therefore not be presented in detail at that stage. After placing our trained staff as Billing Consultants into the client environment, we monitor their performance at the client's customer service department. This second step will be performed by our technicians and Telefona.

We propose that in two years, we initiate a third phase wherein we teach Telefona's Billing staff to take on the role of the Billing Consultant. Our people provide the training and quality reviews.

Excerpt 3 — Requirements document

The Office of Public Works needs to implement a fax solution that enables employees to send and receive faxes from and to their computer workstations. Public Works also wants workers to be able to share faxes among peers electronically.

We can use one of the two broad methods of implementing PC-based fax capabilities in mid-sized offices given our moderate fax volume. The table below illustrates the two approaches and their pro's and con's:

Method	*Advantages*	*Disadvantages*
Dedicated Modem	Provides flexibility Handles large fax traffic	No central control Very expensive
Fax Servers	Provides central control Shares resources	Requires dedicated PC server Increases network traffic

Because of the expense associated with providing a fax modem per user, we do not recommend that course of action, but prefer the server solution.

Technique 8.2   *Ensure each paragraph begins with the point.*

Tip 1   Check each paragraph to be sure you make your point — *and only one point* — in the first sentence.

Make all other sentences logically develop the point.

Use the last sentence in your paragraph to summarize, draw conclusions, or transition to the next paragraph's point.

Warning   Do not bury the point in the middle of the paragraph, or omit it altogether, forcing the audience to infer the correct meaning.

Do not lead up to the point and place it at the end of the paragraph.

Error Trap   If key words do not appear in the first sentence of the paragraph, your paragraph probably does not begin with the point.

Example   Poor: Based on a survey of 10 years' data from 20 countries for children ages 6 to 14 in both rural and urban environments, the committee's findings are statistically significant. (Which of the five points does the paragraph expand?)

Good: The committee's findings are statistically significant.

See also   Sentence outline; content test.

Discussion

Your sentence outline provides key points to develop into paragraphs. Consequently, your audience can skim your discussion by reading the first sentence of each paragraph.

Also, make your point in a short sentence. If you begin with a compound sentence, you have at least two thoughts. Your audience must guess which of the thoughts you intend to develop in the paragraph. Break your compound sentence into a simple sentence, and put the point of the paragraph first.

One can almost inspect a document — *without reading for content* — to see if the author used a sentence outline. If paragraphs begin with long sentences, the author probably did not use an outline.

A paragraph is easier to follow when we know the point. In logically developed paragraphs, each sentence progresses purposefully to the next. However, we can follow the progression only when we know the point.

In rare cases, as a persuasive strategy for a *hostile expert* audience, you might want to lead your audience through your facts before getting to the point of the paragraph. Then you put your point at the end of the paragraph.

Exercise: The first sentence tells the audience the point of the paragraph. A coherent paragraph puts the key point first for emphasis, then logically develops it with following sentences. Why are these paragraphs incoherent? (Answer A-25)

Paragraph 1

The hardware required for the upgrade includes three Amiga® CPUs, each with an extra 256 megabytes of RAM. Peripherals include more than 200 gigs of hard drive. You get one 18-inch flat screen and three high-speed read-writable CD-ROM drives. Including cables and couplings, the cost of the hardware is $18,625. The off-the-shelf security software costs $495 including our discount. Our fee for setting up the system, writing the software patches, building user-friendly screens, and training your staff is $8,200. Therefore, your total investment in the upgrade is $27,320. With this bid, you also get one year of on-site maintenance and a one-year warranty on the hardware we install.

Paragraph 2

The violations cited on the Form FDA 483 and presented to your firm at the conclusion of the inspection are not all-inclusive of deficiencies at your firm. It is your responsibility to ensure that your firm adheres to all the requirements of the Federal Food, Drug, and Cosmetic Act. The specific violations of the Act noted in this letter and the Form FDA 483 may be symptomatic of serious underlying deficiencies in your firm's manufacturing and quality systems. The Act requires you to investigate and determine the causes of the violations identified by FDA. You must promptly initiate corrective action to comply with the Act.

Paragraph 3

When a Universe BankCard credit card customer requests termination of his or her account, the Customer Service Representative (CS) responds by either closing the customer's account or referring the customer to the Customer Retention (CR) department. The CS first determines if the customer is profitable and worth saving. The CS flags the ATTEMPT_SAVE field to indicate to CR that the customer is profitable and worth saving. If the account is profitable and the call is taken during CR's operating hours, the CS transfers the call to CR. If CR is closed, the CS attempts to save the account by explaining the benefits of the Universe BankCard and possibly offering a lower interest rate or eliminating the annual fee. If the account is not profitable, the CS closes the account and makes appropriate monetary adjustments.

Tip 2   Use short paragraphs to emphasize important points, and use long paragraphs to elaborate on those points.

Use key words as a clue when deciding where to break overly long paragraphs.

Warning   Avoid paragraphs longer than 15 lines, and limit one-sentence paragraphs.

Example   We note the repeating key words in italics.

Poor: Thank you for sending me *material* about business writing. I already shared the *material* with NACA Studios employees who indicate an interest in attending one of your workshops. I will call you this week to set the agenda for our *meeting* scheduled next Friday, March 8, 2002. However, based on the information you sent us, we may be able to make a quick decision to schedule training and thereby forgo the *meeting*. I enclosed the results of our internal *needs assessment*. You'll be pleased to see that writing training demand ranks third for employees and second for managers. Please treat our *needs assessment* data as proprietary.

Good: Thank you for sending me *material* about business writing. I already shared the *material* with NACA Studios employees who indicate an interest in attending one of your workshops.

I will call you this week to set the agenda for our *meeting* scheduled next Friday, March 8, 2002. However, based on the information you sent us, we may be able to make a quick decision to schedule training and thereby forgo the *meeting*.

I enclosed the results of our internal *needs assessment*. You'll be pleased to see that writing training demand ranks third for employees and second for managers. Please treat our *needs assessment* data as proprietary.

See also   Audience.

Discussion

A combination of short and long paragraphs keeps the audience's interest. For 8½"x11" paper, keep your paragraphs less than 15 lines long. Use shifts in thought as a chance to break long paragraphs. Your audience can process only so much information at once.

Too many short paragraphs seem choppy. Too many long paragraphs seem dense. Our eyes naturally go to short paragraphs, so put your most important points in the short paragraphs. However, remember that if you have too many short paragraphs, none of them attract attention.

Business letters often use a short initial paragraph, using the purpose statement to grab attention. They shift to longer paragraphs to explain and expand details. Then they close with a short paragraph calling for action.

A one-sentence paragraph states a point but does not develop it. You may occasionally use a one-sentence paragraph for emphasis, but the point must stand by itself.

Exercise: Break these long paragraphs into shorter paragraphs. Look at the repetition of key words as a clue to paragraph structure. (Answer A-26)

1. ARNEWS is the bimonthly newsletter of the Chief, Army Reserve. The Public Affairs office publishes the contents, current events in the Army Reserve. In addition, Public Affairs maintains the mailing list for ARNEWS's subscribers. To create an edition of ARNEWS, the Public Affairs office collects the articles that comprise the newsletter. Articles come from sources within the Army Reserve as well as outside sources contributing for publication. Public Affairs edits the articles and desktop publishes a camera-ready copy of the newsletter. To create a mailing list for ARNEWS distribution, Public Affairs downloads from its membership database an ASCII file containing name, address, zipcode, and member ID. The ASCII file has one record for each line, followed by a page break. The record fields are delimited by commas. Public Affairs sends the camera-ready copy of the newsletter and a 16 BPI tape of the mailing list to the publisher. In turn, the publisher prints the newsletter, creates and affixes Cheshire labels, then mails the newsletter.

2. Acidic and basic cleaners were successful during preliminary testing. We needed to establish an allowable pH range for dense-pack ceramic membranes. The approach for establishing the pH range was to use hydrochloric acid and sodium hydroxide with the appropriate buffer to determine the extreme pH thresholds. These thresholds serve as the endpoints for an allowable pH range as long as the membrane passed the skim milk test. Our pH testing did not establish a pH range for any particular cleaner, but rather set a guideline. Most acidic or basic cleaning solutions exist within a pH range defined as *mild* or *strong*. However, some confusion came from the use of bleach during the tests. The skim milk test requires the use of bleach plus a non-ionic detergent to remove milk from the pores of the membrane. Bleach was also considered as a possible cleaner for membrane restoration. The chemical effects of bleach on the membrane were unknown prior to testing. Therefore, bleach and the non-ionic detergent were added to sodium hydroxide to find a basic pH threshold. We assumed that if the membrane passed the skim milk test with the bleach in the test solution, then any future failure was not due to the bleach, but from pH. Unfortunately, bleach dissociates into two different ions in solution: the hypochlorous ion (HOCL) and the hypocholorite ion (OCL). Each ion has different chemical characteristics, and the ion concentration varies with pH. This variation can range from 5 to 10, and the effects of these ions on a membrane within this pH range are still unknown.

Technique 8.3   Use transition words to help the audience follow the logic.

Tips   Tell the audience if the next point or detail *progresses, recalls, reinforces,* or *contradicts* the previous point or detail. Transition words provide the audience clues to where the point or detail leads.

Warning Do not cut transition words. They are not deadwood.

Do not use *This means . . .* or *It means . . .* to transition.

Error Trap Remember, you can *highlight* good organization by editing, but you cannot *improve* poor organization by editing. If you are straining to find the "right" transition words, chances are the points are irrelevant, redundant, or poorly sequenced.

Example   The following is just a partial list of transition words:

Progress	Recall	Reinforce	Contradict
Therefore	Aforementioned	For example Adv	Although
First, second . . .	Previously Adv	For instance Adv	However
Next	Earlier	In addition Adv	On the other hand
Consequently Adv	As mentioned	Overall	Nevertheless
Subsequently	Remember	In summary Adv	In contrast
Then	Formerly	Moreover	Despite
Because Conjuncto	Before Conjuncto	Specifically	Regardless

Put transition words at the beginning — not the middle — of the sentence or clause.

Poor: The shortfall in revenue, *nevertheless,* allowed us to service our debt obligations.
Good: *Nevertheless,* the shortfall in revenue allowed us to service our debt obligations.

Poor: Our plane landed one hour late in Paris; we made, *however,* our connection to Nice.
Good: Our plane landed one hour late in Paris; *however,* we made our connection to Nice.

See also   Economy; word choice.

Discussion

You cannot overuse transition words. A message obvious to you, the author, is probably new to your audience.

Avoid transition words with multiple meanings. To avoid confusion, use *while* and *since* when referring to time passing. Do not use *while* when you mean *although,* or *since* when you mean *because.*

Transition words are especially important in oral communication.

You may begin a sentence with *Because. Because* introduces a dependent clause (subject and verb structure): *Because we missed the bus . . . .* You must add an independent clause to complete the thought: *Because we missed the bus, we walked home.*

Exercise: Make the following passages more coherent by using transition words from the boxes to the right. (Answer A-26)

Passage 1: Zybase-REMOD Test Result

_____ the custom Zybase file server works independently with other software modules, you may encounter potential problems when running the report module (REMOD) and Zybase at the same time on the network. If the REMOD fails for any reason, the Zybase file server continues to feed records into REMOD. _____ Zybase disregards operator instructions to stop sending records to REMOD. The operator is forced to close the Zybase function completely without the ability to save open files. _____ the error log is lost.

The immediate problem is easy to fix, if we can access the error log; _____, I suggest we write code to permit the operator to save the error log as part of taking Zybase down. _____ I suggest we take REMOD off the network.

moreover
then
consequently
although
therefore

Passage 2: Letter to Drug Manufacturers

Your advertisement citing *in vitro* data misleads, _____ the advertisement presents the data in a way that shows clinical relevance. _____, the statement "it's time to take action," when shown with the *in vitro* data, implies that Timencin is indicated to treat infections caused by each of the pathogens in the advertisement.

_____, the *in vitro* data combines selected pathogens for which Timencin is indicated and pathogens for which Timencin is not indicated. _____, Timencin is not indicated to treat conditions caused by pathogens such as *coagulase-negative Staphylococcus* (methicillin-susceptible), *Enterococcus feacalis*, and *Streptococcus Group B*. _____, your advertisement includes these pathogens.

for example
specifically
because
however
additionally

Technique 8.4   *Use vertical lists and tables to present series.*

Tip 1   Highlight your series of logically related items, statements, commands, or questions by putting them in a vertical list.

Introduce your vertical lists by stating the number of list items and defining how the list items are logically related. Then ensure each list item conforms to your definition.

Ensure list entries have similar importance and are grammatically parallel.

Treat tables the same way you treat lists.

Warning   Do not confuse numbered paragraphs with a list.

Do not append commentary to list items.

Avoid starting a list within a list.

Do not write a list when you need to write a paragraph.

Error Trap   If a single list item requires four lines of text, you may be trying to develop an idea in a list — use a paragraph instead.

Example   My favorite beer has four ingredients:

1. water softened with pinch of gypsum
2. amber malt from roasted barley
3. hops of the Fuggles and Cascade variety
4. liquid ale yeast from Scotland

See also   Transition words; parallelism; economy; readability; punctuation.

Discussion

A list is merely a series of like items. If you need to explain the connection between one idea and the next, write a paragraph, not a vertical list.

Vertical lists call attention to key information. They signal that the information is logically related.

Vertical lists improve readability. A long series strung together into one sentence is hard to read.

Vertical lists within vertical lists are cryptic, often looking like programmers' code. Either create a table, or separate the material into a number of shorter lists. A table is a multi-dimensional list.

Pull commentary out of your list items. Commentary usually belongs in a paragraph.

For lists, tables, figures, graphs, and pictures follow this simple logic: introduce, show, and comment. For example, tell what the picture shows: *The following picture shows the safe handling of molten glass.* Show the picture, then add comments if needed: *Note the safety goggles and the fireproof apron and gloves.*

Bullets have better eye appeal. Numbers are better for reference. Numbers do not necessarily imply order or ranking — your definition of the series implies order or ranking. Use numbers when you have many short lists, lists interrupted with page breaks, or long lists.

Exercise: Use vertical lists to group information for your audience. (Answer A-27)

1. Follow these steps to import line graphs when word processing. First, open an empty frame where you want to put your line graph. Then from the menu bar, choose Graphics, Figure, or Retrieve. The retrieve menu appears and lists the line graphs you may import. Double-click on the desired filename. Your selected line graph appears in the frame. Adjust the position or size of the frame by clicking and dragging a frame handle. Then anchor your frame to the page by double-clicking the anchor icon.

2. Disbursement requests must be properly documented for payment processing. Each disbursement request must contain payment authorization and invoices signed by the approving department. It must also contain a receiving copy of the purchase order and other receipts such as shipping documents, plus a remittance for any merchandise returned. The disbursement system allows some unique purchases on a case-by-case basis. For example, hardware maintenance outside our standard maintenance contracts requires a copy of the estimate and final bill. Advertising requires proof-of-service such as a copy of the advertisement, the order, and authorization.

Exercise: Improve the following list. (Answer A-27)

Follow these steps to download your email:

1. Click on the Mailbox icon.

2. Input your name and password. (If you don't have a password call the customer service line at 1-800-123-4567 between the hours of 9 a.m. and 5 p.m. Pacific Standard Time. Have your employee ID number ready. The service representative will ask you your mother's maiden name.)

3. Your system auto-dials the server and logs into your electronic mailbox.

4. Click the Envelope icon to save the email to your hard disk.

Tip 2   Use tables when you have a series of lists.

Introduce your tables by telling the audience the point: *what the table does for them.* If the table shows some relationship, explicitly state the relationship to look for.

Warning   Do not use tables that lack a point.

Never dump a table of data on your audience without telling the point.

Example   Poor heading: **History of O-Ring Damage on SRM Field Joints**

Launch #	Secondary Ring	Primary Ring	Date	Temperature
51-F	0%	0%	07/29/85	81°
41-D	0%	10%	08/30/84	70°
2	0%	25%	11/12/81	70°
41-C	0%	20%	04/06/84	63°
41-B	0%	85%	02/03/84	57°
51-C	92%	100%	01/24/85	53°

Good heading: **O-Ring Damage Correlates to Temperature**

Poor list:

Follow these two steps to check your voicemail:

Call our secure messaging center
a.   your cell phone, dial (123) 123-4567
b.   any other touchtone phone, dial 1 (888) 555-5678
Access you account
a.   for cell phones, press Message key
b.   for other touchtone phones, press # then input your PIN

Good table:

Follow these two steps to check your voicemail:

From your cell phone	From any touchtone phone
Dial (123) 123-4567	Dial 1 (888) 555-5678
Press Message key	Press #, then input your PIN

See also   Transition words; parallelism; economy; punctuation.

Discussion

Content experts often try to win their arguments by overwhelming the audience with facts. From the content expert's point of view, the facts may seem compelling. This strategy of letting the facts speak for themselves can be disastrous. Ironically, the more overwhelming the facts, the more likely the audience misses the point. Facts, as necessary as they are, do not make the argument. You need to state the point that the facts support.

Exercise: Improve these lists by making them tables. (Answer A-28)

Time Sheet Policy
1. Employees requirements
   - Weekly
   - Use Form FE-10
     - hours
     - charge number
2. Contract labor
   - As required
   - Invoice Form CL-10
     - hours
     - purchase order number

The following section of the Gizmo Test Plan tests the nightly batch runs that match new addresses to the US Post Office address database, merge new addresses into the house file, and purge duplicates.

1. Run pomatch.bat
   A Inputs
     (1) Records for today
     (2) Current week's USPS address file
   B. Process
     (1) Flags exact matches
     (2) Uses US address for 90%+ matches
     (3) Flags < 90% matches for error log
   C. Outputs
     (1) Error file for non-matches
     (2) Matched file with last four Zip appended

2. Run mergepurge.bat.
   Inputs
     (1) USPS-matched file from pomatch.bat
     (2) House file
   Process
     (1) Flags near dupes scoring 3 or more points of commonality
     (2) Deletes exact dupes
   Outputs
     (1) Log of dupes
     (2) Log of near dupes
     (3) Updated housefile
     (4) Backup (old) housefile

Technique 8.5   Apply visual devices.

Tips   Help your audience *skim* by visually highlighting key words, headings, and sentences.

Help your audience *follow* by using different fonts, white space, indentations, ruling lines, boxes, columns, and vertical lists to group and order items.

Help your audience *refer* back to your document with numbers, letters, footers, and headers.

Warning   Do not overuse fonts. Overuse of fonts makes your text look like a ransom note cut-and-pasted from the newspaper.

Example   Visual coherence devices include but are not limited to

Layout	**Typography**
indent, outdent, center, justification	italics, bold, <u>underline</u>
white space	different TYPEFACES
rows and columns	list bullets, numbers, letters
footers and headers	ruling lines and boxes
tabs	icons

See also   Mechanics.

Discussion

Visual devices include page layout and typography. Remember that format follows function.

Don't add visual devices just because your desktop-publishing software allows it.

Consult a style guide or devise your own. A style guide determines visual (and verbal) standards. Professions, companies, projects, and individuals may create their own style guides. Every writer needs access to an appropriate style guide.

A font is defined by typeface and size. Limit your typeface to one serif (like Times) and one sans serif (like Arial). With each typeface, you can make Normal, **Bold**, *Italics*, ***Bold Italics***, and <u>Underline</u>. Limit yourself to five point sizes. Consequently, you have 50 fonts to work with. In addition you can center, justify, indent, and add ruling lines. Assign fonts to specific tasks within your document. Following are five examples of dedicated fonts:

1. Titles = 24pt Bold Times, centered
2. Subheads = 12pt Bold Arial, left justified, outdent .25 inches, ruling line below column width
3. Body Text = 10pt Normal Times, left justified, first line indent
4. Captions = 10pt Normal Helvetica, left justified
5. Citations and references = 10pt Italic Times

Use your fonts for only assigned purposes. Most wordprocessors let you assign fonts, spacing, ruling lines and other visual attributes to create *paragraph styles*.

Exercise: Remember, a document with zero coherence devices is just one huge block paragraph. The following passage is well organized but needs visual coherence devices to make it reader-friendly. Consider paragraph structure and vertical lists. Add visual devices. (Answer A-28)

TO: Senior Management FROM: John Phelps DATE: May 3, 2001 SUBJECT: Long Distance Telephone Credit Cards This memo explains how you can use our new long distance telephone credit cards. Effective immediately, BAP, Inc. will switch from AT&T to TINKERBELL for all credit card calls. Employees traveling on BAP business are eligible to receive a company TINKERBELL credit card. All AT&T credit cards should be returned to Finance & Accounting (3rd floor) by 6:00 p.m. Friday, Tuesday 7, 2001. We will close the AT&T account at that time. The TINKERBELL system requires a different procedure for using the credit card. First, dial the TINKERBELL Travel Number, 1-800-555-4311: you get a voice prompt asking for your code. Enter your four-digit authorization code, then your two-digit travel code, printed on your card. Second, you enter area code and the telephone number that you want to reach. Each business group has its own four-digit authorization code and travel code. Calls are charged against your group's overhead. Finance and Accounting provides group managers with itemized call sheets, so they can track their long distance credit card expenses. Separate cards can be issued for specific contracts, if necessary. I am your principal contact for the new credit card system. I assign authorization codes and travel codes. If you have problems dialing a number or have questions about procedures, contact me. If your credit card is lost or stolen, contact TINKERBELL or me immediately.

Final exercise: Apply coherence devices to help your audience skim, follow, and refer back to the following paper. Put the purpose statement in the right place. Make key words consistent. Suggest headings. Use paragraph breaks and vertical lists. Use other visual devices. (Answer A-29)

Merged Account Legislation: Public law 101-510, enacted November 1999, changed accounting and reporting procedures for obligated and unobligated funds. The legislation eliminated Merged Accounts, and replaced them with a revised definition of Expired Accounts and the newly created Closed Accounts. This paper describes fixed accounts prior to the enacting of Public Law 101-510, how the law changed fixed accounts, and the effect of the law on BAP. Prior to Public Law 101-510, fixed accounts had three situations: Active, Expired, or Merged. Active Accounts have obligation authority. Treasury may record new obligations during this period. Expired Accounts start at the expiration of the active account's obligation authority and last for two years. The Treasury can make obligation adjustments during the two-year period, but can not record a new obligation. When an Active Account expires, the unobligated balances return to the Treasury surplus fund. Merged Accounts begin three years after the obligation authority of the account expires. At this time, the Treasury groups the unspent obligations from all previous budget fiscal years into the merged surplus fund authority. After Public Law 101-510, fixed accounts have three conditions: Active, Expired, and Closed. Each state has a different meaning. Active Accounts stay the same. Active accounts still have obligation authority. Expired Accounts now have a five-year period following the expiration of obligation authority, and they continue for two years. Expired Accounts' unobligated balances do not return to the Treasury as surplus funds, but remain with the obligated balances. During this period, all funds remain for recording, adjusting, and liquidating any obligations properly chargeable to the account prior to the time balances expired. Therefore, the Treasury can make prior-year adjustments. Closed Accounts now replace Merged Accounts. Closed Accounts begin with the sixth year after the obligation authority expires. Then, obligated and unobligated balances return to the Treasury as surplus funds. BAP is affected by the Merged Account Legislation three ways. First, BAP can now file for prior-year adjustments when contracts call for cost-plus-fixed-fee. Second, BAP can more easily contract to perform future work (out to year six) with current funds. Third, for long-term contracts, BAP must carefully track dollars, obligated and unobligated. After funds return to the Closed Account, special legislation is needed to re-authorize the funds.

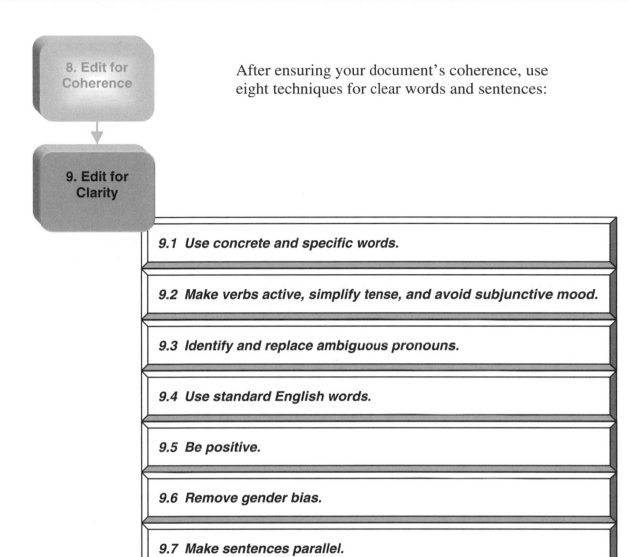

After ensuring your document's coherence, use eight techniques for clear words and sentences:

8. Edit for Coherence

9. Edit for Clarity

9.1 Use concrete and specific words.

9.2 Make verbs active, simplify tense, and avoid subjunctive mood.

9.3 Identify and replace ambiguous pronouns.

9.4 Use standard English words.

9.5 Be positive.

9.6 Remove gender bias.

9.7 Make sentences parallel.

9.8 Ensure each modifier is next to the word you intend to modify.

Discussion

Make clarity your chief editorial concern. You and your audience want one and only one interpretation of your document. Therefore, choose words carefully, and construct sentences carefully.

Never sacrifice clarity for other editorial virtues such as economy. Sometimes you must use more words to express your point clearly or to ensure that you give your audience what they need to know:

Remove the old finish is short, but vague.
Scrape or sand off the four layers of old paint is longer, but clear.

Attack ambiguity at the word level. In fact, you identify ambiguous words by *pattern recognition* rather than context. For example, identify passive voice by the pattern of a *"to be" verb plus another verb*. Identify subjunctive mood by the presence of the words *would, could*, and *should*. Identify ambiguous pronouns by marking the words *it, this, that, these, those,* as well as the pattern *there plus a "to be" verb*.

Technique 9.1   Use concrete and specific words.

Tips   Circle abstract and general words. Change to concrete and specific words.

Warning Don't let abstract and general words diminish your message with vague thoughts.
Abstract and general words leave the impression that the author doesn't know the
subject well.

Example Abstract-general: The artist applied unusual colors to the surface.
Concrete-specific: Andy Warhol splashed hot pink and olive drab on the brick wall.

Abstract-general: The crowd approved their team's success.
Concrete-specific: Dallas fans roared at their Cowboys' 7-0 victory over the Eagles.

Abstract-general: Recently, we have encountered problems in the mailroom.
Concrete-specific: In August, the mailroom misrouted 200 pieces of first class mail.

Abstract-general: The effort was very difficult.
Concrete-specific: Washing your cat took four hours.

See also Economy; readability.

Discussion

Abstract words (such as *contact, purpose, matter*) are intangible; consequently, we interpret the words differently.

General words (such as *recently, expensive, various, several*) are imprecise; consequently, they leave us guessing.

Concrete words appeal to our senses: sight, hearing, touch, taste, and smell.

Specific words include names, dates, places, and measurements.

Your authority as writer comes from your concrete and specific details, not your vocabulary, education, or job title. If your content lacks concrete and specific details, your audience can assume either that you don't know the subject, or that you do know but you are unwilling to share the information. In either case, your audience has reason to distrust you.

Concrete and specific details make business and technical writing more clear, lively, and interesting.

Make your modifiers specific and concrete. Avoid modifiers like *very* and *extremely*.

The author is the only person qualified to replace abstract and general words with specific and concrete words. Therefore, you need to perform this edit on your own documents.

Exercise: Underline the abstract and general words. Suggest concrete and specific words. Use your imagination. Although we can both mark the same abstract and general terms, only the original author can know what the concrete and specific details are. (Answer A-30)

1. Our office has been in communication with your office recently regarding a question about issuing a refund for the remaining portion of your lease on some equipment. There are several reasons why a refund of the whole remaining portion fails to satisfy various material conditions of the lease. However, your office may contact our department to negotiate some amount suitable.

2. A number of factors must be addressed in order to ensure this effort meets its objectives within the proposed timeframe.

3. The government acknowledges your staff's tremendous efforts in incorporating new requirements into the baseline. We are both well aware of the importance of maintaining a high level of progress for the rest of FY 2001. We both recognize there is a point at which any new work may affect that major milestone.

Exercise: Replace abstract and general words with concrete and specific words. (Answer A-30)

1. very difficult
2. subsidy
3. arrange a faster medium
4. contact someone
5. consider
6. finalize the contract
7. a change that can benefit most everyone
8. familiarize yourself with
9. various concerns
10. need a response
11. acquire a new functionality
12. no controlling legal authority
13. devise a means to
14. effect a change
15. some time in the future
16. ASAP
17. by close of business
18. at your earliest convenience

Technique 9.2   Make verbs active, simplify tense, and avoid subjunctive mood.

Tip 1   Use active voice for clear verbs.

Follow three steps to eliminate most passive voice:

1. Find and mark passive voice. Passive voice always has a "to be" verb (*is, are, was, were, been* . . .) plus another verb. For example, The system *is updated* daily.

2. Answer the question *who* or *what* does the action. For example, *Who* or *what* updates the system daily? Answer — *The night shift.*

3. Make the answer the subject of the verb. For example, *The night shift* becomes the subject of the verb *update: The night shift updates the system daily.*

Warning   Do not confuse passive voice with linking verbs. A "to be" verb often links a subject with a noun restating it or an adjective describing it. The "to be" verb acts like an equals sign. *Fred is accomplished* — does not beg the question *accomplished by whom.*

Do not confuse passive voice with progressive tense. *We are hiring 20 new store managers* — does not beg the question *hired by whom.*

Example   Poor: The contract was signed. (by *whom*?)
Good: Our chief operating officer signed the contract.

Poor: The report is automatically generated. (by *what*?)
Good: One-Rite software automatically generates the report.

See also   Dangling modifiers; cut empty verbs.

Discussion

Voice indicates if the subject acts or is being acted upon.

> **Active voice** — Michelle wrote the report. (Subject *Michelle* acts.)
> **Passive voice** — The report was written. (Subject *report* was acted upon.)

Use active voice 90 percent of the time to ensure clarity. You achieve greater precision as you answer *who* or *what* performs each action.

The problem with passive voice is that it begs this question: *who* or *what* performs the action? We guess wrong about half the time.

Some passive sentences quickly answer the question *who* or *what* with a prepositional phrase: *The system is updated daily by Fred.* Although better than not answering the question, the preposition is wordy. The prepositional phrase often identifies the actor too late, forcing the audience to reread the sentence. Also, the phrase *by Fred* is a modifier that you can misplace. For example, in *The system is updated daily to catch errors by Fred,* you accidentally accuse Fred of making the errors.

Passive voice causes expensive misunderstandings in proposals, contracts, design documents, procedures, and user manuals. The blame for ambiguity rightly belongs to the author.

Exercise: Identify passive voice. Convert passive verbs to active. Add a subject by answering the question by *what?* or by *whom?* (Answer A-31)

1. It is pointed out in the article that 13-column spreadsheets help bankers organize their information.

2. Errors that I have been making for years are now more easily seen when I edit.

3. The safety tag must be removed before the toner cartridge can be installed.

4. The addresses must be checked for duplicates, and incomplete addresses must be compared to the US Post Office database.

5. Little attention is being paid to that advertising.

6. The client was invited to review the proposal by us.

7. The verification and validation tests will be conducted after the terabyte of Landsat data is loaded into the database.

8. The insurance investigation is started only after a legal complaint has been submitted.

9. After the contract was won, we met the client to determine how the deliverables are accepted.

10. The sample size must be increased to ensure that the tests are conducted properly.

Exercise: Circle all the passive voice in the following passage from a contracts dispute between BAP, Inc. and the Metropolitan Department of Transportation (MDOT). Change to active voice. You may need to guess *who* or *what* does each action. (Answer A-31)

The contract scope was changed. Soon after, problems were encountered, and the project was delayed. Ultimately the project was suspended until decisions could be made and all issues could be addressed. At that time, the team was scaled back from 40 to 20 members. Contractual and cost accounting matters were also examined. After the contract was renegotiated, the project was restarted approximately three months after it was suspended.

Tip 2   Eliminate passive if you can simply cut the "to be" verb, the second verb, or both.

Eliminate passive voice that occurs after a *who, which,* or *that.* Simply cut the *who, which,* or *that* plus the "to be" verb.

Warning   Don't obsess if you can't fix the passive voice quickly.

Example   Poor: Wait until the door *is opened* completely.
            Good: Wait until the door opens completely. (Eliminate the "to be" verb.)

            Poor: The copier *is located* on the third floor.
            Good: The copier is on the third floor. (Eliminate the second verb.)

            Poor: The test *is intended* to find flaws in system logic.
            Good: The test finds flaws in system logic. (Eliminate the "to be" and second verb.)

            Poor: The system that *was built* in 1979 may have problems in the year 2000.
            Good: The system built in 1979 may have problems in the year 2000.

            Poor: Mr. Smith, who *has been* recently *promoted* to partner, gets a company car.
            Good: Mr. Smith, recently promoted to partner, gets a company car.

See also   Cut empty verbs; cut who, which, that.

Discussion

Passive voice is appropriate only when you want to de-emphasize the actor, because the actor is unknown, unimportant, or embarrassed:

    Unknown actor — *My umbrella was stolen.*
    Unimportant actor — *Coffee and donuts are served after the meeting.*
    Embarrassed actor — *Your account was improperly debited $20,000 instead of $20.*

You can also repair passive voice by rearranging the sentence to make an object of the sentence the subject. Sometimes you must change the verb completely. For example: *The cure for the common cold is to be found in Nature.* You can make an object, *Nature,* the subject and change the verb: *Nature holds the cure for the common cold.*

Poor: An example of passive voice *is presented* on the next page. (Object is *next page.*)
Good: The next page presents an example of passive voice.

Poor: All essential vitamins and minerals *are included* in the new Hamster Chow.
Good: New Hamster Chow includes all essential vitamins and minerals.

In academic writing, you can eliminate much of the passive voice even when you must avoid interjecting yourself into the paper. Let your work speak for you: *the study indicates, the pattern shows, the data suggests, the correlation implies . . . .*

Exercise: Convert sentences to active voice. (Answer A-31)

1. The paint is then allowed to dry overnight.

2. The online help, which is required in the statement of work, has many benefits to the user.

3. This report is supposed to contrast the approval process for generic and brand-name drugs.

4. Upon receiving new data, the system is intended to identify common errors when the program is run.

5. The malfunction that had been reported last night has been corrected by the night shift.

6. The logic is shown in Figure 3.

7. The statistician, who was hired last week, is expected to report to work on May 1.

8. Access the RTP temporary database that is used to sort files by address.

9. All resources that are related must be included in the same file.

10. The process flow is described in Section 2.

Exercise: Circle all the passive voice in the following passage from a user manual. Change to active voice. (Answer A-32)

At present, the daily aging report is produced as part of the daily cash flow statement. Our accounting software is designed to automatically generate new reports and archive the old reports. Then the new report is transmitted to the central database that can be accessed by the accounts receivable staff.

At the end of the month, all daily reports are archived. The accounts receivable staff, who are assigned responsibility for aging reports, are allowed to access the archives. If a report that is archived must be accessed, the accounts receivable staff are expected to notify the Onyx Computer Operations room. Archived tape must be pulled and loaded. Requests are fulfilled in the order in which they are requested.

Tip 3   Simplify tense: stay in present tense when possible.

Mark the future, perfect, and progressive tenses. Change to present or past tense.

Warning   Do not waste time. Either change the tense with ease, or leave the tense alone.

Example   Poor: The technical approach will rely on the OS/9 operating system.
Good: The technical approach relies on the OS/9 operating system.

Poor: We have received your resume.
Good: We have your resume.

Poor: I am enclosing a copy of our audit.
Good: I enclose a copy of our audit.

See also   Parallelism; economy.

Discussion

Simplifying tense has four benefits: your message is more consistent; you avoid grammar problems such as conjugation and faulty parallelism; you use fewer words; you proofread more easily.

Tense tells when the action occurs. English has 12 tenses:

present	I write.
past	I wrote.
future	I will write.
present perfect	I have written.
past perfect	I had written.
future perfect	I will have written.
present progressive	I am writing.
past progressive	I was writing.
future progressive	I will be writing.
present perfect progressive	I have been writing.
past perfect progressive	I had been writing.
future perfect progressive	I will have been writing.

Present tense is clearest, because we live in the present. Use other tenses only when you must emphasize the time of the action.

Except for present tense, all other tenses are a function of one's imagination. The past tense relies on memory. The future tense involves speculation. Even if the action happens in the future, you can describe the action in present tense. Consider cookbooks: they describe future steps in present tense.

Perfect tenses indicate that the action is complete at a particular point in time. Usually your audience doesn't need or won't understand the nuance. A meaningful use of perfect tense might be *The office had closed before we arrived,* to indicate which past action occurred first.

Progressive tenses indicate that the action remains in progress. Usually present tense serves just as well. However, you may want your audience to know specifically that the action remains in progress: *We are working hard to expand service to your neighborhood.*

In most cases, you can simply change the future tense to present; change the perfect tenses to past; and change the progressive tenses to present. However, make the change with ease or leave the tense as is.

Exercise: Put all verbs in present tense. (Answer A-32)

User Manual for Lawnmower

You will need to follow these instructions to operate your lawnmower:

1. First, you will check the oil and gas levels.

2. Then you will ensure no debris is near the blades when you will start the motor.

3. You will next put the choke to the red line as we have shown in figure 2.

4. After you have grabbed the deadman lever with one hand, you will pull the starting rope with the other.

5. If your mower is starting with difficulty, you will need to prime the carburetor.

6. After you have finished mowing your lawn, you will clean grass cuttings from the engine area.

Exercise: Put all verbs in present or past tense. (Answer A-33)

Job Management System Ribbon-Cutting Ceremony

After the guests on stage have taken their seats, the ceremony will open with a welcome statement from the VP of Operations, Mr. Kahn.

A one-hour demonstration of the Job Management System will follow. The demonstration will consist of a brief management overview of our products and services. The demonstration will use multi-media plus a panel of users from the Delaware factory. The panel of users will be playing the appropriate roles of order taking and order fulfillment.

When the demonstration has ended, the stage will be cleared, except Mr. Kahn will remain. The ribbon-cutting ceremony will follow. Joining Mr. Kahn in the ceremony will be the plant manager, and Mr. Stubbs, representing the union.

Closing remarks will be provided by Mr. Stubbs. The remarks will outline the future improvements to the plant that the new system has been making possible.

Light refreshments will be served after the ceremony. We are expecting about 500 employees to attend.

Tip 4   Avoid subjunctive mood.

Cut *would*, *should*, and *could*.

To recommend or request, use *suggest, intend, prefer, need, ask,* and *insist*.
Example: *You should not feed the bears* becomes *We prefer you not feed the bears*.

To give permission, use *may*.
Example: *You may feed the bears*.

To state a possibility, use *might* or *can*.
Example: *The system should run 24 hours per day*, becomes *The system can run 24 hours per day*.

To require or obligate, use *must* or *shall*.
Example: *The system must run 24 hours per day*.

Warning   Do not use the subjunctive mood just to be polite. Use *Please* instead.

Example   Poor: If you work late, you *would* get the next day off — *creates doubt*.
                Good: If you work late, you get the next day off — *clear*.

                Poor: You should notify us if your plans change — *polite but ambiguous*.
                Good: Please notify us if your plans change — *polite and clear*.

                Poor: We could finish painting unless it rains — *lacks conviction*.
                Good: We can finish painting unless it rains — *clear, only condition is rain*.

See also   Parallelism.

Discussion

Verbs express one of the following moods:

Indicative mood — makes a statement of fact or asks a question
Imperative mood — issues a command
Subjunctive mood — expresses a condition (without identifying the condition)

Indicative and imperative moods are clear. Subjunctive mood, with its *would, could,* and *should*, creates ambiguity. Subjunctive mood implies a condition. Do not imply a condition if none exists.

Poor: You *should* be careful with matches — implies a condition where you may be careless.
Good: Be careful with matches — simply states a fact or instruction.

Your audience can interpret *would, should,* or *could* as any condition: recommendation, permission, possibility, requirement, or obligation. Make your conditions explicit.

Poor: *You should send data to support your application* — leaves the matter open to interpretation.
Good: You *must* send data for us to process your application — explicitly tells the cause and effect, that you need your audience's cooperation to process the application.

Do not sign contracts that have ambiguous language, especially passive voice and subjunctive mood. Some writers argue that they must use ambiguous language to leave room to negotiate. We advise that ambiguous language does not protect you, especially when *you* are the author.

Exercise: Change subjunctive mood to indicative. (Answer A-33)

1. Letter

Dear Joe Palmer:

This letter should clear up a misunderstanding about proposed changes to our purchasing policy that would affect your department.

It would appear that you caught a significant typo in our draft guidance. We should have warned you that you had an early draft, which could have saved you some anxiety. Whereas the first draft said vendors should not expect to be paid in less than *600* days, the final policy states vendors should not expect to be paid in less than *60* days.

We would like to thank you for catching the typo. You should note other changes in the final draft of our purchasing policy. We would be grateful if you would address further questions about the new vendor policy to Mr. Smith, (991) 555-1234.

2. Requirement for Solid State Air Conditioner

When needed, we would deploy solid state air conditioners as part of a remote sensor that could detect hazardous materials. The entire unit of sensor plus cooler should meet the following requirements. The unit should be able to operate at ambient temperatures between -10° and +43° C. The weight of the unit should not exceed 80 lbs. The volume of the unit should not exceed 3.375 ft^3. The unit should be designed to operate in harsh industrial environments and most parts should be off-the-shelf.

A thermoelectric (TE) cooler would help satisfy the unit's requirements. The TE cooler would have no moving parts, and therefore, would be lighter than mechanical coolers and should survive better in harsh environments. The TE cooler would exceed the temperature range -10° to +43° C. Even at the extremes, the TE coolers could maintain precise temperatures within +/- 0.1°C. A TE cooler also would serve as a heater by changing the polarity of the DC power. The TE cooler would generate no electrical signature or mechanical noise.

3. Warning Label

Drysalol®
(ninitparo injection)

Skin rashes could be possible when Drysalol® is administered. However, rashes could be rare in patients with no prior exposure to ninitparo. The risk of skin rashes would increase in patients who are re-exposed to Drysalol®. The benefit of Drysalol® to patients undergoing surgery should be weighed against the risk of skin rash should a second exposure be required. Patients should consult their primary physician.

Technique 9.3   *Identify and replace ambiguous pronouns.*

Tip 1   Mark *this, it, that, there*, and other pronouns.

For vague pronouns such as *it*, look backward to the nearest noun. If the *it* doesn't refer to the previous noun, replace the ambiguous pronoun with a noun.

For the words *this, these, those, that*, ask the question *what*? This *what*? These *what*? Those *what*? That *what*? Insert your answer after the pronoun.

Replace phrases like *that's that, this means,* or *this means that* with a transition word such as *therefore*.

Warning   Don't worry about repetition. Replacing ambiguous pronouns causes repetition, but repetition is not necessarily bad. You can eliminate the worst repetition by combining sentences and using vertical lists.

Error Trap If you don't know what noun replaces *this*, go back to revision and evaluate content. Your topic and point might be unclear.

Example   Poor: We did a study of a new drug. It proved ineffective. (the drug or the study?)
Good: We did a study of a new drug. The study proved ineffective.

Poor: Read this.
Good: Read this warning label.

Poor: This means we must store old files in the attic.
Good: Therefore, we must store old files in the attic.

Poor: The client accepted our proposal. It follows that we must increase staff.
Good: The client accepted our proposal. The work requires us to increase staff.
Or: The client accepted our proposal. Therefore, we must increase staff.

Poor: It's not worth it.
Good: The limited increase in machine speed is not worth $5,000.

See also   Key terms; transition words; cut unnecessary repetition.

Discussion

Ambiguous pronouns — *this, these, those, that, it* — make poor subjects for sentences.

Writers often use pronouns to avoid repeating nouns. However, when the pronoun doesn't clearly refer to the noun to its left, confusion sets in. For example, — *Because the firm neglected the project, it failed* — What failed? the firm? the project? Do not sacrifice clarity to avoid repetition.

Replace ambiguous pronouns with concrete and specific nouns.

Exercise: Circle the ambiguous pronouns and suggest changes. (Answer A-34)

1. We do not tear your laundry by using machinery. We do it carefully by hand.

2. This is what's been going on, and everybody knows it.

3. It makes it clear that this is not required.

4. This demands your immediate attention.

5. That does not mean that this can be taken for granted.

6. The inspector found a safety guide dated May 1988 taped to a machine you installed in 1999. Please explain what this means.

7. We adjusted job descriptions after the layoffs. The client requested these.

8. The sample is insufficient for the test. It needs to be completely re-done.

9. The use of Alphadine with a protein diet can cause liver failure. It is not recommended.

10. They cancelled my flight with no explanation, and they still managed to lose my luggage. This is the third time this has happened.

Exercise: Find and replace the ambiguous pronouns in the following document. (Answer A-34)

Integrating a Personal Information Manager into C-Net

The Personal Information Manager (PIM) has six functions to help users manage their time and resources. We surveyed our C-Net users about those and they require only one: PIM Task Manager. It lets each C-Net user maintain a personal calendar. Then it combines those into a master calendar available on the C-Net server. Users can consult it for scheduling meetings.

However, it presents a technical problem. When C-Net calls PIM Task Manager, it must query a PIM resource database without switching between the two applications. This means it must reside on the same file server as C-Net and strain its limited processing capacity.

With this in mind, we researched this and uncovered two problems with it. These include

1. PIM stores the calendar files in its own proprietary format. C-Net must convert that to a format it can read. This means that every time PIM updates a Task Manager file, it must use already strained processing capacity to convert it.

2. Before it can generate the master calendar, it must restore the data into the PIM file format, and then process that back to C-Net format so users can read it. This causes a further strain on its processing capacity.

We considered the cost of converting from C-Net to a PIM-compatible server software, but it was too expensive. This means we must sacrifice server processing capacity to install and use it.

Considering the strain this puts on the server and its limited benefit to the users, installing PIM Task Manager is not worth it.

Tip 2   Eliminate openings that begin with *there* or *it* followed by a "to be" verb.

Determine *who* or *what* does the action and reconstruct the sentence. Tell your audience *who does what* or *what does what*.

Warning   Do not obsess over eliminating these openings. Fixing *there are* openings is more complicated than fixing *this* or *it* pronouns. You may need to rearrange the sentence. Either fix this problem quickly or move on to the next problem.

Example   Poor: At present, *there are* no plans to open a third store.
Good: At present, we have no plans to open a third store.

Poor: *There is* a simple solution to our cash flow problem.
Good: Mega Bank can solve our cash flow problem simply.

Poor: *There might be* an alternative solution to consider for our problem.
Good: We might consider an alternative solution to our problem.

See also   Key terms; concrete and specific words; economy.

Discussion

Mark every instance of *there* plus a form of the "to be" verb: *is, are, were, will be, have been,* and *will have been.*

The noun *there* is abstract. The verb "to be" merely indicates that something exists. Consequently, *there are* just states that something abstract exists.

We use the expressions *there are* and *it is* as a crutch, especially as we sprint through our drafts. As you edit your draft, you can remove the crutch and add value to the sentence.

Who does what and *what does what* force us to be concrete and specific. Consequently, we are clearer and more convincing. For example, *It is known that* lacks credibility. *It is widely accepted that* is pure demagoguery — *widely known by whom?* Instead use phrases like *The medical community knows,* or *the pharmaceutical industry knows,* or *the American public knows,* or *I know . . . .*

Exercise: Replace the abstract and ambiguous *there are* expressions with concrete and specific language. You may need to rearrange the sentence or provide a specific subject for the sentence. (Answer A-35)

1. There are ten key milestones in our management plan.

2. There is a sense of history in Easton, Maryland. There are streets lined with Victorian homes. Each Saturday during the spring, there will be garden tours hosted by the Easton Garden Society.

3. Within the scope of the work, there are three deliverables.

4. At the Jobs Fair, there were 15 applicants for our sales job. There might have been more applicants, but there was poor attendance at the Fair because there were competing events: the Rose Festival Marathon, and the Harbor Festival. The newspaper reported that at those events there was a combined attendance of 137,000 persons.

5. It is our plan to offer many initiatives to improve customer service at ACME Bank.

6. There may have been a misunderstanding about the risks involved when I signed the contract.

7. There was plenty for children to do at the company picnic.

8. If the Fatal Error message flashes on the screen, there is only one course of action.

9. Look at the motherboard. There are four short slots and six long slots. There is a video card in the first long slot. In long slot number two, there is an internal fax-modem. Depending on the configuration of your machine, there might be extended memory in long slot number three.

10. There has been a rumor circulating throughout the company that there are plans to move the headquarters from Dayton, Ohio to the Grand Cayman island. There is no truth to those rumors.

11. It is unnecessary to use a purchase order for office supplies. There is a credit card.

12. Call us when it is convenient.

Technique 9.4   Use standard English words.

Tips   Replace Latin and other non-English words with standard English.

Use English words currently understood by most business and technical professionals.

Avoid the slash: *and/or, he/she*.

Warning   Do not supplement English words with non-English words that add no meaning.
Poor: We need supplies: pens, paper, etc.
Good: We need supplies such as pens and paper.

Don't invent or use slang.
Poor: We functionalized the process taskwise.
Good: We defined the process functions by task.

Example   Ask a roomful of professionals what *i.e.* means, and you get as many as five answers, often vigorously defended. The abbreviation *i.e.* stands for the Latin *id est*, or English *that is*.

People invent words by adding suffixes such as invent*ability*, acceptance*wise*. We also add prefixes to create another class of nonstandard words. Regardless becomes *ir*regardless or even *disir*regardless.

See also   Cut redundancy.

Discussion

Latin and French terms are carry-overs from the 19th century when most professionals knew these languages. Today, most people don't know what the foreign expressions mean. English is hard enough with its 1.2 million words.

As technology expands, so does our working vocabulary. Use recognized technical jargon for the audience identified as having a high knowledge; avoid jargon for the low-knowledge audience.

The expression *A and/or B* is confusing. Most often, pick either the *and* or the *or*. If you must relate the possibilities that only one condition (A or B) or both conditions (A and B) are true, then use the expression *A or B or both*.

Avoid slang. Computer engineers use a lot of slang, such as *system crash*. Often, slang is general or abstract. For example, *system crash* is general. Better: *System software aborted the KERNEL32.DLL module with fatal exception error 0E @ 0167:BFF9DFFF.*

Exercise: Match non-English or non-standard phrases with one of the standard English phrases listed on the right. (Answer A-35)

1.	a la mode	a.	by way of, or by means of
2.	ad hoc	b.	by the day
3.	ad infinitum	c.	that is
4.	alright	d.	and so forth
5.	apropos	e.	consequently
6.	ca.	f.	it does not follow
7.	conceptwise	g.	limitless
8.	departmentation	h.	let people do
9.	e.g.	i.	by the fact itself
10.	ergo	j.	appropriate
11.	et al	k.	to this (purpose)
12.	et cetera	l.	for example
13.	idealize	m.	and others
14.	i.e.	n.	around or approximately
15.	in lieu	o.	in the fashion
16.	in situ	p.	slang for okay
17.	ipso facto	q.	noun meaning department?
18.	laissez faire	r.	namely
19.	non sequitur	s.	face-to-face
20.	per	t.	position reversed
21.	per diem	u.	instead of
22.	quid pro quo	v.	something for something
23.	via	w.	on site
24.	vice versa	x.	verb: to perfect?
25.	vis-a-vis	y.	adverb form of concept?
26.	viz.	z.	through, by or according to

Technique 9.5   Be positive.

Tips   Change a negative statement to a positive statement to improve clarity. Remove the *not*'s, *un*'s, and *anti*'s to express the thought positively.

Warning Do not confuse a negative statement and a negative message.

Negative statement of a positive message: *His excellent efforts did not go unnoticed.*

Positive statement of a positive message: *We noticed his excellent efforts.*

Negative statement of a negative message: *Your application cannot be processed because you did not sign it.*

Positive statement of a negative message: *Please sign your application so we can process it.*

Example   Poor: It is not impossible that we made a mistake.
          Good: It is possible we made a mistake.
          Better: We possibly made a mistake.

          Poor: We are not going to meet the deadline.
          Good: We expect to deliver the manual one week late.

          Poor: Jack lives not far from the airport.
          Good: Jack lives within a mile of Dulles Airport.

          Poor: The Senate was unreceptive to the President's budget.
          Good: The Senate rejected the President's budget.

          Poor: We are not unmindful of the lack of prosecutorial disinterest in this case.
          Good: We know we're about to be indicted.

See also   Economy; adjectives and adverbs.

Discussion

Positive statements are clearer than negative statements, because positive statements tell us what something *is* rather than what it *is not*.

Lawyers use negative statements to create ambiguity, or room for doubt. *Nobody can disprove my client's alibi* means *We desperately need a witness for our alibi*.

Writers sometimes use negative statements to soften the impact of a negative message. *The project is not lacking an extraordinary level of effort* means *We are behind schedule and over budget*. Although such evasive prose may postpone the negative impact, the evasion does not soften, but often amplifies the impact. People often resent the evasion more than the negative message.

Positive statements persuade better than negative statements. Change *Don't take your coffee break before 10:00 a.m.* to *Take your coffee break after 10:00 a.m.*

Most positive statements are more concise than the negative version.

Exercise: Change these negative statements to positive statements. (Answer A-36)

1. It is not an uncommon practice for employers to give employees year-end bonuses.

2. I don't find anything the slightest bit unsettling in those dealings.

3. The Court rejected an appeal by Maryland officials challenging a state law allowing the investment tax credit.

4. We can't hear you.

5. If the operator does not remove the red safety tag from the disk drive, the system will not boot up and software installation cannot continue.

6. The General Partners will not be found liable for non-performance unless the General Partners cannot show that the Limited partners failed to prove that the General Partners did not act in good faith.

7. We were unable to accept your bid because we were unable to justify your higher costs for services not unlike those offered in a less costly bid.

8. Your problem is not being unable to justify the need for a company car, but rather obtaining the necessary funding.

9. I do not intend to appear unreasonable.

10. Her response was not illogical, but it did not include key information.

11. It no longer appears unlikely that your shipment will not arrive late.

12. My comments were not reported in their context, which is inconsistent with journalistic ethics.

13. The two situations are not at all dissimilar.

14. Do not leave your oven on, especially when you are not in the house.

Technique 9.6 Remove gender bias.

Tips   Use the following eight guidelines to remove gender bias:

1. Use a plural pronoun and eliminate the use of the gender pronoun.

2. Substitute *person* for *man* or *woman.*

3. Substitute *one* or *you* for *he* or *she.*

4. Use both genders by writing *he or she*, *his or her.*

5. Avoid unnecessary references to marital status.

6. Be consistent when referring to people by last names and titles.

7. Replace occupational terms ending in *-man* or *-woman* with another word.

8. Use synonyms.

Warning   Avoid ridiculous constructs like *personhole* cover instead of *manhole* cover.

Do not use a plural possessive pronoun *their* with a singular noun such as *the user.*

Do not use *he/she*, *his/her,* or *s/he.* All three are non-standard English.

Example   Poor: Every *employee* selects *their* own health care plan. (grammar error)
              Correct: Every *employee* selects *his or her* health care plan.
              Better: Every *employee* selects *a* health care plan.

              Poor: This model home is a man's ambition and a woman's dream. Mom will love the gourmet kitchen while Dad enjoys the large hobby room.
              Good: This model home is your ambition and dream. Your family will love the gourmet kitchen and large hobby room.

See also Grammar; mechanics.

Discussion

Gender bias occurs when language stereotypes or unnecessarily distinguishes people by gender. We can take advantage of our large vocabulary, gender-neutral plurals, and gender-neutral second-person pronouns to eliminate much of English gender bias. Remove gender bias from your message to avoid these problems:

Practical: *Some of your firemen* are really female firefighters.
Economic: *A family man needs insurance* excludes half of the market.
Legal: *We seek a professional who has her MBA* illegally excludes male applicants.

Exercise: Think of a suitable synonym. (Answer A-36)

1. businessman

2. craftsmanship

3. foreman

4. middleman

5. sportsmanship

6. stewardess

7. fatherland

8. gentlemen's agreement

9. salesman

10. waitress

Exercise: Edit these sentences to avoid gender bias. (Answer A-36)

1. Experienced waiters make dining more pleasant.

2. The average American drives his car every day.

3. A man who wants to get ahead works hard.

4. If a man plans ahead, he can retire at age 60.

5. Each senator selects his staff.

6. Be sure to bring your husband to the D.C. Armory Flower Show.

7. Reagan, Gorbachev, and Mrs. Thatcher dominated politics in the 1980s.

8. The fireman and policeman controlled the crowd.

9. A homeowner can deduct interest expenses from his taxes.

10. The user can make only three attempts to enter his password before the machine locks him out.

Technique 9.7   Make sentences parallel.

Tips   Make sentences and parts of sentences grammatically parallel when they are in pairs, series, and vertical lists.

Pay special attention to sentences that have pairs such as *either . . . or . . .* , *not only . . . but also . . .* , *between . . . and . . . .* Use identical grammar after each member of the pair.

Keep mood and tense parallel in logically equal sentences. Use your ear: most writers recognize a shift in parallelism when they hear it.

Warning   Do not confuse your audience by making unnecessary changes in verb tenses and mood.

Error Trap If you have a difficult time making a list item parallel, consider the strong possibility that the list item is not part of the series.

Example   Poor: Our salesroom is clean, comfortable, and has a lot of space.
                Good: Our salesroom is clean, comfortable, and spacious.

                Poor: Their firm leads not only in production, but also is a leader in marketing.
                Good: Their firm leads not only in production, but also in marketing.

                Poor: With Weatherby software the user can get a weather report, produce reports, zoom in on an area for detail, and the screen displays current aerial photos.
                Good: With Weatherby software the user can get a weather report, produce reports, zoom in on an area for detail, and view current aerial photos.

                Poor: Either you can buy a cat or a dog.
                Good: You can buy either a cat or a dog.
                         Either you can buy a cat or you can buy a dog.

See also   Grammar; punctuation; vertical list.

Discussion

Parallelism refers to using the same grammar for logically similar sentences and parts of sentences.

You have already done much to improve parallelism during your previous edits. By changing your verbs to present tense and eliminating the subjunctive mood, you removed two major causes of faulty parallelism: shifting tenses and moods.

Parallelism helps your audience group information for easier understanding and recall. For example, express a series of instructions in imperative mood: *Put up the signs, arrange the tables, and display the new merchandise.*

Exercise: Make these sentences parallel. (Answer A-37)

1. You can either select the condensed version or the full-text version.

2. The choice between an optimum system design or one that is less than desirable is affected by our R&D budget and how we use commercially available software.

3. Management will assess your job performance by the following criteria. Are you neat and well groomed, did you get your assignments done on time, have you been flexible and are you willing to learn.

4. Our latest magazine issue lost money because we did not fill the advertising space, we needed 2,000 extra copies for promotion, and we pay too much for paper.

5. Based on their requirements, we will either recommend the zoning board approve the plan outright or the review committee request more information.

6. When you make the list, arrange the items in order of importance, write them in parallel form, and all the items should be numbered.

7. We propose the following agenda for the meeting:
   a. calling the meeting to order
   b. set date for next meeting
   c. taking the roll call
   d. election of new officers

8. The tax committee voted to
   a. review the materials being purchased for the tax library
   b. submit a report on new billing rates
   c. client development programs
   d. annual tax department party

9. When you build your database, either use dBase IV for Windows or Altbase for OS/9.

10. The new accounting software package fails to meet our requirements for several reasons:
    1. It is too slow.
    2. Do the menus need to be so complicated?
    3. Should the power fail, it would lose all my data.
    4. Enter a future date, and the ledger will not balance.

Technique 9.8   Ensure each modifier is next to the word you intend to modify.

Tips   Find the modifier. What word does it modify now? What word needs the modifier?

Put a misplaced modifier in the right place, next to the word that needs the modifier.

Give a dangling modifier something to modify.

Warning   Do not trust the sound of the modifier within the sentence. Some modifiers like *only* and *almost* seem to sound better in the wrong place.

Poor: I *only* have eyes for you. — song by A. Dublin and H. Warren
(*only I*, because you're ugly? *only have eyes*, because you're stupid?)

Good: I have eyes for you *only*.
Or: I have eyes for *only* you.

Example   Misplaced: *Although a key ingredient in his wife's meatballs*, Mr. Brody hates pepper.
(Mr. Brody had better stay out of Mrs. Brody's kitchen.)

I am happy to report *in April* no accidents occurred.
(Was April accident free? Or was the report in April?)

Dangling: *Ignoring Mr. Brody's protests*, pepper was added to the meatballs.(The pepper is ignoring Mr. Brody: no wonder he hates pepper.)

See also   Grammar.

Discussion

Modifiers are words we use to describe, limit, or otherwise modify the meaning of other words in a sentence. Modifiers modify the word or phrase they are next to.

Misplaced modifiers confuse, because they are in the wrong place, too far from the words you intended to modify, and too close to words you did not intend to modify.

Dangling modifiers confuse, because a dangling modifier cannot logically refer to another word in the sentence. You repair a dangling modifier by giving it something or someone to modify.

Passive voice and ambiguous pronouns cause many misplaced and dangling modifiers. Fix those two clarity problems and you fix many misplaced or dangling modifiers as well. Three examples follow:

Passive voice — misplaced modifier: "*After entering the password*, the file is updated by the operator," corrects itself when you fix passive voice: "*After entering the password*, the operator updates the file."

Passive voice — dangling modifier: "*Ignoring Mr. Brody's protests*, pepper was added to the meatballs" corrects itself when you fix passive voice: *Ignoring Mr. Brody's protests*, Mrs. Brody added pepper to the meatballs."

Ambiguous pronoun — dangling modifier: "*Being a world leader in telecommunications*, there are many opportunities for individual growth" corrects itself when you replace the ambiguous pronoun: "*Being a world leader in telecommunications*, BAPCO provides many opportunities for individual growth."

Exercise: Correct misplaced modifiers. (Answer A-37)

1. Our department only receives a limited amount of money to spend on office equipment.
2. Our mixing bowl set is designed to please any cook with a round bottom for efficient beating.
3. We want to hire a man to take care of our prize cow that does not smoke or drink.
4. The Fish and Game Club announced tuna are biting off the west coast.
5. Although extremely difficult to understand, Fred needs to consider all the client's competing requirements.
6. A recent White House report was released claiming that acid rain is linked to methane emissions by the President's scientific advisor.
7. For your information, I have enclosed our company's financial statements.
8. Senior managers will meet with the Chairman about the competition in the boardroom.
9. Soaring high above the clouds, we watched the space shuttle fly into space.
10. You only need to turn in your time sheet at the end of the month.
11. Patients can now take a simple test to detect hearing loss in their homes.
12. Please mark your calendars on April 5 for the annual tax meeting.
13. Simutex must only be prescribed for pregnant women when the risk to the fetus is considered.
14. Two campers were found shot to death by the park rangers.
15. I met a man with a wooden leg named Smith.

Exercise: Correct dangling modifiers. (Answer A-38)

1. Operating at 400 Megahertz, we can process your largest files quickly.
2. To determine the final costs, the labor-hours must be totaled and multiplied by the hourly rate.
3. After lying on the bottom of the Atlantic Ocean for 70 years, the photographers brought back pictures of the Titanic.
4. Having studied the client's requirements, the technical approach must include icon-driven menus.
5. To be a successful manager, good writing skills are essential.
6. Having interviewed 100 veterinarians, cats are cleaner than dogs.
7. Using the same concept, it may be a good idea to define defaults for each program.
8. Confident of our success, the proposal was sent to the client.
9. After processing the records, the next step is to print the results.
10. After raining all day, we moved the reception indoors.
11. If dangling, you must give the modifier something to modify.
12. If misplaced, you must put the modifier in the right place.

Final Exercise: Edit for clarity to improve the following passage. Find and fix the vague terms, passive voice, shifting tenses, ambiguous pronouns, Latin phrases, negative statements, gender bias, unparallel vertical list, and misplaced modifiers. (Answer A-39)

Virginia Department of Historical Preservation
111 Broad Street, Richmond, VA 25432

August 20, 2001

Mr. Smith
P. O. Box 2456
Arlington, VA 22145

Dear Ms. Smith:

We are unable to approve your request to register your farm edifice (i.e., a barn) as a historical building. This cannot be approved because it cannot meet minimum requirements for several reasons:

1. Although the barn was originally built in 1927 by an alleged descendent of Lord Fairfax, later improvements to accommodate cows have caused the Historical Society to place the barn's effective date much later, ca. 1954.

2. The barn requires extensive repairs that neither the owner can afford, nor our agency.

3. If the barn were repaired at the owner's expense, the owner would still have to pay for his own insurance.

4. The barn has already been condemned to allow a four-lane highway to be constructed.

This means that there is no way to register your old cow shed as a historical site and use that to impede construction of the new Route 206. Frankly, if it had not been condemned for the road construction, it would have been condemned as a structural hazard. Ergo, the owner would have had to pay for razing the barn instead of the State. Also, you were paid 150 percent of the assessed value of the condemned land.

If you believe you have other edifices of historical interest, e.g. a sheep pen or birdhouse perhaps, please have your findings submitted with proper surveys through your county land management office.

Best regards,

William Fairfax
Commissioner

Step 10. Edit for Economy

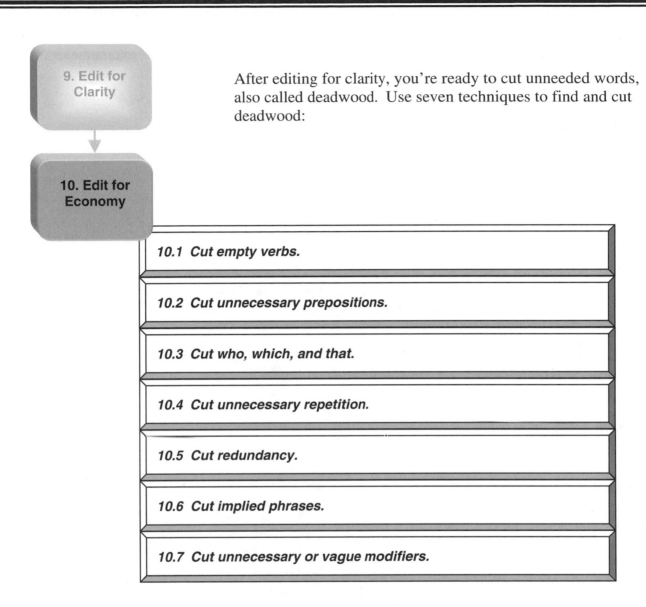

9. Edit for Clarity

10. Edit for Economy

After editing for clarity, you're ready to cut unneeded words, also called deadwood. Use seven techniques to find and cut deadwood:

10.1 Cut empty verbs.

10.2 Cut unnecessary prepositions.

10.3 Cut who, which, and that.

10.4 Cut unnecessary repetition.

10.5 Cut redundancy.

10.6 Cut implied phrases.

10.7 Cut unnecessary or vague modifiers.

Discussion

Editors call words that add no meaning to your sentence *deadwood*. Removing dead branches helps rather than hurts the tree. Just so, removing unnecessary words helps rather than hurts your draft. Deadwood hides your message and slows reading. Deadwood is usually general and abstract, causing your audience to doubt your expertise and sincerity.

Remove deadwood to make your writing clear, efficient, and vigorous. You can probably cut 20-50 percent of the words from your draft with no loss of meaning. Keep track of your most common deadwood habits, and practice editing techniques to eliminate them.

Vague terms, ambiguous pronouns, future tense, subjunctive mood, and passive voice add to deadwood. By editing for clarity, especially by using specific and concrete words, avoiding "to be" verbs, and eliminating ambiguous pronouns, you have already cut some of the draft's deadwood.

After you methodically delete deadwood, only concrete and specific words remain. As an extra benefit, you reduce the number of grammar and punctuation errors. For example, when you cut an unnecessary modifier, you don't need to worry if the modifier is misplaced or dangling.

Technique 10.1 Cut empty verbs.

Tips   Challenge "to be" verbs and other inactive, vague verbs. Know your own habits. *You will be able to . . .* becomes *You can.*

Find the more specific "buried verb" and use it as an active verb in the sentence. *We are in agreement* becomes *We agree.*

Replace many verbs with one. *You will have to decide* becomes *You must decide.*

Warning   Don't try to unbury all the verbs. For example, don't change *We go on vacation* to *We vacate.*

Example   "To be" verb: You need to be sure you have enough fuel.
　　　　　　 Simpler verb: Ensure you have enough fuel.

　　　　　　 Buried verb: We accomplished the system improvement.
　　　　　　 Active verb: We improved the system.

　　　　　　 Many verbs: You will have to input your user ID.
　　　　　　 One verb: Input your user ID.

　　　　　　 Buried verb and
　　　　　　 passive voice: A decision may be reached through consideration of the facts.
　　　　　　 Active verb: Consider the facts before you decide.

See also   Passive voice.

Discussion

Sometimes you find specific, concrete verbs buried in nouns and modifiers. Learn to recognize buried verbs by these common suffixes:

-ation	application — apply
-ion	instruction — instruct
-ment	statement — state
-ness	forgiveness — forgive
-ance	performance — perform
-able	acceptable — accept
-ity	totality — total
-ing	training — train

With the specific verb buried in a longer noun or modifier, the sentence typically uses an abstract or general verb to complete the thought. For economy, cut the abstract verb and unbury the specific verb.

Buried verb	Specific verb	Reduction in syllables
We made a recommendation.	We recommended.	37%
We had a discussion.	We discussed.	50%
We reached a conclusion.	We concluded.	33%
We passed judgment.	We judged.	50%
We discovered its usefulness.	We used it.	62%
We did maintenance.	We maintained.	40%
We find your proposal acceptable.	We accept your proposal.	30%
We are knowledgeable.	We know.	67%
We achieved prosperity.	We prospered.	57%
We are involved in testing.	We test.	72%

Exercise: Cut empty verbs. (Answer A-40)

1. Please give due consideration to approval of an expenditure of $10 for the acquisition of paper clips.

2. It is preferable from the clients' point of view that we hold the meeting at their site.

3. This letter is to notify you of our intention to make an adjustment to our bill.

4. Your efforts failed to meet our criteria for satisfaction.

5. Having conducted an inspection of your factory, we reached a conclusion that your smokestacks are in violation of the Clean Air Act.

6. We make a commitment to the on-time completion of your printing job.

7. This contract is to be signed by the vice president.

8. The cost to make the system enhancements is dependent upon whether you have a requirement that causes us to experience a duplication of efforts.

9. You have to bear in mind that your brakes were not made to bring your car instantly to a stop.

10. Please provide verification of which payment was to be applied to the January invoice.

11. We successfully made an attempt to effect repairs on your motorcycle.

12. The board of directors formed a decision to give notification to employees about this year's pay raises.

13. It was the determination of the auditors that BAPCO remains in compliance with generally accepted accounting principles.

14. This letter is in reference to our May 5 visit when we conducted an investigation of your factory's safety. We came to the conclusion that you are in violation of state and federal law. In our report we made suggestions that you must provide training to remain in compliance. When you are conducting the training, you need to be mindful that safety provides a benefit to your workers as well as provides satisfaction of legal obligations.

Technique 10.2 *Cut unnecessary prepositions.*

Tips Cut *of* when used to show possession.
> *Design of the system* becomes *system design.*
> *House of Tom* becomes *Tom's house.*

Cut cliche prepositions.
> *In accordance with* becomes *following.*
> *In order to* becomes *to.*
> *On a daily basis* becomes *daily.*

Warning Don't sacrifice clarity for economy. Do not remove the prepositions if a confusing noun string results. Consider this sign on the back of a truck: "Free Moving Videos!" Are the videos captive? Are they floating? Do they move you to tears? Or are they "Free Videos *About* Moving!" This sign needs the preposition.

Example Poor: *In order* to review the files *of the* company, I traveled *to* Denver.
Good: To review company files, I visited Denver.

Poor: We have no vacancies *at this point in time.*
Good: We have no vacancies now.
Better: We have no vacancies.

See also Cut implied phrases; English as a Second Language.

Discussion

Prepositions link a noun or pronoun to the rest of the sentence. English uses about 70 prepositions. Most other languages have far fewer prepositions. A non-native English writer may worry whether to say, "The minutes *of the* meeting, *from the* meeting, *about the* meeting, *for the* meeting, *to the* meeting, *on the* meeting . . . ." Cut the preposition and avoid the problem: "The meeting minutes . . . ."

Prepositions express relations such as

direction:	from, to, into, across, toward, down, up
location:	at, in, on, under, over, beside, among, by, between, through
relative locations:	or, against, with, to
time:	before, after, during, until, since
possession:	for, to, of

Ending a sentence in a preposition is not a grammar error; however, the offending preposition may be deadwood. In *Where is the library at?* the preposition sounds bad, because it is deadwood. However, in *Where are you from?* you need the preposition.

Cutting deadwood also removes our regional speech habits and cliches, thereby giving our business and technical documents a more professional and consistent "voice."

Cutting prepositions helps you avoid subject-verb agreement problems. For example, "Decide if any of these values (*need or needs*) to change," is problematic. Is the subject *any* singular or plural? Cut the preposition. "Decide if any value needs to change." The subject *value* is obviously singular.

Exercise: Write alternatives to these prepositional phrases. (Answer A-40)

1. Call *at about* 5 o'clock.
2. *In accordance with* company policy . . .
3. He wrote *with the purpose of* . . .
4. Submit your plan *for the purpose of* . . .
5. Put the phone *on top of* the desk.
6. She is *in the midst of* a big job.
7. *In spite of the fact that* . . .
8. He is an expert *in the area of* finance.
9. . . . *on a daily basis.*
10. *In the event of* . . .
11. Go *in back of* the shed.
12. We are *in receipt of* . . .
13. He worked *over and above* . . .
14. *In the interest of* safety . . .
15. *With regard to* your promotion . . .
16. Indicate *as to whether or not* . . .
17. *Because of the fact that* . . .
18. *Because of this reason* . . .
19. *At this point in time* . . .
20. *In a similar fashion* . . .

Exercise: Cut unnecessary prepositions from the following sentences. (Answer A-41)

1. In order to meet the objectives of this test, XYZ, Inc. has to draw upon the expertise of several people belonging to and part of the staff in the La Jolla Laboratory.
2. The review by Dr. Roger of the draft of the report by the committee is on hold until the DOD review is completed.
3. In the event that you want to qualify for the exemption from taxes to local businesses, your sales of tickets to the series of lectures must conform to each of the following requirements.
4. One of the purposes of the whole project is to ensure that the Navy receives maximum return on its data documentation efforts.
5. Write up the meeting notes, then pass them out to all of the members of the committee.
6. If any of these steps fail to restart the motor, take your lawnmower back to your dealer.

Exercise: Remove prepositions to shorten this 103-word paragraph. (Answer A-41)

Revenues from sale of lumber fell by five percent in the third quarter. Despite the fact of falling revenue, the sale of number of board feet rose by fifteen percent. The fall in revenue was due to the fact that pressure in prices was caused by increased competition from suppliers in Canada. In the event of a further fall in sale of lumber, the dividend to stockholders may be at risk. In the interest of improving relations with stockholders, the report for the third quarter needs to highlight efforts made by the company for the maintenance of profitability by the control of costs.

Technique 10.3 Cut who, which, and that.

Tip   Cut *who, which*, and *that* when combined with a "to be" verb, because the words add no value to the sentence.

Warning Do not cut *that* when used to separate two thoughts.

Poor: Mrs. Martin explained to him her newspaper vanished.
Good: Mrs. Martin explained to him that her newspaper vanished.

Poor: Economists warn business will suffer from new tax rules.
Good: Economists warn that business will suffer from new tax rules.

Example Poor: Our chief engineer, who is an MIT graduate, supervised the factory design.
Good: Our chief engineer, an MIT graduate, supervised the factory design.

Poor: The copier, which is obsolete, must be replaced.
Good: The obsolete copier must be replaced.
Better: Replace the obsolete copier.

See also Passive voice; ambiguous pronouns; cut empty verbs; commas.

Discussion

Who, which, and *that* combined with a "to be" verb link a noun, pronoun, or modifier to the rest of the sentence. Delete the *who, which*, and *that* plus the "to be" verb, and keep the noun, pronoun, or modifier.

Three examples follow:

Change *FastChip, which will be available next year* . . . to *FastChip, available next year* . . . .
Change *FastChip, which is new and improved* . . . to *The new and improved FastChip* . . . .
Change *My article, which was accepted for publication* . . . to *My article, accepted for publication* . . . .

Often, this edit also eliminates passive voice.

We also use the word *that* to connect thoughts. If you can easily cut the *that* without the thoughts running together, do so.

Change *Take all the time that you need* to *Take all the time you need*, because the change is easy.

However, you might resist changing *We fixed the damage that our client discovered*, because you want to separate the words *damage* and *our client*.

Exercise: Cut *who*, *which*, and *that* (plus "to be" verbs) from these sentences. (Answer A-41)

1. Resumes have been received from 11 people who are qualified to fill the job.

2. Ann Jones, who is the leader in our contract negotiations, wants to meet you on the six o'clock air shuttle, which is the first flight of the day.

3. Please select a desk that is more suitable to your work.

4. Work continues on the Vega Project, which is scheduled for completion next summer.

5. He added a requirement that was the same as ours.

6. The policy committee, which is composed of local elected officials from Clark County, chose not to include a request for more road salt in their final budget that was submitted on September 10.

7. Remove the red safety tag, which you will find next to the oil drain plug.

8. Your letter discusses many questions that have been bothering me as well.

9. Access the data that will have already been loaded onto your hard drive.

10. If the customer requests statement copies that are older than six months, you must look in the microfilm library.

11. Employees must report any plant accident resulting in lost labor time to the shift supervisor, who is responsible for safety.

12. Employees who are assigned to the new Jupiter Project must submit a form W-2 that can be found in the introduction packet that was issued during last month's orientation.

Technique 10.4 Cut unnecessary repetition.

Tips Use vertical lists to cut unnecessary repetition of words or phrases.

Combine sentences.

Warning Do not use synonyms to avoid repetition. Coherence demands that you establish and repeat key words to keep your audience on track.

Do not use passive voice or ambiguous pronouns to avoid repetition.

Example Using a vertical list cuts this passage from 57 to 44 words.

Poor: To qualify for the $50 rebate, *you must* accomplish the following four steps. First, *you must* fill out completely and sign the accompanying 3-by-5 card. Second, *you must* attach the bar-code label as proof of purchase. Third, *you must* enclose the original cash register receipt — no photocopies allowed. And fourth, *you must* enclose a self-addressed stamped envelope.

Good: To qualify for the $50 rebate, accomplish four steps:
1. Fill out completely and sign the accompanying 3x5 card.
2. Attach the bar-code label as proof of purchase.
3. Enclose the original cash register receipt — no photocopies allowed.
4. Enclose a self-addressed stamped envelope.

Combine these two sentences to cut the passage from 17 to 13 words.

Poor: Our patented battery can recharge using regular household current. Consequently, our patented battery lasts for two years.

Good: Our patented battery can recharge using regular household current, thereby lasting two years.

See also Key words, passive voice, ambiguous pronouns.

Discussion

Repetition is often useful. Recall from editing for coherence that you use repetition to emphasize key words. However, avoid repeating words and phrases when they draw your audience's attention away from your key points and details.

Some writers mistakenly use passive voice to avoid repeating a subject. In technical writing, repetition is better than guessing *who* or *what* performs the actions.

When you edit for clarity, changing passive voice to active voice and replacing ambiguous pronouns with nouns, you often repeat nouns. If the repetition becomes painful, you probably have a series of like items that you can put into a vertical list.

Do not shift words just for variety. You may think you have improved your message by eliminating repetition, but in fact, you've created worse problems: incoherence and redundancy.

Exercise: Cut the repetition. (Answer A-42)

1. He added an additional requirement.

2. QuickDraw provides a complete set of line-drawing tools for your personal computer. QuickDraw provides free-hand tools as well as common shapes. QuickDraw provides a full palette of 256 colors. QuickDraw provides scaling. QuickDraw also lets you rotate shapes and text. QuickDraw can save your work in GIF, TIP, Acrobat, and most other popular file formats.

3. Each stock item record contains a stocking conversion factor (the stocking conversion factor being the number of end-use units contained in one stocking unit).

4. This regulation is more important than other regulations.

5. The road surface must meet state construction standards, and the road surface must be in good condition.

Exercise: Cut unnecessary repetition from this passage. (Answer A-42)

Training Conferences

We plan three training conferences for government employees. The first training conference occurs approximately 45 days after the contract award. This first training conference starts with a working meeting and review of initial planning documents and requirements documents for training. The second training conference happens at day 90 to coincide with our first deliverable, the draft AIS training and technical manuals. In the second training conference, we review customer comments of the manuals as well as the skills analysis report, plan of instruction, and course outlines. The second training conference also helps resolve any concerns before we design and develop the training courses. The third conference happens about 225 days after contract award for the review and comment of the training materials and schedules. Other training concerns will be addressed as necessary during the third training conference.

Technique 10.5 Cut redundancy.

Tips   Cut words that say the same thing using synonyms.

Cut doubling.

Warning   Do not cut words or phrases that make useful distinctions.
For example, *We offer efficient and proven methods.*

Do not simply paraphrase statements. The expression *In other words . . .* usually indicates redundancy. Instead, add value: define terms, give examples, present analogies, and draw pictures.

Example   Poor: His suit of clothes is a gray color.
                    Good: His suit is gray.

Poor: In the month of June, Wooster Shire condos reported the same vacancy rate as in the month of May.
Good: In June, Wooster Shire condos reported the same vacancy as in May.

Poor: In this case, a refund is right and proper.
Good: In this case, a refund is proper.

Poor: Please approve and accept our offer.
Good: Please accept our offer.

See also   Cut repetition; concrete and specific words.

Discussion

Redundancy often results from using an abstract or general word that means the same as a specific or concrete word. For example, in the phrases *three feet in length*, and *the subject of chemistry, three feet* and *chemistry* are specific, while *length* and *subject* are abstract.

Doubling occurs when writers join two synonyms or almost-synonyms using conjunctions *and* and *or.* For example, *We offer effective and successful methods.* Even when the doubled words are not exact synonyms, the subtle nuances in meaning tend to confuse rather than clarify the message. For example: *Attend this urgent and important meeting* is less direct than *Attend this urgent meeting.*

Doubling is common in English. In medieval England, when half the nobility spoke Anglo-Saxon, the other half French, they wrote key terms in contracts in both languages. Hence, *null and void, cease and desist, complete and full, varied and sundry.*

Trying to sound like the educated lawyer class, early English writers doubled with phrases like *each and every, this day and age, appraise and determine, refuse and decline, clear and understandable . . . .*

Don't let *this* and *that's* run down your page. Beware of word pairs joined by conjunctions *and* and *or.*

Exercise: Cut redundant words and phrases. (Answer A-42)

1. The Duraflex tank is 10 cubic feet in volume and stands 2 feet high from bottom to top.

2. First and foremost, I am sorry and apologize to each and every employee for attempting a little levity and humor now and then.

3. BAMCorp's singularly unique personnel and technical package will completely and professionally fulfill, as well as satisfy, all your complex and challenging requirements. By partnering together with your professional staff and personnel, our teams can become interdependent upon each other. In other words, BAMCorp can solve all your problems.

4. Please read and understand this quick and easy guide of instructions.

5. Doubling can detract from and confuse the message or idea.

6. The company especially wishes to recognize and compliment Mr. Smith for five years of unselfish and generous aid and support to Little League Baseball in Falls Church.

7. The clients asked these following questions in their request for information.

8. Please make sure your tray-tables are fastened and secure in an upright position for landing.

9. Remain securely fastened and buckled in your seat until the plane has come to a full, complete, and final stop.

10. Please make sure your carry-on luggage is of the type and size that can be stored above in the overhead bin compartment or below under the seat space beneath the seat in front of you.

11. Customers can access their account information by modem, that is, go online.

12. Brokers first introduced junk bonds to the general public in the decade of the 1970s.

13. I spent all the years of my youth studying and learning systems engineering.

14. I choose words and vocabulary to sound more educated, sophisticated, and erudite.

Technique 10.6 Cut implied phrases.

Tips   Cut phrases already understood from context.

Cut overly formal courtesies.

Warning   Do not cut meaningful qualifiers.

For example, *When properly used with a seatbelt, airbags save lives.*

Example   Poor: The purpose of this memo is to review the employee health plan.
              Good: This memo reviews the employee health plan.

Poor: Therefore, the question often arises: "Who is most qualified?"
Good: "Who is most qualified?"

Poor: It seems to me that the Purchase Price Parity theory lacks conclusive proof.
Good: The Purchase Price Parity theory lacks conclusive proof.

Poor: On behalf of the entire staff, I would like to take this opportunity to thank you for your many years of outstanding service.
Good: The staff and I thank you for your outstanding service.

See also Cut prepositions.

Discussion

Most documents and activities imply by their existence a purpose, goal, or intent. Therefore you rarely need to write *the goal of this staff study is to compare . . . .*

Use qualifying phrases if you need to be legalistic: *In the opinion of this court . . . .* Also, use qualifying phrases to highlight your lack of conviction: *In this instance, we suggest that . . . .*

However, many qualifying phrases are cliches that you need to avoid:

In accordance with these regulations . . .
One may conclude that . . .
Within the realm of possibility . . .
It is clear that . . .
The intent of the study is to . . .

Implied phrases, like other deadwood, obscure your message and weaken your writing. Cut them for a clearer and stronger writing voice.

Poor: Perhaps it would be wise to take a moment and read these instructions first.
Good: First, read these instructions.

Exercise: Cut implied phrases. (Answer A-43)

1. As you may already know, Lockheed and Martin Marietta merged to become the world's largest defense company.

2. It should be noted that these new theories mark a radical change in the way scientists view the universe.

3. All things considered, our new office manager shows promise.

4. It is suggested that you send an invoice within 30 days of completing work.

5. Please feel free to call me if you have any questions.

6. When you find time, please give me your decision about whether or not you want me to work late.

7. Most experienced experts claim that children need to eat a well-balanced breakfast before going to school.

8. Before we begin our discussion, remember that these remarks are strictly off the record.

9. At this time, we at BAP Industries wish to take this opportunity to thank all our vendors for their support in our on-going activities.

10. You may establish another category for the purpose of recording, adjusting, and liquidating other obligations properly chargeable to the AIS contract.

11. On the form in question, called FX-10, please write your claim number in the blank space provided on line 5.

12. It has come to our attention that you may be in the market to buy a new car. We invite you to test drive the new Hugo Millennium.

Technique 10.7 Cut unnecessary or vague modifiers.

Tips Choose nouns and verbs carefully to convey precise meaning and intensity. If the noun or verb needs help, use concrete and specific modifiers or supporting details.

Cut abstract and general modifiers.

Warning Do not intensify nouns or verbs with vague modifiers.
Avoid words such as *very, great, extreme, various, several . . . .*

Example Poor: Prolonged exposure to this distillate is very dangerous.
Good: Exposure to this distillate is dangerous.
Better: A thirty-minute exposure to this distillate can cause blindness.

Poor: Ms. Jones very carefully read our report.
Good: Ms. Jones scrutinized our report.

Poor: Your access code does not actually appear on the screen.
Good: Your access code does not appear on the screen.

See also Cut redundancy; concrete and specific words.

Discussion

Modifiers are words we use to describe, limit, or otherwise alter the meaning of other words in a sentence.

If you changed abstract and general words into concrete and specific words, you will have already cut most vague modifiers. If you need to make the point that "This task requires a *very* difficult change," define *very* in specific terms such as, "This task requires a difficult two-thousand line change to the code."

Many unnecessary modifiers are cliches.

Exact same — different from just plain same?
Advance reservations — more useful than posthumous reservations
Almost positive — means you're not sure
Mutually agreeable — what other kind of agreeable is there?
Most unique — like unique, uniquer, uniquest?
Join together — to differentiate from joining apart?
Absolutely sure — not quite as sure as positively sure?
Both cooperate — or you cooperate your way, I'll cooperate my way
Previous experience — usually more useful than experience after the fact
Close proximity — can one be close and not in a proximity?
Unexpected surprise — more exciting than the expected surprise
Complete annihilation — worse than partial annihilation
Advance forward — to distinguish from retreat forward or advance backwards
Honest truth — as opposed to the dishonest truth

Exercise: Cut unnecessary and vague modifiers. (Answer A-43)

1. I usually write my first drafts very quickly.

2. Please use extreme caution when removing carry-on luggage from the overhead bins.

3. The client asked the following specific questions about our work that is currently in progress.

4. Please provide a copy of the original receipt so we can close down your account.

5. BAP Industries offers a most unique solution to your complete personal computer needs.

6. Are you absolutely sure you unplugged the coffeepot? I'm almost positive I didn't.

7. Management remains fairly optimistic that we can meet our relatively high sales quotas.

8. Martin's analysis was completely accurate, but his conclusion was totally wrong. The end result was confusion.

9. Sally first debuted her new innovation to the public last month.

10. At last, the market survey was completed in its entirety. The Market Committee reached a full consensus of opinion. They decided to stick to the basic essentials of franchising new retail stores. In concert with the Products Committee, they decided to exactly replicate store layout and merchandise.

11. If you two will both cooperate with each other, we can all achieve our intended goals.

12. Pam and John found it mutually agreeable to join together in the bonds of marriage.

13. When we finally found the car, the battery was completely dead. She left both the headlights turned on, which totally drained the battery of all its power.

14. Employees need to be thoroughly convinced that the mutual goals they share with our management team can form the basis for a lasting long-term job security.

Final exercise: Cut 25-50 percent of the 228 words in the letter. (Answer A-44)

Charles Wiggins
12345 Kings Park
Fairfax, VA 22030

February 20, 2002

Julia Wright
BAPCO, Inc.
Personnel Department
Arlington, VA 22201

Dear Julia Wright:

In the interest of exploring employment opportunities with your organization, I am submitting a copy of my resume for your review and consideration.

As you may know by now, I have a variety of work experience, which includes providing valuable insight into grasping a combination of relational database development products, front-end development, and analysis of microcomputer graphical user interface (GUI) software applications, as well as analytical and technical support of full life-cycle software development projects.

Through my previous experience, I have worked in a myriad of different environments ranging from major corporations to small, start-up companies, holding progressively more responsible positions, which has given me the ability to easily adapt to any situation that might come along. I will work independently, taking a self-starter, hands-on, and self-reliant approach, yet I know the advantages of interdependence and the importance of teamwork.

I am interested in learning more about your company, BAPCO, Inc., and I am confident that we can find a mutually beneficial employment opportunity for both of us. In short, I am confident that I can be an asset as well as a resource to your company. My salary requirements are subject to negotiation.

Perhaps we can arrange a mutually convenient time for an interview so you can meet me and I can meet you to discuss my future with BAPCO. Thank you for your time and consideration.

Sincerely,

Charles Wiggins

Step 11. Edit for Readability

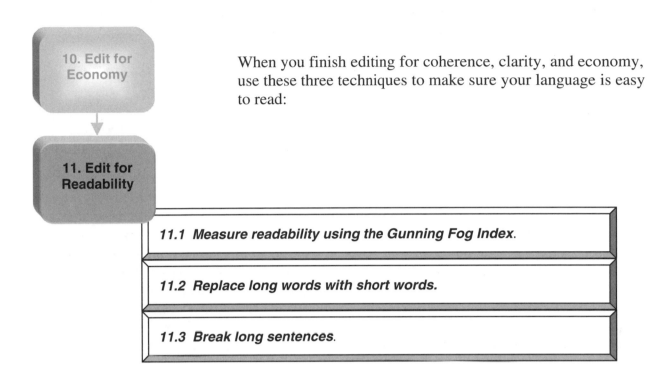

When you finish editing for coherence, clarity, and economy, use these three techniques to make sure your language is easy to read:

10. Edit for Economy

11. Edit for Readability

11.1 *Measure readability using the Gunning Fog Index.*

11.2 *Replace long words with short words.*

11.3 *Break long sentences.*

Discussion

We want to read quickly and accurately. We resent difficult language.

Readability refers to how easy or difficult your audience finds your language. Short sentences and short words are easier to read.

Different measures for readability include Flesch-Kincaid Grade Level, Flesch Reading Ease, and Robert Gunning Fog Index. All the algorithms rely on two variables: sentence length and word length. We prefer the simplicity of the Robert Gunning Fog Index from his book *The Technique of Clear Writing.* McGraw-Hill: New York, 1968. Many wordprocessors provide readability algorithms.

If you follow the writing system, you usually achieve good readability. For example, sentence outlining ensures that the first sentences of your paragraphs are short. Editing for clarity and economy shortens average sentence length. Your specific and concrete words tend to be shorter than abstract and general words.

Nevertheless, check readability after editing, and lower readability, if needed, by using more short words and shorter sentences.

Technique 11.1 Measure readability using the Gunning Fog Index.

Tips Follow this formula:

Average sentence length	(105 words/5 sentences)	21
plus Long words per 100	(12 words/100 count)	+12
		===
		33
multiply by constant 0.4		x 0.4
		===
equals Gunning Fog Index		13.2

The Index value 13.2 is the grade level to which you wrote your document, college freshman in this case.

Omit vertical lists in your sample. Lists cause a false reading for average sentence length. When counting long words per 100, count only words with three or more syllables that are not proper nouns, acronyms, or Arabic numbers like 1998. Do not count *es* or *ed* endings as syllables. Count *ing* endings as syllables. For example, suceed*ed* counts as a two-syllable word, therefore, not a long word, but succeed*ing* counts as a three-syllable word, and therefore, a long word.

Warning Do not use readability algorithms until after you edit for coherence, clarity, and economy.

Do not waste time on false precision. If you miscount a word or a syllable, don't worry.

Example The passage in the discussion box below has 204 words, 17 sentences, and 23 long words total or 11 long words per hundred count. ASL = 12 HW/100 = 11 12+11= 23   23*0.4 = 9.2 Grade, high school freshman.

See also Clarity; economy.

Discussion

Subject matter does not cause language complexity. In fact, if you have a complex subject, you are obliged to make the language simple. Making complex subjects simple is the hallmark of brilliant communication. Lowering the readability score is *not* dumbing down. Rather, readability measures how hard one must work to get your message.

The Fog Index algorithm's variables tell you whether you need to reduce average sentence length or replace long words with short words. As a rule, keep average sentence length to 17 words, and limit your long words to 10 to 15 per 100.

Write at the level that your audience *wants* to read, not at the level that they *can* read. Most technical professionals prefer to read at grade levels no higher than 10 to 13. Newspapers write to grade 8. Even sophisticated magazines write to grade 10, high school sophomore. Professional journals such as the *New England Journal of Medicine* write to grade level 16 or less. This book has a Fog Index of 9. Calculate a Fog Index on a document you admire.

Exercise: Measure readability by calculating the Gunning Fog Index for each passage.
(Answer A-45)

Managing Proposal Commitments

In order to lay a foundation to consider principal issues in managing to proposal commitments, we must first consider and accept that companies in both their government and commercial businesses, lack adeptness in managing the very commitments, and consequently the risks, to which the managers must manage.

In order for the acquisition of adeptness in the management of proposal commitments, companies must understand the imperfections in their currently used management systems. The interrelated areas in which companies seem to appear to experience the preponderance of substandard performance in managing the commitments themselves are inconsistency among commitments and ignorance of the potential negative outcomes of commitments.

Why do companies experience difficulty in managing their proposal commitments, and what effect does that have on companies' abilities in managing to those commitments? The legal community would point to suggestions from our experience adjudicating contracts that a principal reason is that the personnel who write proposals and make the commitments are not the same personnel who eventually provide management of the projects. Companies usually view proposal writing and project performance as discrete tasks rather than part of a continuum.

How to Manage Proposal Promises

To learn how to manage proposal promises, we must accept that firms lack the skills to manage their promises. Therefore, they incur risks.

To acquire the skill to manage proposal promises, firms must understand the flaws in their present management systems. Firms experience poor results in managing promises because they make promises that conflict. Also, they don't know the likely bad outcomes of promises they make.

Why do firms have problems managing their proposal promises? Contract lawyers point to one main reason. The people who write proposals and make the promises are not the same people who later manage the projects. Firms often view proposal writing and project performance as discrete tasks rather than part of a process.

Technique 11.2 *Replace long words with short words.*

Tips Challenge each long (three or more syllable) word, excluding proper nouns. (Disregard *es* and *ed* suffixes.)

Keep the long words that have no good short word substitute, including expected jargon. Replace others with one- or two-syllable words.

Limit your long words to 10-15 per 100 to keep your writing at a high school level.

Trust your natural speaking voice. Long words sound unnatural and overly formal. We react better to a human-sounding voice with simple language. If you wouldn't *say* the word to your intended audience, don't write it.

Warning Do not use long words to impress.
Do not send your audience to the dictionary.
Do not use words ending in *-ize*, such as *prioritize, actualize, finalize, conceptualize, utilize, systematize . . . .*

Example Poor: Management initiated procedures for accident reduction.
     Good: Management took steps to reduce accidents.
         (No short-word substitutes for management and accident.)

     Poor: Verisimilitude equates to pulchritude.
     Good: Truth is Beauty.

     Poor: Individuals who domicile in vitreous edifices must abstain from catapulting petrous projectiles.

     Good: People who live in glass houses mustn't throw stones.

See also Concrete and specific words.

Discussion

Many long words are just cliches from the workplace. Use your dictionary and thesaurus to find short synonyms for long words.

You and your audience are stuck with many long words that have no good short-word substitute such as *civilization, dangerous, helicopter, satellite,* and *computer.* Many professionals use long words that have a precise meaning in their profession. For example, doctors writing for doctors use words like *efficacy* and *toxicity* instead of *helpful* and *harmful.*

You also use long words that take the place of many short words. For example, use *management* instead of *the people who watch over the firm's daily affairs.*

If you can't avoid using a lot of long words, compensate by writing shorter sentences.

Exercise: Replace these long words with short, one-syllable words. (Answer A-45)

1.	accurate	31.	magnitude
2.	actuate	32.	magnanimous
3.	additional	33.	methodology
4.	allocate	34.	minimum
5.	aggregate	35.	modification
6.	apparent	36.	necessitate
7.	ascertain	37.	negative
8.	assimilate	38.	objective
9.	assistance	39.	operate
10.	capability	40.	optimum
11.	circular	41.	preliminary
12.	commensurate	42.	prioritize
13.	consistency	43.	probability
14.	demonstrate	44.	quantity
15.	denominate	45.	remuneration
16.	designate	46.	represents
17.	determination	47.	self-conscious
18.	disseminate	48.	sensible
19.	eliminate	49.	stratagem
20.	enumerate	50.	substantiate
21.	establish	51.	suitable
22.	expeditious	52.	supposition
23.	expertise	53.	terminate
24.	facilitate	54.	uncompromising
25.	functionality	55.	underutilize
26.	generate	56.	utilize
27.	hesitate	57.	variance
28.	identical	58.	verification
29.	initiate	59.	voluminous
30.	legitimate	60.	wonderful

Technique 11.3 Break long sentences.

Tips   If your Fog Index is too high because your average sentences are too long, you can break sentences to improve readability. Try breaking at punctuation marks; they often signal shifts in thought.

Break long series into vertical lists.

Warning   Do not break all sentences. Use long sentences carefully to express complex ideas.

Example

Poor: AAP selected BAP, Inc. to design and develop critical applications for its internal management information system, which requires BAP to manage the construction of a data center, purchase all the necessary software, plan and implement the transition to the new system, integrate all existing records, operate and maintain the new system, then hire and train the new data center personnel. (Fog Index = 32)

Good: AAP selected BAP, Inc. to design and develop critical applications for its internal management information system. Therefore, BAP must manage the construction of a data center and purchase all the necessary software. Then BAP must plan and implement the transition to the new system, integrating all existing records. BAP must operate and maintain the new system, then hire and train the new data center personnel. (Fog Index = 14 by cutting sentence length alone)

Better: AAP picked BAP, Inc. to build tools for its management information system. Therefore, BAP must build the data center and buy the software. Then BAP must migrate current records to the new system. BAP must operate and maintain the new system, then hire and train new data center staff. (Fog Index = 8 by cutting sentences, cutting deadwood, and replacing some long words)

See also Economy; vertical lists.

Discussion

Recall sentence outlining. If you begin your paragraphs with short, 6-to-10-word sentences, you reduce your average sentence length significantly. Recall editing for economy. If you cut your text by 20 percent, you cut your average sentence length by 20 percent.

The average spoken sentence length is 17 to 20 words. Professional writers keep average sentence length to less than 20 words.

Vary your sentence length with a range of 6-to-28-word sentences.

Emphasize key ideas in short sentences, as short as 6 words. People remember short sentences and forget long ones. Develop complex thoughts with long sentences. Use vertical lists to group logically related items, statements, commands, or questions.

Exercise: Break these long sentences to improve readability. Use short sentences for emphasis, vertical lists to group related items, and long sentences to express complex relationships. (Answer A-46)

1. The client had told us that the tanker was purchased in December, 1986, and after fulfilling an existing obligation to act as a storage facility for fuel in the Caribbean, the tanker proceeded to Portugal in May, 1987, where it was dry-docked for barnacle scraping, painting, and repairs.

2. Because the multi-state Rentacar discount is the only discount plan that would require these types of functionality, and no other discount plans have been proposed that might require this functionality, the multiple levels or alternate level credits will not be addressed in any other functional specifications.

3. To meet the Air Force Controller's need for a financial system that would provide a single, consolidated repository of a budget execution, general ledger, and external reporting for Air Force-wide financial management purposes, we developed MegaCount software modifications; developed custom interface programs to provide the MegaCount application software with data from external Air Force budget execution and reporting applications; developed conversion programs to convert existing Air Force data to MegaCount formats and data files; and developed additional custom reports, including external reports for submission to Treasury and GAO.

4. The purpose of the Uniformed Securities Act is to protect investors from fraudulent securities transactions, for which the administrating agency requires securities to be registered with the state; and unless a security is specifically exempt from registration, or the transaction is considered exempt, the security must be registered before it can be sold, or offered for sale within the state.

5. If you get a flat tire, don't panic: using the car jack is safe; however, you must ensure that the car is on a level surface, that the ground can support the weight of the car on a jack, that you retrieve the spare tire and tools from the trunk before raising the car, and that you place the jack at one of the designated phalanges located behind a front wheel.

Final exercise: The following passage is an ad for an Uninterruptible Power Supply in a catalog aimed at small businesses. The ad has 158 words, in three long sentences, for an average sentence length of 53 words. The ad has 63 long words or 40 long words per 100, generating a Fog Index of 37.

Reduce the Fog Index to 12 or lower. Cut deadwood, replace long words with short words, and break long sentences. Use vertical lists if you wish. Recalculate the Fog Index. (Answer A-46)

Uninterruptible Power Supply (UPS)
and Personal Computer Preventive Maintenance

Obviously, the corporation's configuration manager has an obligation to provide his or her corporation an electronically secure environment for the corporation's personal computers, and this advertisement will demonstrate an essential preventive maintenance application that provides reduction in the estimated mean time to failure rate for computer processing units, improvements in hard disk performance, and increased reliability of input/output peripheral devices. The pre-eminent prerequisite for establishing a secure preventive maintenance environment is an unparalleled technology known as the uninterruptible power supply (UPS), and we recommend that you consider purchasing the Microman Standby System with its internal EMI/RFI filters and surge protection capability, which provides the most economical protection for your equipment and your data from all serious electrical power interruptions. Microman's marvelous uninterruptible power supplies (UPS) feature technologically superior power transference rates, a comprehensive set of diagnostic and LED status indicators, intelligent communication interfaces, audible alarms, and attractive casings, virtually eliminating power-related risk to sensitive electronic equipment.

Step 12. Check for Correctness

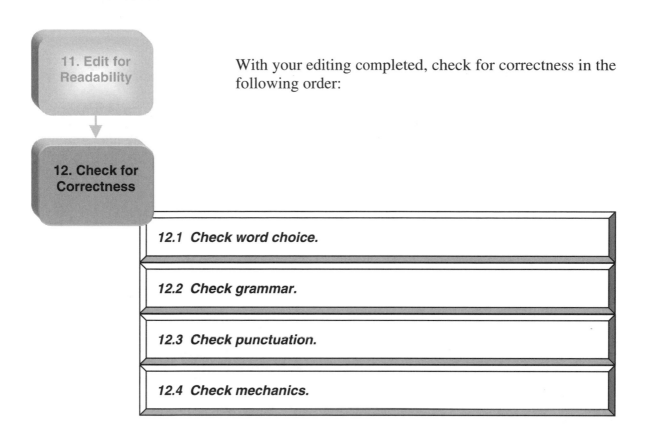

11. Edit for Readability

12. Check for Correctness

With your editing completed, check for correctness in the following order:

12.1 Check word choice.

12.2 Check grammar.

12.3 Check punctuation.

12.4 Check mechanics.

Discussion

Your earlier edits helped make the document correct. Coherence made a high-level pass at consistency and mechanics. Clarity addressed verbs, pronouns, parallelism, and modifiers. Also, clarity addressed matters of word choice as you chose specific and concrete words. Economy took you further into noun forms of verbals, prepositions, and modifiers. Readability made another pass at word choice and sentence structure.

Nevertheless, you need to make a separate pass to check standard word choice, grammar, punctuation, and mechanics. Departures from standards confuse and distract your audience.

Word choice refers to your use of individual words. Grammar is how you put the words together to express your thoughts. Punctuation marks indicate pauses and inflections. Mechanics are other conventions we accept to make our documents consistent. Check correctness in this order, because word choice affects grammar, and grammar affects punctuation.

In his book *In Search of Excellence*, author Tom Peters describes an airline that meticulously cleans the coffee rings from the tray-tables, because some passengers assume that dirty tray-tables mean poor engine maintenance. Mistakes in word choice, grammar, punctuation, and mechanics are like those coffee rings. Your audience may dismiss your message because of errors in correctness.

Technique 12.1 Check word choice.

Tips   Consult a good dictionary to check meaning, spelling, and pronunciation of words.

Check sound-alike words.

Warning   Do not trust your ears. Many word choices in speech are inappropriate for formal documents.

Do not rely on spell-checking or grammar-checking software. For example, *"We can't stand any farther weeping and whaling"* passes both spell-checking and grammar-checking software.

Example   Poor: *Presently*, NIMROD does not operate on PCs.

Good: *At present*, NIMROD does not operate on PCs.
(*Presently* means soon, and *at present* means now.)

Commonly confused sound-alike words include

affect, effect	assure, ensure, insure
council, counsel	compliment, complement
discreet, discrete	everyone, every one

See also   Readability; mechanics.

Discussion

English has more than 500,000 root words (some claim more than 1.2 million) with many multiple meanings. Don't feel inadequate if you fail to memorize them all.

Use your dictionary to build vocabulary. First, own your dictionary — a good one like *The American Heritage Dictionary*. Second, each time you look up a word, put a dot in the margin. When you find three or more dots in the margin, memorize the word. This dictionary-and-dot method ensures that you build your vocabulary with words you and your colleagues use, instead of the lofty and often useless words memorized from vocabulary-building tapes.

English has many sound-alike words, spelled differently, with different meanings. We often confuse these sound-alike words. You avoid sound-alike word confusion and improve readability by using shorter words. For example, "Margaret *(instigates, initiates)* a *(discrete, discreet)* set of commands to put the computer into *(continuous, continual)* operation" confuses. "Margaret *begins* a *distinct* set of commands to *repeat* the computer operation," communicates clearly, simply, and correctly.

Use the first definition of the word when possible. For example, the first three definitions of *since* refer to time. The fourth definition obliquely refers to cause. Therefore, use *since* when referring to time passed and use *because* to show a causal relationship.

Exercise: Match the commonly confused words with the definitions. Some words may have more than one definition. (Answer A-48)

Confused words	**Definitions**

1. adapt
   adept
   adopt

highly skilled
to take as one's own
to adjust to the situation

2. addition
   edition

increase
attachment
publication

3. advice
   advise

a noun meaning counsel given
a verb meaning to recommend

4. alter
   altar

religious table
change

5. awhile
   a while

a short time (adverb)
a period of time

6. basis
   bases

reasons, or foundations
a reason, or a foundation
facilities

7. biennial
   biannual

twice a year
every two years

8. capital
   capitol

seat of government
money owned
the building where legislators meet

9. cite
   sight
   site

to use as proof
to summon to appear in court
act of seeing
that which is seen
place or location

10. compliment
    complement

that which completes
a flattering comment

11. compose
    comprise

include
create or make up the whole

12. continuous
    continual

repeatedly and regularly
without interruption

13. counsel
    council

a group of people
advice (noun)
advise (verb)

14. devise
    device

equipment
plan

15. disapprove
    disprove

have an unfavorable opinion
show to be false

16. discrete
    discreet

tactful
separate or distinct

17. effect
    affect

to influence
a result (noun)
to result in (verb)

Confused words	Definitions
18. elicit	ask for
illicit	illegal
19. eminent	prominent
immanent	about to happen
imminent	inherent
20. envelop	surround
envelope	container for a letter
21. ensure	to promise someone
assure	to make sure
insure	to protect against loss
22. everyone	every person
every one	every person of a group, emphasizing the individual
23. except	to receive with favor
accept	aside from
24. expend	increase
expand	pay out
25. farther	space or distance
further	to a greater degree
26. formally	according to custom
formerly	in the past
27. forward	preface
foreword	at the front
28. illegible	qualified
eligible	unreadable
29. implicit	expressed directly with clarity
explicit	not directly expressed
30. it's	a possessive pronoun
its	contraction of it is
31. lie	to place
lay	to recline
32. lone	the act of lending (verb)
loan	that which is lent (noun)
alone	by oneself
	isolated
33. lose	not fastened or confined
loose	to part with
34. maybe	verb conditionally possible
may be	adverb meaning perhaps
35. past	moved on (verb)
passed	at a former time (adjective)
	former time (noun)
36. parameter	boundary
perimeter	variable or constant

Confused words	Definitions
37. people	a large anonymous group
persons	individuals
38. personal	private
personnel	employees
39. physical	financial
fiscal	of material things
40. presently	now, currently
at present	soon
41. principal	leader, money (noun)
principle	first or highest (adjective)
	rule
42. proprietary	exclusively owned
propriety	introductory
preparatory	appropriateness
43. proscribe	condemn or prohibit
prescribe	set down as a rule
44. respectively	showing respect
respectfully	considered singly
45. stationary	standing still
stationery	writing paper
46. statue	height or level
statute	rule or law
stature	carved figure
47. supplement	add to
augment	increase or magnify
48. than	in comparison with
then	at that time
49. their	possessive pronoun
there	at that place
they're	contraction of "they are"
50. to	toward
too	in addition
two	one more than one

Exercise: In each of the following pairs, identify the word that implies *time* and the other that implies *logic*. (Answer A-50)

1. While   Although
2. Because   Since
3. Then   Than
4. Once   After
5. Hence   Therefore
6. When   If
7. Consequently   Subsequently

Technique 12.2 Check grammar.

Tip 1   Check sentence structure.

Be sure you follow these three standards:
1. Each sentence has at least one subject and verb.
2. Each sentence expresses at least one complete thought.
3. Thoughts join together with standard punctuation.

Warning   Do not mistake incomplete thoughts for complete thoughts.
Connecting words such as *after, when, because*, and *while* make thoughts incomplete.

Incomplete: They postponed the survey. Until we finish the fall budget.
Complete: They postponed the survey until we finish the fall budget.

Example   Each sentence must have at least one subject and verb.
Missing verb: Carol, needing a change.
Complete: Carol, needing a change, returned to college.

Each sentence must express at least one complete thought.
Incomplete: Whenever John arrives late to work.
Complete: Whenever John arrives late to work, he blames traffic.

Thoughts must join together with standard punctuation.
Run-on: Success has a thousand fathers failure is an orphan.
Corrected: Success has a thousand fathers; failure is an orphan.
Comma Splice: A word to the wise is sufficient, don't drink and drive.
Corrected: A word to the wise is sufficient: don't drink and drive.

See also   Clarity; punctuation.

Discussion

A sentence fragment does not express a complete thought, often because the sentence lacks a verb. A run-on is two or more complete sentences joined without punctuation. A comma splice occurs when a comma joins two or more complete thoughts. Check for these common mistakes in sentence structure. For a more detailed grammar review, use grammar handbooks like the *Harbrace College Handbook.*

Learn to override your grammar-checking software. About 40 percent of the errors that your grammar checker identifies are in fact *not* errors. Ironic perhaps, but to use the grammar checker, you need to know grammar well enough that you don't need the grammar checker.

Exercise: Circle the subject(s) and underline the verb(s) of each sentence. (Answer A-51)

1. Thunder is loud, but lightning does all the work.

2. The customer does not know what we can do for her company.

3. Fred and Barney took Wilma and Betty dancing.

4. Your contribution to the project deserves our praise.

5. Sticks and stones may break my bones, but words will never hurt me.

6. You can't win if you don't play.

Exercise: Identify each word group below as a correct sentence (C), incomplete thought (IT), run-on (RO), or comma splice (CS). (Answer A-51)

1. Considering that the competition has reacted strongly to our effort to grab more market share.

2. Can type 25 words per minute.

3. Mr. Johnson, unable to attend the afternoon meeting or evening dinner.

4. Beverly Timmons, project leader for database development, made three unsuccessful requests for government assistance.

5. Whose responsibility is it to clean up the oil spill?

6. Until we found out that Good Food, Inc. had raised its price to cater a cocktail party and the Sheraton Inn had almost doubled the price to rent the ballroom.

7. Now that Sandra has finished her Associate Degree in Accounting.

8. Tax increases choking off economic growth again.

9. The office manager interviews all candidates for staff positions.

10. Friendly, courteous, and always available to answer your questions about our software products.

11. The favor of reply is requested.

12. We have a scheduling conflict for the conference room, Mr. Smith scheduled a news conference at four and the facility engineer planned to re-carpet the floor, please advise.

13. The climb to the top is hard remember that staying at the top is harder.

14. Concentration is the key to economic success, it's also the key to success in life.

Tip 2   Check pronouns.

Be sure you follow these three standards:
1. Subject and object pronouns use correct form.
2. Possessive pronouns use standard spelling.
3. Collective nouns and pronouns agree in number.

Warning   Do not confuse possessive pronouns with contractions.

| **pronoun:** | your | its | whose | their |
| **contraction:** | you're | it's | who's | they're |

Example   Use subject and object pronouns to substitute for a subjective or objective noun.
          We (subject) found *them* (object) in the corridor.

Most possessive pronouns do not use an apostrophe.
          Possessive pronouns include *mine, his, hers, ours, yours, theirs, whose.*

Use a singular pronoun when a collective pronoun acts as a group.
          The *jury* reached *its* verdict in less than two hours.

Use a plural pronoun when the members of a collective noun act separately.
          The *jury* left for *their* homes at day's end.

See also   Ambiguous pronoun; gender bias; punctuation.

Discussion

Recall editing for clarity. You've already eliminated ambiguous pronouns, thus solving many if not most pronoun problems.

Pronouns	**Subjects**	**Objects**
1st person	I, we	me, us
2nd person	you	you
3rd person	he, she, they, it	her, him, them

Use five techniques to choose the right subject or object pronoun:

1. Reverse a sentence that has a "to be" verb to choose the right pronoun. For example, *That is him* is obviously incorrect when reversed to *Him is that.*

2. To test the interrogative pronouns *who* or *whom*, substitute *he* for *who* and *him* for *whom*. For example, *Tell me (who or whom) ordered the pizza? He* ordered the pizza or *him* ordered the pizza? In this case you use the word *he*, so the right choice is *who.*

3. Be careful when using two or more pronouns together or when using a pronoun and a noun. Choose the right pronoun by imagining one of the words left out. For example, *Give it to Mary and I* is obviously incorrect when reduced to *Give it to I.*

4. Complete the sentence with understood words to help you choose the correct pronoun. Use this method when the sentence includes the words *than* or *as.*
          No one loves you more *than* your father and (*I, me*).
          Complete the sentence and it reads — *than* your father and *I* do.

5. Sometimes the pronoun you choose determines the meaning of the sentence. Be sure you communicate the intended meaning.
          She loves chocolate more often than (*he, him*).
          She loves chocolate more often than he (*does*).
          She loves chocolate more often than (*she loves*) him.

Exercise: Circle the correct pronoun. (Answer A-51)

1. The two winners were Jane Swanson and (I, me).

2. Please send Mr. Jenkins and (I, me) to the seminar.

3. Both you and (he, him) should apply for the new position.

4. The telephone technician (who, whom) you sent for has helped us before.

5. Rebecca is taller than (I, me).

6. No one wants to win the AIMS job more than Alice Cairns and (me, I).

7. The company must monitor (its, their) sick leave policy carefully.

8. BAP Industries, Inc. has (its, their) headquarters in Virginia.

9. The team won (its, it's, their) first game of the season.

10. (Its, It's) not (I, me) (whose, who's, who am) responsible for losing the key!

11. (Their, They're) talking about (your, you're) book.

12. (Whose, Who's) in charge of marketing?

13. The committee can't agree what (its, it's, their) responsibilities are.

14. That's (he, him) standing in the lobby.

15. Jerry writes better than (they, them), so (their, they're, there) supervisor asked (he, him) to edit the company newsletter.

16. Everyone cheered for (their, his or her) favorite team.

Tip 3 Check verbs.

      Be sure you follow these two standards:
      1. Subjects and verbs agree in number.
      2. Special verb form *were* expresses unreal ideas.

Warning Do not assume the noun closest to the verb is the sentence's subject.
      Note the italicized subjects and verbs below:

      IBM, like other computer manufacturers, *has* lowered prices.
      Each of the three proposed plans *ensures* good results.
      Skilled *masters* of ceremony *don't* start a speech with a joke.

Example A singular subject uses a singular verb; a plural subject uses a plural verb.
        A *collection* of paintings by the local artists *is* on display.
        Our short-term *goals* and long-term *budget conflict.*

      A collective noun acting as a group uses a singular verb.
        The *faculty uses* the conference room for its meetings.

      When its members act separately, a collective noun uses a plural verb.
        The *faculty wear* their caps and gowns at graduation.

      Use the verb form *were* to express unreal ideas (subjunctive mood) regardless of the
      number of the subject.
        If *he were* more ambitious, John might become president.

See also Clarity; economy.

Discussion

Recall editing for clarity and economy. You already made your prose clearer by using present tense, active voice, and imperative or indicative mood verbs. In addition, you cut deadwood associated with buried verbs. Both edits eliminate many grammar problems associated with verbs.

Exercise: Circle the subject. Write the verb in the form that agrees with the subject. Some sentences are correct. (Answer A-52)

1. Each of the four divisions in the company is responsible for submitting an annual budget.

2. Neither the Army nor the Air Force wants to pull troops out of Europe.

3. The senior scientist and engineer in this company wants to work on the space-station contract.

4. Difficult decisions like the one we must make today takes time.

5. A collection of paintings by three local artists is on display in the lobby.

6. A four-member crew cleans and maintains each UPS truck.

7. Where does the desk, chair, sofa, and filing cabinet go?

8. Shoes, belt, and a tie add a lot to a man's wardrobe.

9. The board of directors agree with management.

10. The carton of typewriter ribbons are sitting on the desk.

11. The duties of the police officer requires courage and self-sacrifice.

12. Attention to details ensure fewer errors.

13. Both have the authority to write checks up to $1,000.

14. George Burns, with his companion Gracie Allen, needs no introduction.

15. Here is the new copy machine and its instruction manual.

16. Half a load of bricks do not satisfy our order.

17. I wish I was your boss instead of your assistant.

18. If wishes were horses, then poor men would ride.

19. If I was a full time employee, I would get a salary with benefits, but I would lose my overtime.

20. ACME Theaters is a large national chain.

Tip 4   Check adjectives and adverbs.

Be sure you follow these two standards:
1. Articles *a* and *an* agree with the *sound* of the word that follows.
2. A negative statement uses only one negative word.

Warning   Do not decide to use *a* or *an* simply on the appearance of the first letter of the next word. Letters can be pronounced in different ways.

an umbrella   a unit   an hour   a hope

Example

Use the article *an* if the following word begins with a vowel sound (a, e, i, o, u). Otherwise, use *a*.

an angle	an egg	an intern	an option
a one-day job	an umpire	a utility	

Pay special attention to the sound of acronyms.

an MBA (em-bee-ay)   an SOW (ess-oh-double-you)
a BMW (bee-em-double-you)   a DMV (dee-em-vee)

Use only one negative word in a negative statement: *He hasn't received any orders.* A double negative results when you use two negative words in a negative statement: *He hasn't received no orders.*

Logically, a double negative equals a positive — not your intended meaning: *We have not scarcely begun* means *We have earnestly begun. The plane barely missed . . .* means *The plane directly hit.*

A sentence with more than one thought can use a negative word in each thought. *If you don't submit your application, we can't consider you for the job.* However, when editing for clarity, make your sentences positive. *If you submit your application, we can consider you for the job.*

See also   Be positive; economy; English as a second language.

Discussion

Recall editing for clarity and economy. You replaced abstract and general words with concrete and specific words, eliminating many adjectives and adverbs. Then you cut unnecessary adverbs and adjectives as part of cutting deadwood.

Negative words include *no, not, neither, never, none, nowhere, nobody, scarcely, rarely, barely, seldom, don't, doesn't, won't, can't, shouldn't, aren't, wouldn't, couldn't, haven't,* and *hardly.*

Exercise: Write *a* or *an* before each word. (Answer A-53)

1.____ten percent raise

2.____action

3.____example

4.____European

5.____hour

6.____hostess

7.____MBA

8.____order

9.____uncle

10.____11 percent drop

11.____balancing act

12.____donor

13.____FBI investigation

14.____history book

15.____icon

16.____one-time write off

17.___SOS

18.___uniform

Exercise: Write *a* or *an* in each blank. (Answer A-53)

1. _____ one-month night shift is followed by _____ 18-day paid leave.

2. Dr. Peters, ___history professor, taught ___ unit about the Civil War.

3. __ ambassador from __ European country made __ unusual request at __ UN meeting.

4. His clock has __ electrical dial, not __ hour, __ minute, or __ second hand.

5. __ aspirin is not always enough for ____ aching head.

6. Jane earned ____ MBA with ____ emphasis on marketing.

7. We need 100 days to complete ___ order, but we have ___ 83-day deadline.

8. The doctor told me to start ___ aerobic activity, which was not ___ answer I wanted to hear.

Exercise: Correct the double negatives in these sentences. (Answer A-53)

1. James couldn't find hardly anyone to invest in his gourmet doughnut shop.

2. We don't want nobody to miss the staff meeting.

3. Peter doesn't know nothing about the value of a dollar.

4. If you don't have a positive attitude, you won't succeed.

5. She couldn't scarcely hope to get a promotion after one week on the job.

6. Wouldn't Jim rather not go?

7. Let's not give no more thought to the unfortunate incident.

8. Phyllis never hardly saw no records to justify Bill's tax deductions.

9. Roger never met nobody that didn't not like his mom's tollhouse cookies.

10. The safety inspector told us that we must not store none of the nitro next to the glycerin.

Technique 12.3 Check punctuation.

Tip 1   Check apostrophes.

Be sure you follow these two standards:
1. Apostrophes show possession correctly.
2. Apostrophes show plural correctly.

Warning   Do not confuse possessives with plurals.

Do not add an apostrophe to the plural of capital-letter abbreviations
(two PCs, three RFPs).

Example   Add 's to a make a singular noun possessive.
> *The sailor's boat sank.*
> I married the *boss's* daughter.
> Exception: If a singular noun ends in *s* and has more than one syllable,
> add only the apostrophe.
> Mr. *Childress'* hat blew off.

Add an ' to make a plural noun that ends in possessive.
> The *soldiers'* relatives waited for news.
> The *Joneses'* home is beautiful. (more than one person named Jones)

Add *'s* to make a plural noun possessive if it does not end in s.
> *Men's* suits can be expensive.
> Your future *sisters-in-law's* dresses arrived two weeks before the wedding.

Use an apostrophe for the plural of letters, words, and numbers.
> How many *t's* did you count?
> Watch the use of *and's* in your writing.
> Cross out the *2's.*

See also   Mechanics; English as a second language.

Discussion

An apostrophe and *s* are often used to indicate possession.

Possessive relationships include
1. personal — *John's* friend
2. ownership — the *women's* volleyball team
3. time — a *year's* leave
4. authorship — the *accountant's* report
5. type or kind — a *men's* clothing store

Exercise: Write the singular possessive and the plural possessive. For example, *player* has singular possessive — *player's* and plural possessive — *players'*. (Answer A-54)

1. clerk   2. Jones   3. day   4. business   5. man

6. facility   7. area   8. boss   9. knife   10. advisor

11. fence   12. city   13. guest   14. line of credit   15. loss

16. waitress   17. year   18. lunch   19. brother-in-law   20. friend

Exercise: Insert an apostrophe and an *s* to show a possessive noun. Make other nouns plural if necessary. (Answer A-54)

1. The employee attend lectures where they learn techniques to improve their plant efficiency.

2. We investigated Bill complaint.

3. All of the question were answered in turn.

4. The Treasurer recommendation is that we cut overhead cost.

5. If we build a men locker room, we'd better build a women locker room too.

6. We hired several new employee for the Jason project.

7. Fred office will need two coat of paint.

8. It's the office manager responsibility to make sure the light work in the conference room.

9. The toxic waste response team must respond in a minute notice.

10. Please evaluate Avis proposal to discount our company large car rental fees.

Tip 2   Check commas.

Be sure you follow these three standards:
1. Commas separate items in series.
2. Commas separate introductory expressions from main idea.
3. Commas set off parenthetical expressions.

Warning   Do not forget the second comma in a pair of commas.

Poor: Senator Foghorn, our senator runs for re-election this year.
Good: Senator Foghorn, our senator, runs for re-election this year.

Example   Use commas to separate items in series of three or more, including a comma before the *and*.

Betty wrote, edited, proofread, and produced the manual.

Use a comma to separate most introductory expressions from the main idea of the sentence.   Use commas after introductory expressions that contain any form of a verb.

If she calls, take a message.
Planning ahead, Marty packed his tennis shoes.

Use a comma after an introductory expression of five or more words.

In the back of the computer, the serial port connects to the printer cable.

When an introductory expression has fewer than five words and has no verb form, decide if a comma is needed to avoid confusion.

In our county, taxes are high.   (comma distinguishes county from county taxes)

Use commas before and after a non-essential expression — details that add to a sentence but do not change its meaning.

The result, however, was disastrous.
Thomas, a chemical engineer, took the night shift.
Refer to the letter, which I sent last week, for your answer.

See also   Clarity; English as a second language.

Discussion

Commas indicate a short pause to separate items. To help yourself place commas correctly, consider where you pause briefly in speech.

English delimits each item in a series with commas: *a, b, and c*. European languages omit the comma before the *and*. Do not use a comma to separate pairs: *a and b*.

Use *which* when the expression is non-essential, and set off with commas. You can remove non-essential expressions without changing the sentence's meaning. Use *that* for an essential expression and do not set off with commas.

Read my letter, which I sent March 11. (Non-essential — I sent you only one letter.)
Read my letter that I sent March 11. (Essential — I sent you other letters.)

Commas and periods go inside ending quotation marks. *The contract allows "a 45-day extension," so we can "verify and validate the system."*

Exercise: Insert commas where needed. (Answer A-54)

1. The Smith Foundry Tool and Die Company was started by Thomas Smith an inventor and entrepreneur.

2. I want to see last quarter's income statement balance sheet and cash flow statement.

3. Margery Elizabeth Susan and I can just barely fit in her new sedan.

4. IBM Compaq Apple and a host of other personal computer manufacturers are struggling to define their marketing strategies.

5. Employee benefits include paid vacation holidays sick leave bereavement leave and unpaid maternity leave.

6. The new copy machine is faster cleaner more reliable and more versatile.

7. We can buy industrial grade fire retardant carpet in either beige dark blue green gray or burnt orange.

8. Our lounge always keeps pots of regular and decaffeinated coffee with cream and sugar.

9. Your flight has stops in Atlanta Denver Los Angeles and Melbourne.

10. Because the air conditioner broke down we're releasing the workers at 2:00 p.m.

11. After I just got a $2 million construction loan you've got a lot of nerve telling me you underestimated the job.

12. Although they finished paving the parking lot they have not painted the lines yet.

13. Gigamega the most powerful computer ever built has been programmed to invent video games.

14. Our new vice-president for engineering Dr. Potts will lead the discussion on cryogenics.

15. William's plan even though it made no sense to us won high praise from the Navy.

16. If I had to learn a second language all things being equal I would study FORTRAN.

17. Patriots Day a paid holiday in Massachusetts does not merit a day off in Virginia.

18. *Slick* magazine boasting a circulation of five million paid subscribers charges $1,600 for a quarter-page ad.

19. In the past success came easily for George.

20. In conclusion we use commas to separate parenthetical expressions from the main idea of the sentence.

21. Before a conversion starts the system downloads the source data into three files.

22. Send the blue yellow and pink copies of the purchase order to accounting.

Tip 3   Check semicolons.

Be sure you follow these two standards:
1. Semicolons join two complete thoughts correctly.
2. Semicolons separate list items that have internal commas.

Warning   Do not use semicolons to join a complete thought with an incomplete thought or phrase.

Poor: Although Inga lives in Maryland; she works in Virginia.
Good: Although Inga lives in Maryland, she works in Virginia.

Poor: The project manager met with the client; because the contract requires weekly reviews of schedules, costs, and deliverables.

Good: The project manager met with the client, because the contract requires weekly reviews of schedules, costs, and deliverables.

Example   Use a semicolon to join two closely related, complete thoughts.
Ms. Kim's references were excellent; we offered her the job.
Bob likes the car; he can not afford it.

Transition words such as *therefore, however, nevertheless,* and *rather* often relate ideas. Use a semicolon before these transitional expressions to join complete thoughts. Use a comma after the transition word.
Bob likes the car; however, he can not afford it.

If either side of the transition word is not a complete thought, separate the transition word with commas.
Bob likes the car. He cannot, however, afford it.

Use semicolons to separate items in a series when the items already have commas.
We have offices in Atlanta, Georgia; Tampa, Florida; and Mobile, Alabama.
Choose one of the three dates: May 1, 2002; June 15, 2003; or July 8, 2004.

See also   Parallelism.

Discussion

The semicolon marks a pause longer than a comma, but shorter than a period — easy to remember because the semicolon consists of a period over a comma. A semicolon often takes the place of the word *and.*

Semicolons go outside ending quotation marks. *Read "The Employee's Handbook"; adhere to the policies.*

Exercise: Insert semicolons where needed. (Answer A-55)

1. The receptionist area needs new carpet, however, we'll wait until we remodel the entire floor.

2. Although the receptionist area needs new carpet, we'll wait until we remodel the entire floor.

3. Dr. Latrobe, a propulsion expert, designed a rocket motor that runs on normal jet fuel, nonetheless, liquid hydrogen remains our preferred fuel, because it has a better thrust to weight ratio.

4. Francis will meet us at O'Hare Airport, however, 30 minutes later than expected.

5. Luck is where preparation meets opportunity, so keep your eyes open and be prepared.

6. We won the contract, now we have to do the work.

7. Karen Kelly brought us some of our most profitable accounts, for example, she landed both the Hechinger and the Safeway accounts.

8. We've added four new sales districts, which are Atlanta, Georgia, Mobile, Alabama, New Orleans, Louisiana, and Houston, Texas.

9. Our company has but one mission, that is, to provide our clients the best value in video home entertainment.

10. Megatech bid the highest price, nevertheless, they won the contract on technical merit.

11. Conglomerator, Inc.'s most recent acquisitions were Catfish Farms, Ltd. on April 10, 1999, and Carlisle Cosmetics, Inc. on December 2, 2001.

12. Although Mr. Derickson is younger than the other applicants, he deserves to get the job because of his superior performance record.

13. Our company's policy is to promote from within, for instance, Mr. Jacobs started as a clerk and rose to be chief executive officer.

14. Because John Heath just came to us from the Department of Transportation, where he was a special assistant to the Secretary, we mustn't bid him on the Highway Study Project.

15. As long as sales continue to increase at the present rate, we can absorb the rising cost of labor without raising our prices.

Tip 4　Check colons.

Be sure you follow these two standards:
1. Colons come after a complete thought when a supporting thought, phrase, word, or series follows.
2. Colons come after a complete thought when a list follows.

Warning　Do not use colons after an incomplete thought.

Poor:　After the blades have stopped completely: remove the cover to inspect the roller bearings.

Good:　After the blades have stopped completely, remove the cover to inspect the roller bearings.

Poor:　The exercise room has: free weights, stationary bikes, and a sauna.

Good:　The exercise room has free weights, stationary bikes, and a sauna.
　　　　The exercise room has equipment: free weights, stationary bikes, and a sauna.

Example　Use a colon after a complete thought when a sentence, phrase, word, or series follows.

Sentence:　You must save for retirement: contribute the maximum to your 401K plan.
　　　　　Remember Churchill's advice: Never give up.
　　　　　The President made this point: "We must all pull together."

Phrase:　We have one option to stay competitive: reducing prices.

Word:　His answer was simple: no.

Series:　We suggest these furnishings: a desk, chair, table, and lamp.

See also　Clarity; grammar.

Discussion

As a good rule of thumb, put a colon only where you can put a period. A colon indicates that the thought ends — not that a series begins. After the colon you can add supporting details: a word, phrase, series, or even another sentence.

Use colons after a complete thought that introduces a vertical list. Use a colon after a complete sentence that introduces a quote. Use quotation marks unless the quote is famous.

Colons go outside ending quotation marks. *We found two errors in the article "Home Repair": transposed letters and misplaced modifiers.*

Capitalize the first word after the colon if the statement that follows is an independent complete sentence, formal resolution, question, or quoted material that also began with a capital. Use lower case if the following statement is a subordinate sentence, phrase, word, or series.

Put one space after the colon.

In letters, use the colon after the salutation for business: *Dear Tom Jones:* Use the comma after the salutation if personal: *Dear Tom,*

Exercise: Insert colons where needed. Check capitalization. (Answer A-56)

1. Next time, give that pushy salesman an evasive answer, tell him to take a long walk off a short pier!

2. Note well the company would have posted a substantial loss in 2000 except for the one-time sale of the Occoquan property.

3. Our company has but one mission to provide our clients the best value in video home entertainment.

4. Conglomerator, Inc. made two acquisitions Catfish Farms, Ltd. on April 10, 1999; and Carlisle Cosmetics, Inc. on December 2, 2001.

5. You must add one procedure to lower your worker's compensation insurance you must aggressively prosecute fraud.

6. Eric made a significant breakthrough in his research he discovered a new graphite compound.

7. Doc Watson put a sign on his briefcase Moon or Bust!

8. The odor from the paper mill smoke smells bad, but it's harmless.

9. Managing inter-personal conflict is like the law of thermal dynamics you can't win, you can't break even, and you can't get out of the game.

10. The employee lounge has three simple rules for everyone's mutual enjoyment no smoking, no alcoholic beverages, no radios without earphones.

Tip 5   Check dashes and parentheses.

Be sure you follow these two standards:
1. Dashes emphasize details or thoughts.
2. Parentheses de-emphasize details or thoughts.

Warning   Do not confuse a hyphen with a dash. A dash is as wide as a capital letter 'M' or twice as wide as a hyphen. If you can't print an M-dash, make your dash with two hyphens.

Do not overuse dashes. When everything screams for attention, nothing gets noticed. Too many dashes fragment and disorganize thoughts.

Example   Dashes emphasize. Commas are neutral. Parentheses de-emphasize.

Our firm — *having earned a large profit last year* — hopes to expand into new markets. (emphasized)

Our firm, *having earned a large profit last year*, hopes to expand into new markets. (neutral)

Our firm (*having earned a large profit last year*) hopes to expand into new markets. (de-emphasized)

Use dashes to separate a nonessential expression that contains one or more commas. However, to de-emphasize the word group, use parentheses.

The neighbors — Mr. Johnson, Mr. Black, and Mrs. Smith — attended the party.
The neighbors (Mr. Johnson, Mr. Black, and Mrs. Smith) attended the party

Use a dash after a series or a single word that comes before a complete thought.

Looks, brains, talent — she had them all.

Use ending punctuation inside parentheses only when the parenthetical expression is outside a sentence.

The safety valve (see figure 1) is red.
The safety valve is red (see figure 1).
The safety valve is red. (See figure 1.)

If the parenthetical expression is outside a sentence, the parenthetical expression itself needs to be a complete sentence, beginning with capitalization.

See also Hyphens.

Discussion

Limit the use of parentheses in technical and business documents. If the information is truly less important, considering cutting it. Otherwise, remove the parentheses.

Typesetters typically do not put spaces between the dash and the word. We add the space to compensate for the word-wrap function of wordprocessors.

Use parentheses to introduce acronyms: *The Food and Drug Administration (FDA).* Use parentheses — not dashes — to enclose directions. *The figures (see page 2) indicate modest gains in 1998.*

Exercise: Insert dashes, parentheses, commas, or colons. Some sentences can be punctuated several ways. (Answer A-56)

1. The invoice for $215.00 not $21.50 needs your prompt attention.

2. Writing and editing ability that's what we want in our senior technical staff.

3. The partnership usually pays a portion of the net profits for example, $670 per limited partner in 2000 to help cover the limited partners' tax liability.

4. Jeff must fix the rear projector in the conference room today tomorrow is too late.

5. The Penultimate II cordless phone you won't find a better value offers the following features speed dialing, auto call back, conference calling, and much more.

6. The offices on the sixth floor Treasury, Marketing, and Human Resources will be moved to the new building in May.

7. Dorothy had it all a dog, ruby slippers and Kansas.

8. Rebecca requested a four-week vacation she won a cruise and she has no choice as to dates.

9. Sales rose see figure 4, page 32 to a record high however return on sales fell slightly.

10. A high school diploma, three years' experience, good references these are the minimum requirements.

Tip 6   Check hyphens.

Be sure you follow these two standards:
1. Hyphens separate parts of a word.
2. Hyphens join parts of a compound adjective.

Warning   Do not confuse a hyphen with a dash.

Example   Use a hyphen to separate parts of a word.

twenty-two
self-taught

Use a hyphen to join the parts of a compound adjective (an adjective made up of two or more words). In a compound adjective, the first adjective describes the second adjective.

a computer-generated graphic (computer describes generated)
a top-to-bottom analysis (the words *top, to*, and *bottom* must work together)

Use a hyphen when a compound adjective appears before the noun or verb. Do not use a hyphen when the phrase appears after the noun and verb, or if the first word in the phrase ends *with ly, er,* or *est.*

The graphic is computer generated.
The analysis runs top to bottom.
The slowly opening door caught his attention.

See also   Dash.

Discussion

Use a hyphen in other compound words as indicated by your dictionary or company style manual. Some common compound adjectives have dropped the hyphen, such as *high school* student and *real estate* broker.

Some technical terms have evolved to drop the hyphen. For example *data-base* evolved to *data base* without the hyphen. Now *database* is standard.

Modern style guides also drop hyphens from words. *Co-operate* becomes *cooperate*. *Bird-like* becomes *birdlike*. The dropped hyphens may irk traditionalists, but remember at one point the word *today* was hyphenated, *to-day*.

Exercise: Punctuate compound adjectives with hyphens. (Answer A-57)

1. We graduate a hundred odd students each year.

2. John sent a carefully worded letter to IRS to explain his highly irregular filings for 1998 and 1999.

3. Send an up to date roster of security clearances to Lt. Avery.

4. The security inspector, Lt. Avery, said our security clearance roster was not up to date.

5. We received a well-written proposal to build an off site data entry system.

6. He wished his off the record remarks had stayed off the record.

7. Alice made a reasonably good attempt to send the package before five o'clock.

8. John and Martha sublet a one-bedroom apartment in a not so nice part of town.

9. Thelma told the interior decorator she wanted eggshell white paint in the dining facility, but when the paint dried, she swore the color was coffee stain brown.

10. Mrs. Stern won't tolerate a gum-chewing receptionist.

11. Please follow the simple step by step instructions.

12. Be sure to follow the instructions step by step.

Tip 7   Check vertical list punctuation.

Be sure you follow the standards established by your style guide, or use these three standards:

1. Use a colon after an introductory sentence, but omit the colon after an introductory phrase.
2. If list items are complete sentences, begin each with a capital and punctuate them as complete sentences with ending period, question mark, or exclamation mark.
3. If list items are not complete sentences, omit ending punctuation.

Be consistent.

Warning   Do not vary the way you punctuate lists.

Example   With Pert Plan software you define each task three ways:

1. Give task with a firm deadline.
2. Estimate the range of time for completion.
3. Estimate the average time to completion.

The project start-up team must
- provide a work plan
- negotiate definitions for deliverables
- hire and train project staff

Three symptoms of allergic reactions include the following:
- itchy nose and throat
- sinus headaches
- tearing eyes

See also   Vertical lists; parallelism; colons.

Discussion

Treat the list introduction and the list items separately for punctuation. For example, the introduction may be a complete thought with the colon, while the list items are phrases without punctuation.

Make each item in your list grammatically parallel. Make punctuation at the end of each item consistent.

A vertical list is not a long sentence, but a series of like items. Therefore, a list does not follow the same punctuation rules as a sentence.

Modern business and technical writers favor using less punctuation in vertical lists for a cleaner, more streamlined style. Punctuating a vertical list with ending semicolons and period is outdated.

Exercise: Correct the punctuation in these lists. (Answer A-57)

1. We need to address two conversion issues for Design Release 2.2, including:

    1) conversion of information from the VAX to IBM environment; and,
    2) initialization and maintenance of the operator's manual.

2. Avoid ambiguity with three techniques:

    1) choose words carefully
    2) place modifiers close to words they modify
    3) use active voice

3. Before you turn off the LAN host computer, you must:

    Close any open files and exit any active programs
    Run the backup to tape procedure
    Run the LAN check to warn users of system shutdown
    Input a valid LAN operator ID# then end the LAN program

4. The strengths of the Shazbot system include:

    a. error trapping prevents faulty data entry
    b. online help functions decrease training time

5. The flag's three colors are:

    1. Red;
    2. Green; and,
    3. Gold.

6. The flag has three colors:

    1. Top field is red;
    2. Bottom field is green, and:
    3. Star in the center is gold.

Technique 12.4 Check mechanics.

Tips   Follow or establish standards for visual mechanics: spelling, layout, and typography.

Use or create a style guide.

Be consistent.

Warning   Do not vary mechanics without a logical reason.

Example   *Numbers:* Spell zero through ten. Use numerals for 11 and above. Spell approximate numbers: *almost a thousand applicants*. Always use numerals for measurements (*8½"x11" paper*). Use numerals for percentages (*20 percent*), and spell the word percent, except in tables. Use numerals in tables or when space is limited. When several numbers appear in the same paragraph, either spell or use numerals for all. Spell numbers that begin a sentence: *Twenty students enrolled*. When numbers run together, spell one number; use a numeral for the other: *sixteen 3-day weekends*. Write fractions as numerals when used with whole numbers: *8½"x11" paper*. Use numerals for numbers with decimals: *6.12 parsecs*.

Acronyms are the first letters or parts of words combined to make a new word: *Local Area Network* becomes *LAN*; *first in first out* becomes *FIFO*. Capitalize acronyms except for the few that have become common nouns, such as laser or zipcode. Initializations combine first letters but do not make a new word; rather, they are pronounced as the letters: *cash on delivery* becomes *C.O.D.*; *personal computer* becomes *PC*. Not all initializations use capital letters: *ante meridian* and *post meridian* are *a.m.* and *p.m.* Spell out acronym or initialization the first time it appears in the document, except when it is better known in its shorter form: *HTML* is better known than *Hypertext Markup Language*. Make acronyms and initializations plural by adding a lower case *s* with no apostrophe: *two PCs*.

Abbreviations: When in doubt, spell it out. For states, use postal abbreviations in addresses — *VA*, otherwise spell state name — *Virginia*. Spell *United States* except when used as a prefix for an agency. Do not add a second period if the abbreviation ends the sentence.

See also   Visual devices.

Discussion

Although standards for word choice, grammar, and punctuation remain fairly constant, standards for mechanics vary. Pick a style guide appropriate for your profession, company, project, or document. An Internet search confirms that you have many style guides to choose from. They tend to fall into the following four categories:

1.   Academic, often associated with a university: Chicago Manual of Style, MLA, Turabian
2.   Discipline, often associated with an association or professional journal: IEEE, APA
3.   Journalism, often associated with a news agency or newspaper: AP, *The New York Times*
4.   Organization: Government Printing Office (GPO), National Labor Relations Board

Ask your clients if they use a particular style guide and consider using theirs.

Supplement the published style guide with your own style sheet. At a minimum, keep a list of key words, acronyms, and abbreviations to ensure consistency. Determine page layout and assign fonts, spacing, alignment, and ruling lines for visual devices such as titles, subheads, body text, captions, and footnotes.

Be consistent. Remember that unnecessary shifts in mechanics, just like unnecessary shifts in key words, confuse the reader.

Exercise: Improve the mechanics of these sentences. (Answer A-58)

1. At our 9:00 AM meeting we reviewed the 4-month extension through 9/01. We learned yesterday that DoD (Dept. of Defense) will request another two month extension. We decided to submit the extension to DOD for 2 months with two one month options.

2. Beginning 3/19/02 Ben Brown will handle any material and/or supplies request through the MS/Plus computer system.

3. The mayor introduced former pres. Bush at the local Veteran's day celebration in Alex., VA.

4. Enter your userid in the ibm; then transmit your lotus files from the pc's hard-disk to your own floppy disk.

5. 250 people attended the air force convention in Palm springs, CA.

6. Mr. Smith called this morning. (He left his telephone and fax #.)

7. The order was for 12 6 inch pipes; We shipped them to Joe's hardware inc. yesterday at 5PM.

8. See figure four on page nine.

9. My favorite book is How to Repair Your Volkswagen: a step-by-step manual for the complete Idiot.

10. This occurrance only strengthens our commitment to proceding with BAP industries' expansion into nickle mining.

Final exercise 1: Circle the correct word. (Answer A-58)

1. We are (adapt, adept) at software design.

2. Please indicate your (ascent, assent) by signing the contract.

3. The improved lighting has had a good (affect, effect) on productivity.

4. Careful pre-writing (assures, ensures, insures) effective writing.

5. Dewey, Cheetham, and Howe serves as (council, counsel) to the city (council, counsel).

6. The salad makes a fine (compliment, complement) to the broiled fish.

7. It helps to break the problem into (discreet, discrete) topics.

8. (Everyone, Every one) must attend the safety briefing.

9. We cannot discount our hourly rates any (farther, further).

10. Can we (forego, forgo) the interview process?

11. Mr. Smith was (formally, formerly) self-employed.

12. The operator must get (past, passed) the shut-off valve before seeing the display.

13. We will not allow an employee administrative leave unless we believe there is a serious (personnel, personal) problem.

14. The key to persuasive writing is seeing the reader's (perspective, prospective).

15. The students felt sure of success because they had a (principal, principle) at stake.

16. Please examine each cost item (respectfully, respectively).

17. Please (sit, set) yourself a place at the table.

18. What harm is a couple of beers (between, among) friends?

19. The Fairfax County Symphony gave a (credible, creditable) performance.

20. Doctors recommend we eat a (healthy, healthful) breakfast.

21. There are (less, fewer) than six days left to complete the work.

22. We moved our offices to the suburbs (since, because, due to) the lease expired and (since, because of, due to) the high prices in the city.

23. As the company's founder, Mr. Adam Smith raised the company to a (respectable, respectful) position in the steel industry.

24. Refer to the letter, (that, which) I sent last Tuesday.

25. The lawyer had no (further, farther) questions for the witness.

Final exercise 2: Punctuate these sentences correctly. (Answer A-59)

1. If ever you've nothing to do and plenty of time to do it in why don't you come up and see me.
    — Mae West in the movie *My Little Chickadee.*

2. In his best selling book *Wabbit Hunting* the author Elmer Fudd discusses a hundred ways to trap snare or shoot cwazy wabbits.

3. Our bookkeeper Teresa impressed the auditors with her accurate files.

4. The temporary services agency Temps & Co. will give us eight hours of temp services at no charge just so we can evaluate their company.

5. Erica the company expert on time management suggests that we conduct all staff meetings standing up.

6. We billed four hours at the principal rate of $180 per hour and eight hours at the staff rate of $42 per hour.

7. Lorna Ewald Ph.D. in computer sciences started her own company in 1985 but she sold her interest to Logicon Inc. and then she came to work for us.

8. Population growth in the United States according to the latest census data has fallen if you take out immigration.

9. The qualities we seek include good people skills willingness to learn and willingness to travel.

10. Sam's motto cash is king made a lot of sense in the 90s when so many companies struggled with debt.

11. Steel, oil, and railroads the great monopolies of the 19th Century changed the face of capitalism forever.

12. Dr. Nathan our only nuclear engineer decided that the company's research into cold fusion is a poor investment.

13. A typical engine overhaul is a one day job.

14. Red, white and blue will wrap our Fourth of July Sale in the flag.

15. The telecommunications van must be able to operate in the tropics therefore we added a dehumidifier to its on board equipment.

16. Dr. Harold Brown chairman of the Loudon Board of Trade met with the Loudon County Zoning Commission to attempt a compromise between local environmentalists and developers.

17. AMTRAK's Metroliner runs between Washington, D.C. and New York in 2 hours and 52 minutes with stops in New Carrolton Maryland Baltimore Maryland Wilmington Delaware and Philadelphia Pennsylvania.

18. Any member of our cross trained staff that includes me can help you solve your most difficult files management problems.

Final exercise 3: Find and correct the word choice, grammar, punctuation, and mechanics errors in this excerpt. (Answer A-60)

Implementation of b-2 module

This plan outline's the requirements, for the successful *B-2* module implementation, in a MBE application. This document describes the (high level) requirements, according to agreed standards within BAPCO's marketing dept.. The b2 module supports 2 users, vp of Marketing — Mr. John, and its supervisor, the treasurer, Mr. Bynum.

The b-*2* module serves three purposes:

1. Management of assignment for sales representatives;
2. Appraisal of success rate for each sales representative, and;
3. Determination of commissioning level for each sales representative.

However, a one time event report must firstly be set-up. While the report lists the prospects respectfully by sale's representatives Mr. Bynum also want to see all prospects even those not retrieved by the *B2* module. Therefore, we must create a report to show the relevant info of those prospects as a base-line. Presupposes Mr. Bynum's agreement to this plan.

Relevant prospects has the following 3 *prospect criterion*

1. Lead (prospestat_id="LEAD");
2. Hot (prospestat_id="HOT"), and;
3. Inactive (prospestat_id="INACT".)

Everyone of the sales representatives work in three countries (Canada, Mexico and the US.) Retrieved prospects have a cite located in a city which corresponds to *ZIPcode* ranging from 00000 to 99999. (*4000<prospect.zip_code<7900*). A valid prospect has a *sight type* designated commercial (*prospect.sitetype_id="COM".*)

Since the report also shows the contact persons first and last name, the queries need to excess: the *prospect* table, the *contact_link* and *contact* tables. The keys to success is: *prospect_no*, and the *contact_no*. Each have links from the *prospect_link* to prospect tables and from the *contact_link* to the contact tables.

Step 13. Proofread

12. Check for Correctness

13. Proofread

After correcting your document's word choice, grammar, punctuation, and mechanics, use these two techniques to proofread accurately and quickly:

13.1 Proofread in a series of readings.

13.2 Check live copy against dead copy.

Discussion

Proofread after you have checked for correctness, when you think the document is standard and consistent. Look for errors that you missed. Look for errors that crept into the current, *live* copy.

Proofreading, the final step in the writing system, demands patience and disciplined attention to detail.

Often, poor proofreading occurs because writers try to combine editing and correcting with proofreading. Consequently, they lose focus.

Technique 13.1 Proofread in a series of readings.

Tips   In a series of readings, look for typing errors and check accuracy.

Use proofreading tools: spellchecking and grammar-checking software, dictionary, and style guide. Use a straightedge to check columns and alignment.

Mark corrections in the text, then note them in the margin. Count the corrections per page and put the number at the top right corner of the page.

Transcribe corrections into *live* copy.

Warning   Do not try to check everything at once.

Do not re-edit while you proofread. You will introduce errors.

Example   Look for these common typing errors:

- Incorrect spacing
- Duplicated or omitted letters, words, or lines
- Mistyped numbers in dates, statistics, formulas, or money
- Missing punctuation marks that usually come in pairs such as commas, parentheses, quotation marks, and dashes
- Typos in material outside the body text such as titles, captions, table of contents, headings, addresses, and signature lines
- Faulty spellchecker word substitution
- Transposed letters — *form* instead of *from*

Look for these common accuracy errors:

- Inaccurate page citation — sending reader to wrong page
- Inaccurate table of contents and index
- Inaccurate detail (Baltimore, Virginia's chief port city)

See also   Correctness.

Discussion

Know the strengths and weaknesses of your software. Wordprocessors use algorithms to break and hyphenate words. The algorithms make mistakes. Your spellchecker doesn't help if you have the wrong word spelled correctly. If you transpose letters — *two* becomes *tow* or *from* becomes *form* — use your wordprocessor's find-and-replace function to correct your most common errors. Grammar checkers make mistakes. Use your grammar-checker to check eye-straining details like spaces between sentences.

After using your software tools, print your document for final proofreading. Paper documents are easier to check; therefore, accuracy improves.

Proofread slowly — more slowly when the content is technical, is highly formatted, or uses varied fonts. Be careful at the end of long lines and in the middle of long words. If you find one error, look back for others, because errors often cluster. Take breaks to stay alert.

Exercise: Even professionals make mistakes. Find and fix the errors. (Answer A-61)

"Welcome to the Writing Center! This unique area is designed to help you improve the style, presentation, and effectivenes of your writing. Whether your writing reports for work, term papers for school, or you working on that first novel, you'll discover amazingly useful information onevery aspect of writing well." Prodigy Writing Center, 1997.

"When you turn on Gammar-As-You-Go, Spell-As-You-Go is turned on as well." Corel WordPerfect Documentation, 1977.

"Go To Class — It' a Blast!!!" Washington, DC School Board's advertisement to combat truancy, 2001.

Exercise: Proofread the following letter. Identify errors as word choice, grammar, punctuation, mechanics, typing, or accuracy. (Answer A-61)

12 June 2002
Graphics Leasing Corp.
Attn: Accts. Receivable Manager
VGS Park Dept A
5701 N.W. 9th Ave.

Dear Sir:

Below is a list of Alcor Corp. check numbers, invoice dates and amounts in payment of the lease and maintenance agreement on our POS-320 camera. We obtained this information through our disbursement summery report for fiscal year 1898.

Because these items are old, we can find neither cancelled checks nor duplicate copies for your review. I suggest, that you check your deposit records for the time in question to varify the amounts.

Check #	Invoice Date	Ammount paid
037614	4/25/98	932.04
043569	4/25/98	804.12
0128476	4/28/98	804.04
019383	5/14/98	425.12
019383	5/14/88	425,12
03600	07/3/98	445.12
03600	18/15/8	388.24
037455	0/11/98	432.17
045672	11/22/19	. 464.25
Total Paid		$ 5,110.25

These problem occured because of   your inaccurate files.The discrepency is one and one half and one half and one half years old. Therefore, we are not responsibile fore proving any farther the payment of these items. I consider this matter closed with this letter.

Sincerely,

Accounting Supervisor

Technique 13.2 Check live copy against the dead copy.

Tips Make sure your live copy now includes corrections marked on the dead copy. Count corrections and compare to the total recorded at the top right corner of the dead copy.

Make sure no new errors crept in. Mark or disfigure the dead copy and put it away when you are through checking. Thereby, you ensure pages of dead copy don't accidentally find their way back into the live document.

Check legibility, the quality of print — *faded? smeared? dark? streaking? wrinkled paper? misaligned paper or any other printer mechanical problems?* Are graphics clear and crisp? Do you have adequate margins for binding?

Check completeness: page sequence, auxiliary material such as appendices and enclosures.

Warning Do not proofread if tired or rushed. Rushed proofreading tends to introduce errors. Plan time for proofreading.

Do not assume that boilerplate is perfect. You must proofread boilerplate too.

Example Dead copy: Pete, Don and Mike met today to discuss out Spring schedule.
Live copy: Pete, Don,and Mike met today to discuss our spring schedule.

The proofreader found and corrected three errors in the dead copy: an omitted comma, misspelled word, and unnecessary capital. However, he introduced a new error to the live copy: an omitted space before the word *and*.

See also Correctness.

Discussion

Editors refer to the current copy as "live copy" to distinguish it from the previous "dead copy." Establish procedures to keep track of your proofreading. Otherwise, you waste time with unnecessary re-reading, or you forget to make the corrections marked.

Proofreading ensures the physical quality of the document. Check the paper, type, layout, graphics, and binding. Even the best laser printers occasionally double-feed sheets, wrinkle paper, put pages out of order, streak, and fade. Ensure everything is included in the right order with nothing duplicated.

Exercise: Check live copy against the dead copy. What errors were corrected? What errors remain? Did new errors creep in? (Answer A-62)

Dead copy

Before beginning this tutorial for the System Administrator of the Blue System, be sure that your have already finished the tutorial for the Tech Controller. That tutorial lays the foundation on which all Blue System tutorials are based. This tutorial describes only those administrative tasks that are relevant to the Blue System operated on a SUN Workstation.

Also, before beginning this tutorial, be sure that you are comfortable using the vi editor described in detail in Chapter 6 of *Getting Stated with UNIX — Beginners Guide*, available from your instructor. Recall that some men have items that are not selectable, because they are limited to user's with certain privileges, who are

    1. System Administrator
    2. Circuit Connectivity Modifier
    3. Pin Connectivity Modifier
    4. Technical Controller.

A privileged user may access only certain windows. An individual who has been assigned only System Administration privileges, will be able to open only the System Administration Window, the Console Window, the Message Window, and the RED Messages Window. This tutorial for System Administrators assumes that you have been assigned only System Administrator privileges. This tutorial will describe each window that you you may access and its functions and tasks.

Live copy

Before beginning this tutorial for the System Administrator of the Blue System, be sure that your have already finished the tutorial for the Tech Controller. That tutorial lays the foundation on which all Blue System tutorials are based. This tutorial describes only those administrative tasks that are relevant to the Blue System operated on a SUN Workstation.

Also, before beginning this tutorial, be sure that you are comfortable using the vi editor described in detail in Chapter 6 of *Getting Started with UNIX — Beginners Guide*, available from your instructor. Recall that some menues have items that are not selectable, because they are imited to users with certain privileges, who are

    1. System Administrator
    2. Circuit Connectivity Modifier
    3. Pin Connectivity Modifier
    4. Technical Controller

A privileged user may access only certain windows. An individual who has been assigned only System Administration privilegeswill be able to open only the System Administration Window, the Console Window, the Message Window, and the RED Messages Window. This tutorial for System Administrators assumes that you have been assigned only System Administrator privileges. This tutorial will describe each window that you you may access and its functions and tasks.

Final Exercise: Proofread this memorandum. (Answer A-62)

INTEROFFICE CORESPONDANCE

To: Distributoin
From: Mary Poole
Date: 2 Setpember, 2000

Re: Briefing for Training Faciltators

You have been assigned training resp onsibilities in conjunction with next years MGR training effort. The two short tapes which will be used for the the 2001 training willbe "Timekeeping" and "Harrassment. The tapes were all ready in production and will be   shipped at you approximately October 1, 2000.

A briefing session will be held 11 AM on June 28, 1998 at headqurters to reveiw the to review the content of the tapes, identify expected discussion topics, and to provide some direction for leading the discussion periods. I look forward to seeing at the meeting. Although we may extent into the noon hour, you may exspect that we will be finished by 2 p.m..

Pleese move forward with scheduling trianing sessions at your employees locations,   with goal of completing all training bythe end of Auguest.

Distribution: Presedent,   Controllers Office,   All Senior technecal staff

Appendix A

Answers to Exercises

Step 1. Analyze Purpose

(From p.9) Exercise: Evaluate these scenarios and identify your purposes for writing.

1. You must write a required monthly status report to your client, the City of Boston, who hired your company to clean the water in Boston Harbor.
    Your purpose for writing: to get credit for accomplishments, inform about pending work, and identify new issues.

2. After receiving many phone queries, you decide to write a memo to your plant employees describing procedures for getting their monthly parking sticker from their shift supervisor.
    Your purpose for writing: provide accurate guidance so you won't be bothered with calls.

3. As office manager, you write a staff study to your immediate supervisor, recommending leasing rather than buying a copy machine.
    Your purpose for writing: to persuade that leasing the copy machine is better than buying.

4. You organized the annual holiday party. You write a thank-you note to the hotel manager who helped you host a particularly successful party.
    Your purpose for writing: to continue the goodwill you enjoy with the hotel.

5. As the lead editor for a large documentation effort, you write a style guide for the many contributing authors.
    Your purpose for writing: to standardize submissions, which helps your editing for consistency.

6. As project manager you must write an annual job review for each employee assigned to your project.
    Your purpose for writing: to document your reasons for personnel actions.

(From p.11) Exercise: For each scenario, determine what the audience does with the information in the document. If you have more than one audience, consider each audience in terms of what each does with the information.

1. As project manager you must write an annual job review for each employee assigned to your project.

Audience	Employee	Management
What audience does with the info	Improve performance	Promote employees; award raises

2. You must write a required monthly status report to your client, the City of Boston, who hired your company to clean the water in Boston Harbor.

Audience	Boston project manager
What audience does with the info	Approve payment for work completed and authorize next phase of work

3. After receiving many phone queries, you decide to write a memo to your plant employees describing procedures for getting their monthly parking sticker from their shift supervisor.

Audience	Employees	Shift supervisor
What audience does with the info	Request parking sticker	Issue and account for parking stickers

4. As office manager, you write a staff study to your immediate supervisor, recommending leasing rather than buying a copy machine.

Audience	Supervisor
What audience does with the info	Decide how to procure a copy machine

5. You organized the annual holiday party. You write a thank-you note to the hotel manager who helped you host a particularly successful party.

Audience	Hotel manager
What audience does with the info	Thank the hotel staff

6. As the lead editor for a large documentation effort, you write a style guide for the many contributing authors and your staff of copy editors and proofreaders.

Audience	Contributing authors	Copy editors and proofreaders
What audience does with the info	Write drafts using document standards	Edit and proofread using document standards

(From p.13) Exercise: Identify the audience(s) and their purposes for reading in each scenario. Based on how the audience uses the information, decide if the audience is expert, manager, operator, or general. Thereby, decide how to begin the body of your document.

1. You write a safety manual for your employees who install and maintain high voltage air conditioning equipment.

Employees

Safely install high voltage air conditioners

Operator audience

Result at the beginning

2. You must write a detailed design for building software to automatically switch and bill calls among cellular phone networks. The contract states that the client must approve the detailed design.

Technical staff	Client
Write the code to build the system	Approve the design

Operator audience	Manager audience
Result at the beginning	Recommendation at the beginning

3. You send a letter with your resume to a company that just advertised your dream job.

> Company human resources
> development

Decide whether to invite me for an interview

> Manager audience

> Recommendation at the
> beginning

4. The boss, Dr. Ann Smith, asks you to research the history of glass manufacturing as it applies to the healthcare industry, so she can include some details in a paper she presents next month at the American Medical Association convention.

> Dr. Ann Smith

Include in a speech about glass manufacturing and the healthcare industry

> Expert audience

> Data and methods at the
> beginning

5. You must write the section of a proposal called *Technical Approach for Building the Wilson Bridge*, in which you must prove to the Federal Highway Safety Board that building an eight-lane drawbridge to span the Potomac River is technically sound, although the drawbridge serves the busiest stretch of interstate highway in the United States.

> Federal Highway Safety Board

Recommend approval or rejection of the bridge design

> Expert audience

> Data and methods at the
> beginning

6. You send an email to all company employees announcing that the company henceforth gives each employee the option of either free parking worth $100 or a mass transit subsidy worth $100.

> Employees

Decide which benefit to take

> Manager audience

> Recommendation at the
> beginning

7. You work at Universal Laboratories for Occupationally Safe Environments. You conclude a three-year study on the effect of breathing printer's ink and paper dust at large newspaper printing plants. The American Lung Foundation, which commissioned the study, requests that you provide a report to the unions and Congress, and publish your findings on the Internet.

American Lung Foundation	Unions	Congress	Public
Recommend legislation and other measures to improve air quality at printing plants	Lobby Congress for new legislation	Decide whether to introduce legislation to improve health of printers	Be aware of health risks at printing plants
Expert audience	Operator audience	Manager audience	General audience
Data and methods at the beginning	Result at the beginning	Recommendation at the beginning	Conclusions (if any) at the beginning

8. You are working on an advanced degree in International Finance. Your term paper topic is Economic and Cultural Challenges for the European Union. (Instead of writing your paper to the professor, imagine an audience that might use the information, such as Central Banks.)

Central Banks
Anticipate changes to European banking regulations
Manager audience
Recommendation at the beginning

(From p.14) Final exercise: List and contrast the writer's and the audiences' purposes associated with this writing task.

Your purpose for writing: document the requirement, record the changes from requirement through implementation, identify potential technical problems, justify the costs for billing, and provide detailed instructions to your technical staff — programmers.

Who are your *four* audiences, and what is each audience's purpose for reading? What do you learn about organizing your document?

Telefona Users	Telefona Systems Administrator	Telefona Comptroller	Programmer
Approve or reject new or changed functions	Determine if change affects other Telefona systems	Approve costs and release funds with a work order	Make changes to the code
Manager audience	Expert audience	Manager audience	Operator audience
Recommendation at the beginning, followed by discussion	Data and methods at the beginning, followed by findings, then conclusions	Recommendation at the beginning, followed by discussion	Result at the beginning, followed by instructions and discussion

You learn that you must partition the document, because the four audiences have incompatible needs.

Step 2. Analyze Audience

(From p.17) Exercise: For the following two scenarios, fill in the chart to determine what the audience does with the information, and what the audience needs to know.

Scenario 1

Audience	**Venture Capital**
What audience does with the info	Raise capital
What audience needs to know	How much must one invest How much can one lose How much profit can one make What is the schedule of payback

Scenario 2

Audience	**Tri-Skalion management**	**Insurance underwriters**
What audience does with the info	Decide whether to drop the collision rider	Advise management on the best course of action
What audience needs to know	Risk versus the benefits	Actuarial profile of the company Comparisons of expected payouts for each option Assumptions for cost of capital for twenty years

(From p.19) Exercise: For the following ten scenarios determine whether the audience has a high or low level of knowledge. In other words, does the audience need you to define terms, give examples, provide analogies, or draw pictures?

1. A financial manager HIGH — understands leasing and buying.

2. A financial manager LOW — doesn't understand the Cray technology.

3. The client plant manager HIGH — understands workflow and opportunities to streamline.

4. Employees LOW — need an example of a correctly submitted form.

5. The project manager HIGH — understands tasks; doesn't need to understand complex systems integration problem to know that you are late.

6. Venture Capital, Inc. HIGH — understands capital formation; doesn't need to know robotics.

7. Management LOW — doesn't understand the legal and technical aspects of insurance; provide examples. (Your manager might in fact be HIGH. I'm just reflecting on my lack of technical knowledge about insurance.)

8. Programmers HIGH — understand data formats, processes, and outputs; if not, you may need to hire new programmers.

9. Client managers HIGH — understand how to track the requirement to the detailed design. They don't need to know the specific technology used in the detailed design.

10. Bill Gates reading instructions on how to assemble a tricycle LOW — wants lots of pictures of the parts and how to assemble them.

(From p.21) Exercise: For the following ten scenarios, determine whether the audience believes you as you tell them what they need to know, or whether they want you to prove your points.

1.   Your manager BELIEVE — you are the expert on lease versus buy, after all.

2.   A financial manager PROOF — you're just an intern.

3.   BAP Industries BELIEVE — they brought you back *because* they believe you.

4.   Employees BELIEVE — although you are a modest clerk, you are the authority when processing requests.

5.   Project manager BELIEVE — unless you've given the manager a reason to doubt the integrity of your status reports.

6.   Venture Capital, Inc. PROOF — you may have a reputation as a genius in quantum physics applied to robotics, but you don't have a reputation, good or bad, regarding business start-ups.

7.   Management PROOF — maintenance is your area of expertise, not insurance.

8.   Programmers BELIEVE — you are on the same team, after all.

9.   Client managers BELIEVE — You need only index requirements to the detailed design paragraphs.

10.   Bill Gates BELIEVE — I admit that I've assembled many tricycles — usually on Christmas Eve between 2 and 3 in the morning. I always *started* by believing the instructions. Occasionally, my beliefs were challenged.

(From p.23) Exercise: Plan how to accommodate this multiple audience.

Audience	FDA	Public (label)	Press	Stockholders
What audience does with the info	Approve or reject Wonder Pill for over-the-counter use	Take Wonder Pill safely	Write an article about Wonder Pill	Evaluate their investment in SP
What audience needs to know	Intended uses, protocol followed, results, adverse events . . .	Intended uses, side effects, warnings	What is new about Wonder Pill, who ought to take Wonder Pill and why, side effects	The potential market for Wonder Pill, expected sales growth
Audience's level of knowledge	HIGH	LOW	LOW	HIGH
Audience believes you or wants proof	PROOF	BELIEVE	BELIEVE	BELIEVE

Your plan to accommodate the audiences can be the following:

FDA expert staff gets a drug application divided into sections: intended uses, test protocols, results, adverse effects. The review has an executive summary for FDA managers and a set of appendices that tabulate the test data. In a separate document submit your proposed language for the label.

The press release is a one-page story that must balance the claims with the risks to comply with regulations. The stockholders get a letter signed by the president of Salubrious, in which she forecasts sales and rate of return.

(From p.24) Final exercise: Analyze purpose and audience in this scenario, and plan how to accommodate each audience by partitioning the subject matter.

Use your techniques to analyze purpose and audience, then partition the subject matter. How do you accommodate this multiple audience: separate documents, sections, front and back matter?

Sesquatch management	Sesquatch marketing and production	Sesquatch warehouse personnel	Sesquatch plant engineers	Retailers
Manage the new automated process	Coordinate retail demand with production	Fulfill orders	Keep the plant operating	Place and track orders online
Process overview, responsibilities	How to receive retail orders, calculate economic order quantities, and place factory orders	How to barcode and sort shoe boxes, pack pallets, and ship	How to inspect and maintain machinery	How to determine order quantity, secure web site pages with order forms, fulfillment status, and balances
HIGH	HIGH	LOW	LOW	LOW
BELIEVE	BELIEVE	BELIEVE	BELIEVE	BELIEVE

Divide the manual into four sections, one for each Sesquatch audience. Write the retailers' manual as a separate document. Therefore, you can distribute the retailers' document freely without disclosing your proprietary process. You ought to put much of the retailers' manual on your web page as well. Include the retailers' manual as attachment to the larger Sesquatch manual.

Consider adding appendices for experienced warehouse staff and engineers. Whereas their sections need to provide examples of the process and show pictures of the machinery, the appendices can provide a quick reference or checklist.

Step 3. Write Purpose Statement

(From p.27) Exercise: Write a purpose statement after analyzing purpose and audience.

Scenario 1: Your purpose for writing is to avoid the problems of towing, fees, and angry employees. Your audience is all employees who use the parking lot. Because they read to make plans, they read as managers. (Or, they may read as operators, following your instructions.) They have little interest in background or theory or parking lot maintenance, but they might profit from a diagram.

Audience	Employees (who drive)
What audience does with the info	Plan accordingly
What audience needs to know	Schedule of parking lot closings
Level of knowledge	HIGH
Believes you or wants proof	BELIEVE

Memo	notifies	employees	schedule of parking lot closings	make other plans
Actor	Action	Audience	Topic	Outcome

Purpose Statement: This memo notifies employees who drive about the parking lot closings, September 11 through 16. Please plan accordingly.

We chose *notifies* to set a more authoritative tone. You may prefer a less authoritative tone such as *inform*.

Scenario 2: Your purpose for writing is to get the $88,000 additional work. Your audience is Universe Bank management. Because they read to make a decision, they read as managers. They have little interest in background or theory.

Audience	Universe Bank management
What audience does with the info	Decide whether to expand scope of the contract
What audience needs to know	Cost and schedule impact of adding a web-based commercial account function
Level of knowledge	HIGH
Believes you or wants proof	BELIEVE

Change proposal	presents	Universe Bank management	cost and schedule impact of adding commercial account functions	decide whether to expand the scope of the contract
Actor	Action	Audience	Topic	Outcome

This change proposal presents the cost and schedule impact of adding the web-based commercial account function so Universe Bank management can decide whether to expand the scope of the contract. (We changed the order of audience and object to avoid the repetition in *Universe Bank management . . . so management can . . . .*

You may prefer to write the outcome as *so Universe Bank management can decide to expand the scope of the contract.* This more forceful outcome is what sales people call *the assumptive close*, which means you assume the reader makes the decision you want. The assumptive close is a clever way to present the reader your recommendation early. The assumptive close is more effective when you have a good relationship with the reader.

Scenario 3: Your purpose for writing is to keep customers.

John Lee uses your letter to decide whether to continue buying your bagels. Therefore, he reads as a manager. He probably doesn't care for all the details on why you discontinued his favorite sandwich. The fact that the marketplace didn't share his enthusiasm for *gc&c on a jb* is no consolation to John.

Audience	John Lee
What audience does with the info	Decide whether to remain our valued customer
What audience needs to know	Babahuma replaces the *gc&c* on *jb*, our commitment to serve
Level of knowledge	HIGH
Believes you or wants proof	PROOF

Coupon	gives	(you)	a free Babahuma (commitment) that replaces the *gc&c on a jb*	so you continue as our valued customer
Actor	Action	Audience	Topic	Outcome

Please accept this coupon (actor) offering (action) you (audience) a free Babahuma Sandwich that replaces the *gc&c on a jb* (topic). We hope you remain our valued customer (outcome).

(From p. 29) Exercise: Evaluate these ten purpose statements. Are all five parts included? Do the five parts clearly and logically state the document's purpose?

1. This magazine article (actor) explains (action) to the general reader (audience) the advantages of recycling paper (topic) so residents know how to cooperate in the county's recycling program (outcome).

   Clear but not logical. The outcome *know how to cooperate* doesn't result from explaining advantages.

2. This user guide informs new employees about procedures for using email so they can send and receive email.

   Clear and logical.

3. This proposal explains our technical approach for the client users, and it presents our concept for the management plan, schedule, and costs for the financial department, and it justifies our bid in terms of time and materials, so you have the necessary information to evaluate our qualifications to successfully complete your project.

   > Actor — proposal
   > Action — explains, presents, justifies
   > Audience — client users, finance department, you (understood)
   > Topic — approach, plan, schedule, costs, bid
   > Outcome — so you can evaluate our qualifications

   Not clear, not logical. We have four purpose statements merged into one, and each lacks parts of a purpose statement:

   - We have a section explaining to users our technical approach with no apparent outcome.
   - We have a section presenting to the finance department the plan, schedule, and cost with no apparent outcome.
   - We have a section justifying to reader (you understood) the time and materials.
   - We probably have a section that helps the reader evaluate our qualifications, perhaps a discussion of our experience and resumes.

4. I thought I'd like to write down some thoughts and concerns for you in regard to the TDMS as we approach trials. We need to be constantly aware of several things, monitor their progress, and/or verify the fix.

   > Actor — omitted
   > Action — omitted
   > Reader — you (understood)
   > Topic — thoughts and concerns — vague
   > Outcome — omitted, or possibly so you can be aware, monitor, and fix?

Not clear. Fill in omissions.

5. This letter is a follow-up to our phone conversation today regarding the above captioned.

>   Actor — letter
>   Action — follows up
>   Reader — you (understood)
>   Topic — omitted
>   Outcome — omitted

Not clear. Fill in omissions.

6. Please find attached to this email the cost data you requested for your proposal effort.

>   Actor — email
>   Action — provides (understood)
>   Reader — you (understood)
>   Topic — cost data
>   Outcome — for your proposal effort

Clear enough. The email is a transmittal device. Often transmittal letters, memos, and messages are nothing but a purpose statement explaining the purpose of the attachment.

7. Are you over 65, in good health, and looking for a way to reduce the high cost of health insurance? Call our toll-free number and get answers today.

>   Actor — advertisement (understood)
>   Action — invites (understood)
>   Reader — persons over 65 in good health
>   Topic — our toll-free number
>   Outcome — to get answers to reduce high cost of health insurance

Clear and logical.

8. A representative from Image Tech, Inc. will give a lecture in the boardroom next Tuesday at 3:00 p.m.

>   Actor — omitted
>   Action — omitted
>   Reader — omitted
>   Object — vague lecture; specific place and time
>   Outcome — omitted

Not clear. Too vague.

9. This is in reference to your application, NDA #40235, submitted January 20, 1999.

>   Actor — this what? This letter?
>   Action — does what? refers?
>   Reader — omitted
>   Topic — omitted, or perhaps your application, NDA #40235, submitted January 20, 1999
>   Outcome — omitted

Not clear. Too vague.

10. This letter will orient you, officers of the higher echelons, in the principles of command, combat procedure, and administration which obtain in this Army, and will guide you in the conduct of your several commands. (Patton's General Order, Third Army — March 6, 1944)

>   Actor — letter
>   Action — orients
>   Reader — officers of the higher echelon
>   Object — in the principles of command, combat procedure, and administration which obtain in this Army
>   Outcome — conduct of your several commands

Clear and logical.

(From p.31) Exercise: Help your assistant write a purpose statement.

In the present form, B. Guirre's letter accomplishes nothing except complain. Kay Kemnick won't know if Guirre wants a refund, an apology, or revenge. The key is to focus on what Kay Kemnick does with the information in the letter. A purpose statement can tell Kay Kemnick what to do.

Purpose statement: This letter informs ACME Temps about your employee's unsatisfactory performance so you can investigate her behavior, improve your quality control, and remove the associated charge from your next invoice.

With a well-crafted purpose statement, the assistant can write a focused letter.

(From p.32) Final exercise: Analyze purpose and audience, then write a purpose statement for the system design.

1. Fill in the chart as you analyze your three audiences.

Audience	Technical staff (programmers)	Client Informations Systems manager	VP sales
What audience does with the info	Write, compile, and test code	Approve the design for implementation	Anticipate changes to the business process and need to train
What audience needs to know	Required modifications to the UNIX-based system	Pinnacle's requirements with functions detailed in the design	The new system's improvements on the slow paper-based method
Audience's level of knowledge	HIGH	HIGH	LOW
Audience believes you or wants proof	BELIEVES	BELIEVES	PROOF

2. Plan your strategy for partitioning the subject matter by audience. Who gets the core document? Do you use separate documents, sections, or front and back matter for the others?

Write the core document to the technical staff, but include an appendix for the client IS manager. Write a separate document, or perhaps prepare a briefing for the nervous VP of sales. Because the VP has a low level of knowledge, you need to give many examples. Unfortunately, the proof the VP wants is in the discussion of the technology. The VP won't understand the technical discussion — the proof — even if you provide it. Either refer the VP to Pinnacle's IS manager, the VP's staff expert, to provide the proof by means of an endorsement, or cite other catalogue companies that benefited from similar technology.

3. Write purpose statements for each of the three audiences.

Detailed design	describes	technical staff	required modifications to the UNIX-based system	write, compile, and test code
Actor	Action	Audience	Object	Outcome

This detailed design describes for the technical staff the required modifications to the UNIX-based system. Follow the design to write, compile, and test code.

Appendix A matches Pinnacle's requirements with functions detailed in the design so Pinnacle's IS manager can approve the design for implementation.

The briefing explains to the VP of sales the new system's improvements on your old paper-based method. You can anticipate the changes to your business process and train accordingly.

Step 4. Gather Information

(From p.35) Exercise: Describe how the following purpose statements focus information gathering.

Scenario 1 (two purpose statements describing the same subject matter)

1. This bid request specifies to ACME Carpet Co. the dimensions of eight vacant offices at 123 Maple Avenue, so your carpet company can bid on installing wall-to-wall carpeting.

> Actor — bid request implies first step toward contract
> Action — suggests precise details
> Reader — ACME Carpet, reading as manager, a knowledgeable reader who believes
> Object — suggests eight groups of measurements
> Outcome — suggests a formal reply describing work and price

2. This brochure outlines for prospective renters the features and benefits of our vacant offices at 123 Maple Avenue, so prospective renters can decide whether to schedule an appointment to view the office space.

> Actor — suggests a marketing piece
> Action — suggests a general discussion, informal, less precise
> Reader — suggest people who already know they want rental space
> Object — suggests a limited discussion of the offices' good points, not costs
> Outcome — suggests that brochure need only say enough to entice prospect to call

Scenario 2: These minutes describe the status of each proposed change to help members of the Change Management committee track proposed changes through the process of technical approval, budget approval, scheduling, execution, and final testing.

> Actor — suggests a record
> Action — suggests precision for a knowledgeable audience
> Reader — suggests content matter experts
> Object — suggests an order to the document
> Outcome — suggests that the information helps one audit the work

(From p.37) Exercise: Ask *who, what, where, when, why,* and *how* questions to generate details for documents with these purpose statements.

For each document, we thought of questions. You may have different questions.

1. This tech-report describes the repairs and tests we conducted on your PDQ Laserprinter to stop the intermittent errors you reported, so you know what we cover by warranty and what service you must pay for.
    Who repaired and tested? Whom do you call for more help? What repairs? What errors? What warranty? What do we check next if intermittent errors continue? Where did we make the repairs — shop or on site? When did we receive the call? make the repairs? When do you get the invoice? When is payment due? Why are some repairs under warranty, others not? How do we know if the repairs are effective?

2. This guide provides you, the new owner of a Megawheel plastic tricycle, simple step-by-step assembly instructions, so you can quickly put your little tyke on his Megawheel trike.
    Who manufactured trike? Who assembles trike? Whom do I call for help? What tools do I need? What time do I need — really? Where is the bag of nuts and bolts? When do your tech-support staff answer calls? Why are there eight bolts and seven wing nuts? How do I start? How do I know when I'm finished? (Lots of questions need to be answered here.)

3. This letter notifies LD Cellular Phone Co. billing office about $12,456.56 of unauthorized calls charged to our account, so you can change our phone access code, investigate the fraudulent calls, and remove the charges from our account.
    Who is responsible for unauthorized calls? What measures did we take to avoid this form of theft? Where were

the calls made? When did we notice the unauthorized calls? Why are we asking you to change our phone access code? How do we prove the calls are unauthorized?

4. Are you over 65, in good health, and looking for a way to reduce the high cost of health insurance? Call our toll-free number and get answers today.
   Who answers my call? What does the insurance cover? What does it cost? Where are you located? When is a good time to call? Why is age 65 special? How do I apply?

5. This memo describes to employees the new health care coverage, rights and benefits, preventive medicine programs, co-payment policies, and procedures for submitting claims. With this information you and your family can take advantage of our quality health care program and live healthier lives.
   Who qualifies? Full-time and part-time employees? Dependents? What are the benefits and preventive medicine programs? Where can I go for care? Doctors? Hospital? Emergency care? When do I submit claims? When do I pay the premiums? How much are the premiums and the co-pays? How do I submit claims? Why do some people pay more for coverage than others do?

(From p.38) Final exercise: Use your purpose statement and the questions *who, what, where, when, why,* and *how* to focus information gathering.

1. How does your analysis and the purpose statement focus your information gathering?
   The analysis limits my research. I need to know about *Pet Arama's* business, hiring practices, compensation, and job opportunities. Also, I need to know how to apply online. I know or assume the reader has a high level of knowledge, so I don't need to think of examples or analogies, or invest the time devising pictures. For example, the reader must fill in a simple form asking for basic personal data such as date of birth. Because the reader believes me, I don't need to go into detail. For example, I don't have to prove that our entry-level position pays more than minimum wage. I simply tell them our starting wage.

2. Give an example of data you don't need to gather.
   I don't need to gather data about the Internet. I don't need to research the details of franchising. I don't need to research the opportunities for senior managers.

3. Ask *who, what, where, when, why,* and *how* to determine the information you gather for your audience.
   Who should apply? What are the minimum qualifications? What are the pay and benefits? Where are the hiring stores located? Where do you go for the interview? When does the job start? When are the store hours? When can one expect advancement? Why is *Pet Arama* a good place to work? How do you apply?

Step 5. Write Sentence Outline

(From p.41) Exercise: Using gathered information as your source, write points for a sentence outline. Use short words in short sentences.

1. Generality: Many competent applicants with a wide range of experience applied.

2. Assertion: Job sharing advantages outweigh the disadvantages.
   Or generality: Job sharing has three key advantages and three key disadvantages.

3. Generality: Companies across the United States use job sharing.
   Or generality: Companies in the Great Lakes region or Mid-west are twice as likely to job share as the rest of the United States.

4. Generality: Job sharers set a schedule to satisfy their needs and the company's needs.
   Or generality: Each job-sharing partner works a half-week.

5. Generality: Applicants offered different reasons for wanting to job share.

6. Assertion: Job sharers must carefully communicate their new working arrangement to others.
   Or generality: Job sharers used every opportunity to communicate their new working arrangement to others.

(From p.43) Exercise: Evaluate the following points against the purpose statement. Eliminate irrelevancies.

1. ~~Ninety percent of Fortune 500 companies use data security systems.~~ (irrelevant although possible for introduction)

2. Our professionals keep a lot of valuable information on our computers. (cost)

3. We rely on computers now more than ever to be profitable. (relates to cost)

4. Losing data can severely reduce profits. (relates to benefit of securing data)

5. The proposed system uses three optical drives tied to our local area network. (relates to cost of equipment)

6. ~~The next-best alternative uses old technology, a 16 BPI tape drive.~~ (irrelevant)

7. The three optical drives, ten cartridges, optic fiber cables, and software cost $6,490. (cost of equipment)

8. ~~Causes for data loss range from employee error to natural disaster.~~ (irrelevant)

9. Industry surveys provide statistics on industry-wide information loss. (relates to benefit of securing data)

10. The proposed system limits data loss to a worst case 24 hours. (benefit)

11. Last year, lost data cost our company more than 3,500 labor hours at an average $40 per labor-hour. (relates to benefit or cost)

12. Our costs for losing data exceeded industry averages. (relates to benefit of securing data)

13. ~~We generate almost 800 megabytes of critical data per month.~~ (irrelevant)

14. ~~Eighty percent of the monthly data overwrites old records; however, 20 percent is new.~~ (irrelevant)

15. Expect our proposed data security system to reduce data losses by 99 percent. (benefit)

16. Lost data results in misplaced or late orders, hence angry customers. (relates to benefit of securing data)

17. Our proposed data security includes state-of-the-art protection against computer viruses. (benefit)

18. ~~Perpetrators of computer viruses are seldom found or prosecuted.~~ (irrelevant)

19. Our data security system can rebuild our entire online database in less than a day. (benefit)

20. We require data security to protect our company's profitability. (benefit)

21. The Systems Steering Committee recommends investing in this data protection system. (recommendation always relevant)

(From p.45) Exercise: We continue with the exercise from page 41. You have eliminated the irrelevancies. Now evaluate the remaining points to eliminate redundancies.

1. ~~Our professionals keep a lot of valuable information on our computers.~~ (redundant to 3)

2. ~~We rely on computers and data now more than ever to be profitable.~~ (redundant to 3)

3. Losing data can severely reduce profits.

4. ~~The proposed system uses three optical drives tied to our local area network.~~ (redundant to 5)

5. The three optical drives, ten cartridges, optic fiber cables, and software cost $6,490.

6. ~~Industry surveys provide statistics on industry-wide information loss.~~ (redundant to 9)

7. The proposed system limits data loss to a worst case 24 hours.

8. Last year, lost data cost our company more than 3,500 labor hours at an average $40 per labor-hour.

9. Our costs for losing data exceeded industry averages.

10. Expect our proposed data security system to reduce data losses by 99 percent.

11. Lost data results in misplaced or late orders, hence angry customers.

12. Our proposed data security includes state-of-the-art protection against computer viruses.

13. ~~Our data security system can rebuild our entire online database in less than a day.~~ (redundant to 7)

14. ~~We require data security to protect our company's profitability.~~ (redundant to 3)

15. The Systems Steering Committee recommends investing in this data protection system.

Note: When you find redundancies, do not be overly concerned which sentence you keep. In our exercise we had four sentences that communicated the same point:

1. Our professionals keep a lot of valuable information on our computers.
2. We rely on computers and data now more than ever to be profitable.
3. Losing data can severely reduce profits.
14. We require data security to protect our company's profitability.

We chose to keep sentence 3. You may think sentence 3 is too blunt and therefore prefer sentence 14.

(From p.47) Exercise: Identify major points and group minor points below them.

Purpose statement: This staff study details for the board of directors *the business climate, the transportation network, and the living environment* for building a can manufacturing plant in Tuscaloosa, Alabama. The board must decide where to locate the new plant.

14. Tuscaloosa's transportation is geared for manufacturing companies like ours.

    1. The Black Warrior River-Tombigbee Waterway offers easy access to the Port of Mobile.

    6. The Tuscaloosa Airport requires connections through Atlanta.

    15. Tuscaloosa serves as a minor hub for both highway and rail traffic.

2. At present, Tuscaloosa's business climate meets or exceeds our needs.

    7. The local area costs are low for our business.

    9. Recent layoffs in local chemical, rubber, paper, and iron factories make an abundance of cheap, skilled labor.

    12. Alabama offered us a five-year tax holiday to move to Alabama.

16. Tuscaloosa presents a major change in living environment for our New Jersey transplants.

    3. Tuscaloosa provides many big-city amenities.

4. Tuscaloosa has no big-city costs.

5. The University of Alabama offers many cultural opportunities.

8. Personal income, property, and sales taxes are low.

10. Tuscaloosa has many recreational facilities: lakes and parks.

11. Tuscaloosa has mild winters and hot summers.

13. Local public schools are rated below the national average, but improving.

17. The search committee recommends building the new factory near Tuscaloosa, Alabama.

(From p.49) Sequence the main and minor points.

Purpose statement: This staff study details for the board of directors *the business climate, the transportation network, and the living environment* for building a can manufacturing plant in Tuscaloosa, Alabama. The board must decide where to locate the new plant.

The search committee recommends building the new factory near Tuscaloosa, Alabama.

At present, Tuscaloosa's business climate meets or exceeds our needs.

   The local area costs are low for our business.

   Recent layoffs in local chemical, rubber, paper, and iron factories make an abundance of cheap, skilled labor.

   Alabama offered us a five-year tax holiday to move to Alabama.

Tuscaloosa's transportation is geared for manufacturing companies like ours.

   The Black Warrior River-Tombigbee Waterway offers easy access to the Port of Mobile.

   Tuscaloosa serves as a minor hub for both highway and rail traffic.

   The Tuscaloosa Airport requires connections through Atlanta.

Tuscaloosa presents a major change in living environment for our New Jersey transplants.

   Tuscaloosa has mild winters and hot summers.

   Local public schools are rated below the national average, but improving.

   Personal income, property, and sales taxes are low.

   Tuscaloosa has no big-city costs.

   Tuscaloosa provides many big-city amenities.

   The University of Alabama offers many cultural opportunities.

   Tuscaloosa has many recreational facilities: lakes and parks.

(From p.51) For each purpose statement below, identify the natural patterns you can use to order points. You may combine one natural pattern within another.

1. This test plan provides for each software module the scenario, data, and expected result so the quality assurance team can verify that the system operates correctly.

    Because the plan looks at modules, the pattern of thought is functional. Then, within each function we see three topics: scenario, data, and expected result.

2. This policy outlines the rules employees must obey when using the company gymnasium.

    A list of rules is mostly topical. Each rule is a topic. The author may impose more order on the list of topics. For example, the Ten Commandments group into two areas: proscriptions regarding the Deity, and proscriptions regarding human relationships. Also, within the two groups, the proscriptions are ranked.

3. This guide provides you, the new owner of a Megawheel plastic tricycle, simple step-by-step assembly instructions, so you can quickly put your little tyke on his Megawheel trike.

    Step-by-step implies ordinal. Again, you can find imbedded patterns. The steps may group into a spatial pattern, front to rear. First, we follow steps to assemble the front wheel and handlebars. Second, we follow steps to assemble the seat and mid-section. Third, we assemble the rear wheels. Fourth, we add the decals.

4. This letter notifies your company of the safety violations and systemic deficiencies found during your annual factory inspection. To avoid a substantial rate increase in your insurance premium, you must correct the violations within 30 days and provide a plan to address the systemic violation.

    The topic of the letter, *safety violations and systemic deficiencies,* indicates two topics. Again, within the topics, you might rank the sub-topics by severity, or you might group them by factory function.

5. This memo describes to employees the new health care coverage, rights and benefits, preventive medicine programs, co-payment policies, and procedures for submitting claims. With this information you and your family can take advantage of our quality health care program and live healthier lives.

    Again, the topic of the letter, *rights and benefits, preventive medicine programs, co-payment policies, and procedures for submitting claims* indicates four topics. The four topics can have a different pattern of thought:
    1. rights and benefits — sub-topics
    2. preventive medicine programs — features and benefits
    3. co-payment policies — functional
    4. procedures for submitting claims — ordinal

6. This change proposal outlines the equipment and direct labor costs to add an alternate power generator for your business. As soon as you authorize the purchase, we can schedule the installation.

    The topic of the letter, *equipment and direct labor costs,* indicates two topics. Within the two topics, one may use a general-to-specific pattern typical of cost breakdown.

7. This memorandum outlines our three main reasons for purchasing the Dulles land parcel early, so the chief financial officer can inform the board of directors.

    The topic of the letter, *three main reasons,* indicates three topics ranked, probably beginning with the most important.

(From p.54) Final exercise: Write a sentence outline.

1. Analyze purpose and audience:

Your purpose for writing is to dissuade your client from accelerating implementation, or at least warn of the risks and insulate yourself from a potential disaster.

Profile of the two audiences:

Audience	Universe Bank's IS manager	Universe Bank's senior management
What audience does with the info	Make a recommendation to senior management	Decide when to deploy the new Visa Card system
What audience needs to know	Technical risks of acceleration	Business risks of acceleration
Audience's level of knowledge	HIGH	HIGH
Audience believes you or wants proof	BELIEVE	PROOF

Senior management has a high level of knowledge about business risks, but has a woefully low level of knowledge about the complex system.

Senior management may believe you. However, for this exercise, let us assume they invested some ego in their request for acceleration, and they now want proof. Unfortunately, the proof behind the business risks is a discussion of the technical risks. Instead of educating the senior managers in computer science, you refer them to their staff expert, the IS manager.

2. Plan how to partition subject matter to accommodate each audience: Write a letter to senior bank management with an appendix for the IS manager. The proof of the business risks is in the appendix about technical risks, if senior managers insist on reading the proof.

3. Purpose statements:
This letter alerts senior bank management about the business risks of accelerating the new Visa Card system deployment, so management can decide when to deploy the system.

This appendix details the technical risks of accelerating the new Visa Card system, so the IS manager can recommend a course of action to senior management.

When the senior manager who wants proof finishes the short letter and turns to the appendix, your purpose statement manages expectations and prevents frustration. The senior manager immediately sees that you did perform a technical analysis and that the IS manager will soon translate the technical discussion into a recommendation.

4. Write a sentence outline for the *primary* audience:
    We recommend you keep the original contract schedule.
    The business risks outweigh the potential gains.
    Acceleration may cause a loss of $1.3 million in revenue.
    You might lose customers if we accelerate deployment.
    You might hurt your reputation.
    To accelerate, we must modify the contract and increase our fees.

Step 6 Write Draft

(From p.61) Exercise: Match the following purpose statements with corresponding conclusions.

1. This memo announces to all employees changes in the cafeteria hours and services. Please plan your lunch breaks accordingly.

2. This letter alerts Universal Bank management of the serious business risks of accelerating deployment of the Visa system, so management can decide when to rollout the new system.

3. This staff study details for the board of directors *the business climate, the transportation network, and the living environment* for building a can manufacturing plant in Tuscaloosa, Alabama. The board must decide where to locate the new plant.

4. Attention animal lovers! We welcome prospective employees to our web site. Learn about *Pet Arama*, and determine if you want a future with us. Plus you can follow five simple steps to apply online.

5. This guide provides you, the new owner of a Megawheel plastic tricycle, simple step-by-step assembly instructions, so you can quickly put your little tyke on his Megawheel trike.

6. This section describes the data inputs and conversion algorithms to the operators who build the new taxpayers database.

7. This article describes for BAP's regional managers how the BAP Northeast Region recently implemented a successful pilot program for job sharing. Managers can see if job sharing can help your region attract and keep qualified employees.

c. We look forward to serving you.

f. If you decide to accelerate the rollout of the system to November, we must renegotiate our contract with you immediately. Otherwise, we shall proceed with the original schedule.

e. The site-selection committee looks forward to your decision.

a. If you qualify, we will contact you directly to arrange an interview.

g. Now, you and your child can enjoy hours of fun, but remember to ride safely, and always wear a helmet.

b. Upon completing the database, be sure to send the new record and field layouts to the testing team.

d. To learn more about the legal or employee benefits aspects of job sharing, please contact Human Resources at the BAP Northeast Region Office in Tyson's Corner, Virginia.

(From p.63) Exercise: Critique the following introductions. Identify any essential elements missing.

1. The purpose statement is missing. We see a vague clue that the document is organized in three parts: violations, questionable practices, and safety deficiencies.

2. The topic in the purpose statement, *how you install,* does not indicate the organization. The introduction needs another sentence explaining the document's organization.

3. The introduction has both essential parts.

4. This introduction begins with background and has neither a purpose statement nor a clue to the document organization. Ironically, all the background about the SEPO filter seems pointless without the purpose statement.

5. This short 15-word introduction states both a purpose and organization — *the five simple steps.*

6. The introduction has both essential parts. Having defined the sections, the author can use the same words in the titles of the five sections:
   Section 1 Experience and qualifications
   Section 2 E-commerce business process for Collectibles, Inc.
   Section 3 Technical solution
   Section 4 Management and quality assurance plan
   Section 5 Follow-on support

7. The reader doesn't know the point of the reference until he or she reads a purpose statement. This introduction flounders between background and the information the reader needs to know.

8. The introduction has both essential parts. The topic suggests the organization: *step-by-step assembly instructions.*

(From p.65) Exercise: This introduction lacks one of the seven parts. Identify the six parts it has and the one missing.

1. Purpose statement: missing.

2. Organization of document : . . . optimum flowchart layout of the monthly cycle. Each step has a corresponding chapter. Follow the cycle each month and refer to the appropriate chapter as you work through this manual.

3. Background and significance of topic: Each month company executives view a set of charts, or slides, which have more current information than those of the previous month. Very basically, the new data comes in and is checked, then slides are generated . . . .

4. Description of target reader: designed specifically for Executive Support Personnel in the Product Support area of BAP, Inc. . . .

5. Information sources and research methods: Oracle software, generic graphics, manuals in the Product Services library . . . .

6. Definitions of key terms: The set of characters <<ENTER>> stands for Enter Key. FDBA stands for Functional Database Administrator.

7. Limitations of the document: This manual assumes that the reader has a working knowledge of the Slide Presentation system in the VAX environment . . . .

Are any parts out of order? Yes. The organization of the document comes too late. Put the organization immediately after the purpose statement.

(From p.69) Exercise: Which of the following two passages is an abstract, and which is an executive summary? How can you tell?

Quazel Prion in Armadillidium is an abstract that highlights key words from the paper and uses technical jargon such as armadillidium, cytoplasm, morbidity. The passage follows the format for abstracts:

Topic	This paper examines the reaction of the Quazel prion (QP) on crustaceans of the species armadillidium.
Significance	QP strengthens cytoplasm, theoretically making cells more resistant to disease and aging.
Methods	At the Yuseat Laboratory, half the armadillidium were injected with QP. Subgroups were later exposed to various parasites, yeast, bacteria, and viruses.
Findings	The QP treated armadillidium showed significant resistance compared to the untreated control group. However, the treated armadillidium eventually suffered rapid morbidity when the QP-affected cytoplasm crystallized. The experiment shows that although QP prevents disease, QP cannot prevent aging.
Conclusion	Therefore, QP must remained a controlled substance until science can provide a corresponding enzyme to control effect of Quazel hardening.

Extending Life with Quazel Proteins is an executive summary that uses non-technical language such as *pill bugs*, *membranes*, and *died*. The passage follows the format for executive summaries:

Purpose statement	This report describes the Yuseat Laboratory findings of a self-replicating protein, Quazel, to strengthen cell membranes and slow aging, so Jod management can decide whether to extend the research effort.
Recommendation	We recommend that Jod purchase the rights to manufacture Quazel, then invest in Yuseat's research to find the corresponding enzyme necessary to market Quazel.
Findings	Lab results proved that Quazel makes organisms resistant to most disease. Quazel protein also appears to correct certain genetic defects. Quazel-treated pill bugs were more vigorous than the control group. However, as protein finished replicating, cell membranes became brittle and the pill bugs died more quickly than the control group. The body does not have an enzyme to manage the Quazel protein. Yuseat Laboratory proposes a series of studies to find the enzyme in nature. After finding the enzyme, they may be able to replicate it.
What happens next	Yuseat Laboratory sends a research proposal under separate cover.

Step 7. Revise Content and Organization

(From p.73) Exercise: Apply the content test to this letter. Suggest ways to improve content.

> Is the topic focused? We added a purpose statement with key words: disputed transaction on VISA bill.
> So what? We crossed out assertions that failed the *so what?* test.
> Adequately supported? We italicized the unsupported statement.

This letter informs you of a disputed transaction on our VISA bill that you need to adjust.

~~We have been doing business with your bank for more than 10 years and this incident is our first cause for complaint that we have had in that time. We have substantial demand deposit, money market, sweep, and payroll accounts at the McLean branch.~~

~~We were shocked and dismayed to see a charge on our statement that we did not authorize.~~ Enclosed please find a copy of our recent VISA bill. The transaction that I have circled is the transaction we are disputing. The date of the transaction was March 5th and the date it was posted was March 8th. The company was Greenspan & Co. in El Paso, Texas. ~~I have never heard of this company before.~~ The amount charged was $520.97.

~~I queried our accounts payable department. They have no idea where this bill has come from.~~ We did not place an order with Greenspan & Co. ~~We have a purchase order system and I would have known if I had approved any request involving Greenspan & Co. I didn't. It is possible that our number was mistakenly used or punched into Greenspan's computer. I personally know how easy it is to transpose numbers.~~

~~Your help in any way would be very appreciated in this matter.~~ Change to *Please remove the $520.97 charge from my account before the next billing cycle.*

(From p.75) Exercise: Apply the organization test to this letter. What advice can you give?

> Reads like a data dump? No.
> Reads like a story? Yes. I learned about job, got excited . . . .
> Filled with *I, me, mine*? Yes. Letter tells writer's story, not what Mr. Stark needs to know.

Joan can't edit her way out of this problem. She needs to analyze purpose and audience, write a purpose statement, then write a brief sentence outline. She focuses on her purpose, but ignores the audience's purpose. Consequently, the audience will likely ignore or be put off by her letter.

Remember, when applying for a job, the purpose of your cover letter is to get your audience to look at your resume; the purpose of your resume is to get an interview; and the purpose of your interview is to get an offer.

(From p.77) Exercise: Use your sentence outlining techniques to revise this boilerplate letter.

First, write each point you find in the letter as a short sentence.

1. Thank you for your good service.
2. Some suppliers give customers gifts during the holidays.
3. We think suppliers should not provide gifts.
4. We don't think you're crooked.
5. We want you to spend your money improving your services.
6. Thank you for not giving us gifts.
7. Happy Holidays.

Second, analyze purpose and audience.

Writer's purpose for writing: encourage compliance with strict federal ethics laws.

Audience's purpose for reading: your policy regarding federal ethics laws about gifts.

Purpose of the work: prevent favoritism.

Audience is suppliers who want to maintain good relations with the company. They may or may not know company policy concerning gifts. They are open to the message, and do not need or want background information to follow instructions.

Third, write a purpose statement for the letter. (Don't try to make your purpose statement accommodate all the original points.)

This letter informs our suppliers of our policy of not accepting holiday gifts, so we can all comply with federal ethics guidelines.

Fourth, using your purpose statement, evaluate and sequence points in a sentence outline.

1. Please do not send gifts (omitted in original letter).

2. Thank you for your good service.

3. Happy Holidays.

Other assertions are irrelevant (even insulting) or redundant.

(From p.78) Final exercise: Apply the content and organization tests. Recommend ways to improve the letter.

Content test:
Is the topic focused? Not stated at the beginning of the letter.
So what? We crossed out assertions that failed the *so what?* test.
Adequately supported? We italicized the unsupported statement.

Organization test:
Reads like a data dump? No.
Reads like a story? Yes. The life and hard times of my battery . . .
Filled with *I*, *me*, *mine*? Yes. Letter tells how writer is affected.

On February 1 of this year, we asked for reimbursement for an alternator repair ~~to our new company car, which we purchased through a dealer who sold us~~ your extended warranty. (See attached letter.) *Now as a result of the defective alternator, the company car's battery died, and had to be replaced.* (Specify which alternator: the former or the latter?)

When the service center replaced my alternator, they had trouble recharging the battery. They suggested I keep the old battery for a while to see if it would hold a charge over a period of time. As it turned out, ~~cold weather did not kill the battery~~ two weeks after the alternator was replaced, the battery died. Cold weather did not kill the battery. The battery died as a direct result of the previous defective alternator running it down over a period of time.

~~Unfortunately, the battery died at a most inopportune time. The company treasurer missed a flight to New York and consequently a meeting with our creditors, who did not readily accept the "dead battery excuse."~~

~~I realize that the battery is not specifically covered under our warranty, but~~ because it died as a direct result of the malfunctioning alternator, ~~I think it's only fair that~~ you replace the battery. ~~It was only 17 months old. We shouldn't have had alternator or battery problems in the first place~~. *Please call me if you have any problems with this.* (Specify how and when.)

Recommend ways to improve the letter:

Write a purpose statement. Use sentence outlining techniques to revise the letter. Always close business letters with *what happens next*, often a specific call to action.

Step 8. Edit for Coherence

(From p.81) Exercise: Improve coherence by identifying shifting words and replacing them with consistent key words in these three excerpts.

Excerpt 1 — Regulatory letter

Shifting words: For each set of shifting words, we selected a consistent key word:

firm, company, establishment, corporate = firm
deficiencies, problems = deficiencies (We assume a violation is different than a deficiency.)
Act, law, regulation, federal standards = Act (From the context, we guess that the Act and regulation are synonymous.)

> The violations cited on the Form FDA 483 and presented to your firm at the conclusion of the inspection are not all-inclusive of deficiencies at your firm. It is your responsibility to ensure that your firm adheres to all the requirements of the Federal Food, Drug, and Cosmetic Act. The specific violations of the Act noted in this letter and the Form FDA 483 may be symptomatic of serious underlying deficiencies in your firm's manufacturing and quality systems. The Act requires you to investigate and determine the causes of the violations identified by FDA. You must promptly initiate corrective action to comply with the Act.

Excerpt 2 — Deliverables for training

Shifting words: For each set of shifting words, we selected a consistent key word:

Telefona, client site, environment, customer service department = Telefona customer service department
Temp Staff, Inc., we, our technicians, our people, staff = Temp Staff
Billing Consultant, Telefona's Billing staff, our staff = Telefona Billing Consultant
two phases, steps, first step, phase one, follow-up phase, second step, stage = phases, phase one, phase two
role, scope, responsibilities, job functions, tools, job descriptions = job functions
monitoring performance, quality review = monitoring performance

Deliverables for Training Temp Staff employees to become Telefona Billing Consultants

Telefona outsourced to Temp Staff the task of augmenting Telefona's customer service department. Temp Staff's personnel will work under a new job title: Telefona Billing Consultants.

Temp Staff's training program for Telefona Billing Consultants is divided into two phases. In phase one, Temp Staff defines the job functions for the Telefona Billing Consultant. In this phase, Temp Staff identifies and hires qualified Telefona Billing Consultants. Temp Staff trains those new Telefona Billing Consultants before Temp Staff sends them to Telefona's customer service department.

In phase two, Temp Staff implements the job functions defined in phase one. Because phase two depends on phase one, Temp Staff presents few details here. After placing trained Telefona Billing Consultants at Telefona's customer service department, Temp Staff monitors the Telefona Billing Consultants' performance. Both Temp Staff and Telefona technicians perform phase two.

Temp Staff proposes that in two years, Temp Staff and Telefona initiate a third phase wherein Temp Staff teaches Telefona's customer service staff to take on the job functions of Telefona Billing Consultant. Temp Staff trains and monitors performance.

Excerpt 3 — Requirements document

Shifting words:

Office of Public Works, Public Works = Office of Public Works
employees, workers, peers = employees
solution, methods, approaches, course of action = solution
pro's and con's, advantages and disadvantages = advantages and disadvantages
dedicated modem, fax modem = fax modem
fax servers, PC server, server = fax servers (Change dedicated PC server to dedicated PC.)
fax volume, fax traffic = fax volume (Let fax volume contrast with network traffic.)

The *Office of Public Works* needs to implement a fax *solution* that enables *employees* to send and receive faxes from and to their computer workstations. The *Office of Public Works* also wants *employees* to be able to share faxes electronically.

We can use one of the two broad *solutions* of implementing PC-based fax capabilities in mid-sized offices given our moderate fax *volume*. The table below illustrates the two *solutions* and their *advantages* and *disadvantages*:

Solution	Advantages	Disadvantages
Fax modem per user	Provides flexibility	No central control
	Handles large *fax volume*	Expensive
Fax server	Provides central control	Requires *dedicated PC*
	Shares resources	Increases *network traffic*

Because of the expense associated with providing a *fax modem* per user, we do not recommend that *solution*, but prefer the *fax server solution*.

Note: The key word repetition emphasizes the key points of the memo: Office of Public Works, employees, solution, advantages and disadvantages, fax modem, fax server, and fax volume.

(From p.83) Exercise: The first sentence tells the audience the point of the paragraph. A coherent paragraph puts the key point first for emphasis, then logically develops it with following sentences. Why are these paragraphs incoherent?

Paragraph 1 Start with the generality, then follow with specifics.

Your total hardware and software upgrade costs $27,320. The hardware required for the upgrade includes three Amiga™ CPUs, each with an extra 256 megabytes of RAM. Peripherals include more than 200 gigs of hard drive. You get one 18-inch flat screen and three high-speed read-writable CD-ROM drives. Including cables and couplings, the cost of the hardware is $18,625. With this bid, you also get one year of on-site maintenance and a one-year warranty on the hardware we install. The off-the-shelf security software costs $495 including our discount. Our fee for setting up the system, writing the software patches, building user-friendly screens, and training your staff is $8,200.

Paragraph 2 Aside from the legal facts, the point is that the cited firm has responsibilities.

You are responsible to ensure that your firm adheres to all the requirements of the Federal Food, Drug, and Cosmetic Act. The violations cited on the Form FDA 483 and presented to your firm at the conclusion of the inspection are not all-inclusive of deficiencies at your firm. The specific violations of the law noted in this letter and the Form FDA 483 may be symptomatic of serious underlying problems in your firm's manufacturing and quality systems. The Act requires you to investigate and determine the causes of the violations identified by FDA. You must promptly initiate corrective action to comply with the Act.

Paragraph 3: The first sentence has three points: *customer requests termination, Customer Service closes account, and Customer Service refers customer to Customer Relations.* Change the first sentence to one general point.

Customer Service Representatives (CS) follow these steps when a Universe BankCard credit card customer requests termination of his or her account. Determine if the customer is profitable and worth saving. Flag the ATTEMPT_SAVE field to indicate that the account is profitable and worth saving. If the Customer Retention (CR) department is open, transfer the call to CR. If CR is closed, attempt to save the account by explaining the benefits of the Universe Bankcard and possibly offering a lower interest rate or eliminating the annual fee. If the account is not profitable, cancel it.

(From p. 85) Exercise: Break these long paragraphs into shorter paragraphs. We note some of the repeating key words in italics.

1. *ARNEWS* is the bimonthly newsletter of the Chief, *Army Reserve.* The Public Affairs office publishes the contents, current events in the *Army Reserve.* In addition, Public Affairs maintains the mailing list for *ARNEWS'*s subscribers.

    To create an edition of ARNEWS, the Public Affairs office collects the *articles* that comprise the newsletter. *Articles* come from sources within the Army Reserve as well as outside sources contributing for publication. Public Affairs edits the *articles* and desktop publishes a camera-ready copy of the newsletter.

    To create a mailing list for ARNEWS distribution, Public Affairs downloads from its membership database an *ASCII file* containing name, address, zipcode, and member ID. The *ASCII file* has one record for each line, followed by a page break. The record fields are delimited by commas.

    Public Affairs sends the camera-ready copy of the newsletter and a 16 BPI tape of the mailing list to the publisher. In turn, the publisher prints the newsletter, creates and affixes Cheshire labels, then mails the newsletter.

Note: The repeating key terms are *pH range*, *bleach*, and *ion*.

2. Acidic and basic cleaners were successful during preliminary testing. We needed to establish an allowable *pH range* for dense-pack ceramic membranes. The approach for establishing *the pH range* was to use hydrochloric acid and sodium hydroxide with the appropriate buffer to determine the extreme pH thresholds. These thresholds serve as the endpoints for an allowable *pH range* as long as the membrane passed the skim milk test. Our pH testing did not establish a *pH range* for any particular cleaner, but rather set a guideline. Most acidic or basic cleaning solutions exist within a *pH range* defined as mild or strong.

    However, some confusion came from the use of *bleach* during the tests. The skim milk test requires the use of *bleach* plus a non-ionic detergent to remove milk from the pores of the membrane. *Bleach* was also considered as a possible cleaner for membrane restoration. The chemical effects of *bleach* on the membrane were unknown prior to testing. Therefore, *bleach* and the non-ionic detergent were added to sodium hydroxide to find a basic pH threshold. We assumed that if the membrane passed the skim milk test with the *bleach* in the test solution, then any future failure was not due to the *bleach*, but from pH.

    Unfortunately, bleach dissociates into two different *ions* in solution: the hypochlorous *ion* (HOCL) and the hypocholorite *ion* (OCL). Each ion has different chemical characteristics, and the *ion* concentration varies with pH. This variation can range from 5 to 10, and the effects of these *ions* on a membrane within this pH range are still unknown.

(From p.87) Exercise: Make the following passages more coherent by using transition words.

Passage 1 **Zybase-REMOD Test Result**

Although the custom Zybase file server works independently with other software modules, you may encounter potential problems when running the report module (REMOD) and Zybase at the same time on the network. If the REMOD fails for any reason, the Zybase file server continues to feed records into REMOD. *Moreover*, Zybase disregards operator instructions to stop sending records to REMOD. The operator is forced to close the Zybase function completely without the ability to save open files. *Consequently*, the error log is lost.

The immediate problem is easy to fix, if we can access the error log; *therefore*, I suggest we write code to permit the operator to save the error log as part of taking Zybase down.
Then I suggest we take REMOD off the network.

Passage 2 **Letter to Drug Manufacturers**

Your advertisement citing *in vitro* data misleads, *because* the advertisement presents the data in a way that shows clinical relevance. *Specifically*, the statement "it's time to take action," when shown with the *in vitro* data, implies that Timencin is indicated to treat infections caused by each of the pathogens in the advertisement.

Additionally, the *in vitro* data combines selected pathogens for which Timencin is indicated and pathogens for which Timincin is not indicated. *For example*, Timencin is not indicated to treat conditions caused by pathogens such as *coagulase-negative Staphylococcus* (methicillin-susceptible), *Enterococcus feacalis*, and *Streptococcus Group B*. *However*, your advertisement includes these pathogens.

(From p.89) Exercise: Use vertical lists to group information for the reader.

Follow these six steps to import line graphs when word processing:

1. Open an empty frame where you want to put your line graph.

2. Choose Graphics, Figure, or Retrieve from the menu bar.

3. Select and import line graphs from the menu by double-clicking on the desired filename.

4. Confirm that your selected line graph appears in the frame.

5. Adjust the position or size of the frame by clicking and dragging a frame handle.

6. Anchor your frame to the page by double-clicking the anchor icon.

Disbursement requests must be properly documented for payment processing. Each disbursement request must contain the following five pieces of information:

1. payment authorization

2. invoices signed by the approving department

3. receiving copy of the purchase order

4. other receipts such as shipping documents

5. remittance for any merchandise returned

The disbursement system allows some unique purchases on a case-by-case basis. For example, hardware maintenance outside our standard maintenance contracts requires a copy of the estimate and final bill. Advertising requires proof-of-service such as a copy of the advertisement, the order, and authorization.

(From p.89) Exercise: Improve the following list.

Follow these *three* steps to download your email:

1. Click on the Mailbox icon.

2. Input your name and password.

3. Click the Envelope icon to save the email to your hard disk.

The machine's action of autodialing does not belong in the list of the steps you perform. Either eliminate the sentence, or place it outside the list. The commentary about getting a password belongs outside the list. When introducing the list, tell the reader the number of steps — *three*.

(From p.91) Exercise: Improve these lists by making them tables.

Employees and contract labor have different requirements for filling out time sheets.

Labor category	File time sheets	Use form	Necessary information
Employees	Weekly	Form FE-10	Hours Charge number
Contract labor	As required	Form CL-10	Hours Purchase order number

The following section of the Gizmo Test Plan tests the nightly batch runs that match new addresses to the US Post Office address database, merge new addresses into the house file, and purge duplicates.

Run batch program	Inputs	Process	Outputs
pomatch.bat	Records for today Current week's USPS address file	Flags exact matches Uses US address for 90%+ matches Flags < 90% matches for error log	Error file for non-matches Matched file with last four Zip appended
mergepurge.bat	USPS matched file from pomatch.bat House file	Flags near dupes scoring 3 or more points of commonality Deletes exact dupes	Log of dupes Log of near dupes Updated housefile Backup (old) housefile

(From p.93) Exercise: Remember, a document with zero coherence devices is just one huge block paragraph. The following passage is well organized but needs visual coherence devices to make it reader-friendly. Add visual devices.

TO: Senior Management
FROM: John Phelps
DATE: May 3, 2001
SUBJECT: Switching Credit Cards for Long Distance Calls

This memo explains how you can use our new long distance telephone credit cards. Effective immediately, BAP, Inc. will switch from AT&T to **TINKERBELL** for all credit card calls. Employees traveling on BAP business are eligible to receive a company **TINKERBELL** credit card. All AT&T credit cards should be returned to Finance & Accounting (3rd floor) by 6:00 p.m. Tuesday, May 7, 2001. We will close the AT&T account at that time.

The **TINKERBELL** system requires a different procedure for using the credit card:

1. Dial the **TINKERBELL** Travel Number, 1-800-555-4311: you get a voice prompt asking for your *code*.
2. Enter your four-digit authorization *code*, then your two-digit travel *code*, printed on your card.
3. Enter the area code and the telephone number that you want to reach.

Each business group has its own four-digit authorization *code* and travel *code*. Calls are charged against your group's overhead. Finance and Accounting provides group managers with itemized call sheets, so they can track their long distance credit card expenses. Separate cards can be issued for specific contracts, if necessary.

I am your principal contact for the new credit card system. I assign authorization *codes* and travel *codes*. If you have problems dialing a number or have questions about procedures, contact me. If your credit card is lost or stolen, contact me or **TINKERBELL** immediately.

(From p.94) Final exercise: Apply coherence devices to help readers skim, follow, and refer back to the following paper. Put the purpose statement in the right place. Make key words consistent. Suggest headings. Use paragraph breaks and vertical lists. Use other visual devices.

Merged Account Legislation Affects BAP

This paper describes fixed accounts prior to the enacting of Public Law 101-510, how the law changed fixed accounts, and the effect of the law on BAP. Merged Account Legislation: Public law 101-510, enacted November 1999, changed accounting and reporting procedures for obligated and unobligated funds. The legislation eliminated **Merged Accounts**, and replaced them with a revised definition of **Expired Accounts** and the newly created **Closed Accounts**.

Prior to Public Law 101-510

Prior to Public Law 101-510, fixed accounts had three conditions: **Active, Expired**, or **Merged**.

1. **Active Accounts** have obligation authority. Treasury may record new obligations during this period.

2. **Expired Accounts** start at the expiration of the active account's obligation authority and last for two years. The Treasury can make obligation adjustments during the two-year period, but can not record a new obligation. When an **Active Account** expires, the unobligated balances return to the Treasury surplus fund.

3. **Merged Accounts** begin three years after the obligation authority of the account expires. At this time, the Treasury merges the unspent obligations from all previous budget fiscal years into the merged surplus fund authority.

After Public Law 101-510

After Public Law 101-510, fixed accounts have three conditions: **Active, Expired**, and **Closed**. Each condition has a different meaning.

1. **Active Accounts** stay the same. Active accounts have obligation authority.

2. **Expired Accounts** now have a five-year period following the expiration of obligation authority, and they continue for two years. **Expired Accounts'** unobligated balances do not return to the Treasury as surplus funds, but remain with the obligated balances. During this period, all funds remain for recording, adjusting, and liquidating any obligations properly chargeable to the account prior to the time balances expired. *Therefore, the Treasury can make prior-year adjustments.*

3. **Closed Accounts** now replace **Merged Accounts**. **Closed Accounts** begin with the sixth year after the obligation authority expires. Then, obligated and unobligated balances return to the Treasury as surplus funds.

Effect on BAP, Inc.

The Merged Account Legislation has three effects on BAP:

1. BAP can now file for prior-year adjustments when contracts call for cost-plus-fixed-fee.

2. BAP can more easily contract to perform future work — out to year six — with current funds.

3. BAP must, for long-term contracts, carefully track dollars: obligated and unobligated. After funds return to the **Closed Account**, special legislation is needed to re-authorize the funds.

Note the shifting terms:
condition, situations, states = condition
group, merge = merge

The dash provides a stronger visual device than parentheses for — *out to year six* —

Step 9. Edit for Clarity

(From p.97) Exercise: Underline the abstract and general words. Suggest concrete and specific words.

1. Our office (who?) has been in communication (how?) with your office (with whom?) recently (when?) regarding (huh?) a question (which one?) about issuing a refund (how much?) for the remaining portion (how many months left?) of your lease (any reference number?) on some equipment (my water cooler or my Caterpillar tractor?). There are (what are?) several (how many?) reasons why a refund (how much?) of the whole remaining portion (time or money; how much?) fails to satisfy (how?) various material conditions (how many and how material?) of the lease (which one — I've got four leases with you). However, your office (who?) may contact (how? smoke signals okay?) our department (who?) to negotiate some amount suitable. (what?)

    BAP's accounting office wrote Ace Co. last Friday, March 8, 2001 regarding your request for a $300 refund for the last two months remaining on your photocopier lease. Two material lease conditions preclude a full refund. You may contact Ms. Cook at our Finance Department, (800) 555-4561, to negotiate a lease buy-back price.

2. A number of factors (how many? what's a factor?) must be addressed (how? by whom?) in order to ensure (how?) this effort (what effort?) meets its objectives (how?) within the proposed timeframe. (when?)

    Acme, Inc. must approve the cost and schedule of the new fax server so Software, Inc. can provide fax capability on your company's intranet before April 18, 2001.

3. The government (which agency?) acknowledges (how?) your staff's (which part of our staff?) tremendous (oooh!) efforts (what did we do?) in incorporating (how?) new requirements (which ones?) into the baseline (of what?). We (who's we?) are both well (how well? *really* well?) aware (how did we become aware?) of the importance of maintaining (how?) a high level (how high? *tremendously* high?) of progress (how much?) for the rest of FY 2001. We (who's we?) both recognize (how?) there is (where is?) a point (where is it? Oh, yes, it's back there) at which any new work (which new work?) may affect (how?) that major milestone (which one?).

    The FAA thanks your project manager, Ms. Barbara Jones, for working over the Labor Day weekend to amend her project plan. She added FAA's new requirement for a standard keyboard as an upgrade to the baseline. By sacrificing her weekend, Ms. Jones adjusted the schedule for 34 subtasks to keep her technical staff and our contract officers on schedule for delivery of the computer upgrade by September 2001.

    Note that we drop the last sentence because it says nothing. Usually, if every phrase in a sentence is abstract and general, cut the whole sentence.

(From p.97) Exercise: Replace abstract and general words with concrete and specific words. (We offer two possible answers for each.)

1. very difficult — needs 1,000 lines of code — exceed our budget by one million dollars
2. subsidy — a weekly allowance of $5 — a 4-year tax holiday
3. arrange a faster medium — add a 800Mz server — lease a cable modem
4. contact someone — phone technical support — write your senator
5. We consider it in violation — Your ad violates — We believe that your ad violates
6. finalize the contract — deliver the system — sign the contract
7. a change that can benefit most everyone — lower prices for car buyers — 401K plan for fulltime employees
8. familiarize yourself with — read — study
9. various concerns — risk of cost overrun — physical security of data from fire or theft
10. need a response — return the signed contract — call us to schedule an interview
11. acquire a new functionality — build the fax server subsystem — borrow your brother's car
12. no controlling legal authority — no law or regulation — no jury that would convict me
13. devise a means to — write a plan to train your drivers — install a local area net to link your computers
14. effect a change — sell your leaky houseboat — plant wheat instead of soybeans
15. some time in the future — next Tuesday at 7:00 a. m. — in the third quarter
16. ASAP — before you exhale — by 5:00 p.m.
17. by close of business — by 6:00 p.m. Eastern Standard Time — before last Fedex pickup
18. at your earliest convenience — when you return from your honeymoon — before you can graduate

(From p.99) Exercise: Identify passive voice. Answers show passive voice in italics. Convert passive verbs to active. Add a subject by answering the question by *what?* or by *whom?* Note that the active voice is usually more concise as well as more specific.

1. It *is pointed* out in the article that 13-column spreadsheets help bankers organize their information.
    The article points out that 13-column spreadsheets help bankers organize their information.

2. Errors that I have been making for years *are now more easily seen* when I edit.
    I now more easily see errors that I have been making for years when I edit.

3. The safety tag *must be removed* before the toner cartridge *can be installed*.
    Remove the safety tag before you install the toner cartridge.
    Or Remove the safety tag to install the toner cartridge.

4. The addresses *must be checked* for duplicates, and incomplete addresses *must be compared* to the US Post Office database.
    The system must check for duplicates and compare addresses to the US Post Office database.

5. Little attention *is being paid* to that advertising.
    Students pay little attention to that advertising.

6. The client *was invited* to review the proposal by us. (The phrase *by us* is a misplaced modifier.)
    We invited the client to review the proposal.

7. The verification and validation tests *will be conducted* after the terabyte of Landsat data *is loaded* into the database.
    BAP, Inc. conducts the verification and validation tests, after NASA loads the terabyte of Landsat data into the database.

8. The insurance investigation *is started* only after a legal complaint *has been submitted*.
    State Farms starts the insurance investigation only after you submit a legal complaint.
    Or The insurance investigation starts after a legal complaint.

9. After the contract *was won*, we met the client to determine how the deliverables *are accepted*.
    After we won the contract, we met the client to determine how they accept deliverables.

10. The sample size *must be increased* to ensure that the tests *are conducted* properly.
    Increase the sample size to ensure that you conduct the tests properly.
    Or Increase the sample size to conduct the tests properly.

(From p. 99) Exercise: Circle all the passive voice in the following passage from a contracts dispute between BAP, Inc. and the Metropolitan Department of Transportation (MDOT). Change to active voice.

The contract scope *was changed*. Soon after, problems *were encountered*, and the project *was delayed*. Ultimately the project *was suspended* until decisions *could be made* and all issues *could be addressed*. At that time, the team *was scaled* back from 40 to 20 members. Contractual and cost accounting matters *were* also *examined*. After the contract *was renegotiated*, the project *was restarted* approximately three months after it *was suspended*.

MDOT changed the contract scope. Soon after, BAP encountered problems, and MDOT delayed the project. Ultimately MDOT suspended the project until both BAP and MDOT made decisions and addressed all issues. At that time, MDOT scaled the team back from 40 to 20 members. BAP also examined contractual and cost accounting matters. After BAP and MDOT renegotiated the contract, MDOT restarted the project approximately three months after they suspended it.

(From p.101) Exercise: Convert sentences to active voice. Note that active voice is usually more concise than passive voice.

1. The paint *is then allowed* to dry overnight.
    The paint dries overnight.

2. The online help, which *is required* in the statement of work, has many benefits to the user.
    The online help required in the statement of work has many benefits to the user.

3. This report *is supposed* to contrast the approval process for generic and brand name drugs.
    This report contrasts the approval process for generic and brand name drugs.

4. Upon receiving new data, the system *is intended* to identify common errors when the program *is run*.
Upon receiving new data, the system identifies common errors when the program runs.

5. The malfunction ~~that had been~~ *reported* last night *has been corrected* by the night shift.
The night shift corrected the malfunction reported last night.

6. The logic *is shown* in Figure 3.
The logic is in Figure 3.
Or Figure 3 shows the logic.

7. The statistician, ~~who was~~ *hired* last week, *is expected* to report to work on May 1.
The statistician hired last week reports to work on May 1.

8. Access the RTP temporary database ~~that is~~ *used* to sort files by address.
Access the RTP temporary database used to sort files by address.

9. All resources ~~that are~~ *related must be included* in the same file.
Include all related resources in the same file.

10. The process flow *is presented* in Section 2.
The process flow is in Section 2.
Or Section 2 presents the process flow.

(From p.101) Exercise: Circle all the passive voice in the following passage from a user manual. Change to active voice. Note that active voice is usually more concise.

At present, the daily aging report *is produced* as part of the daily cash flow statement. Our accounting software *is designed* to automatically generate new reports and archive the old reports. Then, the new report *is transmitted* to the central database that *can be accessed* by the accounts receivable staff.

At the end of the month, all daily reports *are archived*. The accounts receivable staff, who *are assigned* responsibility for aging reports, *are allowed* to access the archives. If a report that *is archived must be accessed*, the accounts receivable staff *are expected* to notify the Onyx Computer Operations room. Archived tape *must be pulled and loaded*. Requests *are fulfilled* in the order in which they *are requested*. — 118 words

At present, the daily aging report is part of the daily cash flow statement. Our accounting software automatically generates new reports and archives old reports. The new report transmits to the central database accessed by the accounts receivable staff.

At the end of the month, the system archives all daily reports. The accounts receivable staff responsible for aging reports can access the archives. To access an archived report, the staff notifies the Onyx Computer Operations room that pulls and loads the archive tape. The operations room fulfills requests in the order requested. — 92 words or 23 percent fewer

(From p.103) Exercise: Put all verbs in present tense. In the answer, we cut a few unnecessary words and rearranged instructions 5 and 6 to improve the parallelism. We improve coherence by telling the number of steps: *six*.

User Manual for Lawnmower

Follow these six instructions to operate your lawnmower:

1. Check the oil and gas levels.
2. Ensure no debris is near the blades when you start the motor.
3. Put the choke to the red line as shown in figure 2.
4. Grab the deadman lever with one hand, then pull the starting rope with the other.
5. Prime the carburetor if your mower starts with difficulty.
6. Clean grass cuttings from the engine area, after you mow your lawn.

Original version had 108 words. Improved version has 80 or 26 percent fewer words.

(From p.103) Exercise: Put all verbs in present or past tense.

Job Management System Ribbon-Cutting Ceremony

After the guests on stage take their seats, the ceremony opens with a welcome statement from the VP of Operations, Mr. Kahn.

A one-hour demonstration of the Job Management System follows. The demonstration consists of a brief management overview of our products and services. The demonstration uses multi-media plus a panel of users from the Delaware factory. The panel of users plays the appropriate roles of order taking and order fulfillment.

When the demonstration ends, the stage clears, except Mr. Kahn remains. The ribbon-cutting ceremony follows. Joining Mr. Kahn in the ceremony is the plant manager and Mr. Stubbs, representing the union.

Mr. Stubbs provides closing remarks. The remarks outline the future improvements to the plant that the new system makes possible.

Light refreshments are served after the ceremony. We expect about 500 employees to attend.

Note that simplifying tense also makes the text more concise. The original version was 157 words. Simplifying the tenses cuts the text to 136 words, a 13 percent reduction.

(From p.105) Exercise: Change subjunctive mood to indicative. Note where we simply eliminate the subjunctive mood and where we substitute a more precise condition. You may have different answers.

1. Letter

Dear Joe Palmer:

This letter clears up a misunderstanding about proposed changes to our purchasing policy that affect your department.

You caught a significant typo in our draft guidance. We neglected to warn you that you had an early draft, which might have saved you some anxiety. Whereas the first draft said vendors must not expect to be paid in less than *600* days, the final policy states vendors must not expect to be paid in less than *60* days.

Thank you for catching the typo. Please note other changes in the final draft of our purchasing policy. Please address further questions about the new vendor policy to Mr. Smith, (991) 555-1234.

This edit for subjunctive mood cuts this passage from 126 to 109 words or a 13 percent reduction.

2. Requirement for Solid State Air Conditioner

When needed, we deploy solid state air conditioners as part of a remote sensor that detects hazardous materials. The entire unit of sensor plus cooler must meet the following requirements. The unit operates at ambient temperatures between $-10°$ and $+43°$ C. The weight of the unit must not exceed 80 lbs. The volume of the unit must not exceed 3.375 ft^3. The unit must operate in harsh industrial environments, and most parts must be off-the-shelf.

A thermoelectric (TE) cooler helps satisfy the unit's requirements. The TE cooler has no moving parts, and therefore, is lighter than mechanical coolers and can survive better in harsh environments. The TE cooler exceeds the temperature range $-10°$ to $+43°$ C. Even at the extremes, the TE coolers maintain precise temperatures within +/- 0.1°C. A TE cooler also serves as a heater by changing the polarity of the DC power. The TE cooler generates no electrical signature or mechanical noise.

This edit for subjunctive mood cuts this passage from 171 to 156 words or a 9 percent reduction.

3. Warning Label (We fixed some passive voice as well.)

Drysalol®
(ninitparo injection)

Skin rashes are possible when you administer Drysalol®. However, rashes are rare in patients with no prior exposure to ninitparo. The risk of skin rashes increases in patients re-exposed to Drysalol®. If a patient undergoing surgery requires a second exposure, the physician must weigh the benefit of Drysalol® against the risk of skin rash. Patients must consult their primary physician.

(From p.107) Exercise: Circle the ambiguous pronouns and suggest changes. These examples represent extreme ambiguity. Your wild guess probably differs from our wild guess.

1. We do not tear your laundry by using machinery. We wash your laundry carefully by hand.

2. This rumor has been circulating, and everybody knows the truth.

3. The analysis clearly shows we do not require a company car.

4. This crisis demands your immediate attention.

5. Therefore, you can't take this cool weather for granted.

6. The inspector found a safety guide dated May 1988 taped to a machine you installed in 1999. Please explain this discrepancy in dates.

7. We adjusted job descriptions after the layoffs. The client requested these adjustments.

8. The sample is insufficient for the test. The sample needs to be completely re-done.
    Or, You must completely re-do the test with a sufficient sample.

9. The use of Alphadine with a protein diet can cause liver failure. Do not use Alphadine during a protein diet.
    Or, To avoid risk of liver failure, do not use Alphadine during a protein diet.

10. They cancelled my flight with no explanation, and they still managed to lose my luggage. This instance is the third time they lost my luggage.

(From p.107) Exercise: Find and replace the ambiguous pronouns in the following document. We show our changes in italics.

Integrating a Personal Information Manager into C-Net

Personal Information Manager (PIM) has six functions to help users manage their time and resources. We surveyed our C-Net users about those *functions,* and the *users* require only one: PIM Task Manager. It lets each C-Net user maintain a personal calendar. Then *PIM Task Manager* combines those *personal calendars* into a master calendar available on the C-Net server. Users can consult the *master calendar* for scheduling meetings.

However, *installing PIM Task Manager* presents a technical problem. When C-Net calls PIM Task Manager, *C-Net* must query a PIM resource database without switching between the two applications. *Consequently, PIM Task Manager* must reside on the same file server as C-Net and strain the *server's* limited processing capacity.

Therefore, we researched *the strain on server capacity* and uncovered two problems:

1. PIM stores the calendar files in its own proprietary format. C-Net must convert *PIM files* to *C-Net* format. *Therefore,* every time PIM updates a Task Manager file, *PIM* must use already strained processing capacity to convert the *file.*

2. Before *PIM Task Master* can generate the master calendar, the *server* must restore the data into the PIM file format, and then process the *PIM calendar files* back to C-Net format so users can read the *calendars.* This *constant formatting* causes a further strain on the *server's* processing capacity.

We considered the cost of converting from C-Net to a PIM-compatible server software, but the *conversion* was too expensive. *To summarize*, we must sacrifice server processing capacity to install and use *PIM Task Master.*

PIM's limited benefit is not worth the strain on the server.

(From p.109) Exercise: Replace the abstract and ambiguous *there are* expressions with concrete and specific language. You may need to rearrange the sentence or provide a specific subject for the sentence.

1. Our management plan has ten key milestones.

2. Easton, Maryland evokes a sense of history. Victorian homes line the streets. Each Saturday during the spring, the Easton Garden Society hosts garden tours. (33 to 25 words or 25 percent fewer)

3. The scope of the work includes three deliverables.

4. At the Jobs Fair, we received 15 applicants for our sales job. We might have received more applicants if the Fair had better attendance. The Fair competed with two events: the Rose Festival Marathon, and the Harbor Festival. The newspaper reported those events attracted a combined attendance of 137,000 persons.

5. Telefona plans to offer ten initiatives to improve customer service at ACME Bank.

6. I misunderstood the risks involved when I signed the contract.

7. The company picnic provided children 15 activities.

8. If the Fatal Error message flashes on the screen, you have only one course of action.

9. Look at the motherboard. You see four short slots and six long slots. A video card sits in the first long slot. An internal fax-modem sits in slot number two. Depending on the configuration of your machine, extended memory may sit in long slot number three.

10. The rumor circulating throughout the company that we plan to move the headquarters from Dayton, Ohio to the Grand Cayman island is false.

11. You don't need to use a purchase order for office supplies. Use the credit card.

12. Call us when convenient.

(From p.111) Exercise: Match non-English or non-standard phrases with one of the standard English phrases listed on the right.

1.	a la mode	o.	in the fashion
2.	ad hoc	k.	to this (purpose)
3.	ad infinitum	g.	limitless
4.	alright	p.	slang for okay
5.	apropos	j.	appropriate
6.	ca.	n.	around or approximately
7.	conceptwise	y.	adverb form of concept?
8.	departmentation	q.	noun meaning department?
9.	e.g.	l.	for example
10.	ergo	e.	consequently
11.	et al	m.	and others
12.	et cetera	d.	and so forth
13.	idealize	x.	verb: to make perfect?
14.	i.e.	c.	that is
15.	in lieu	u.	instead of
16.	in situ	w.	on site
17.	ipso facto	i.	by the fact itself
18.	laissez faire	h.	let people do
19.	non sequitur	f.	it does not follow
20.	per	z.	through, by, or according to
21.	per diem	b.	by the day
22.	quid pro quo	v.	something for something
23.	via	a.	by way of, or by means of
24.	vice versa	t.	position reversed
25.	vis-a-vis	s.	face-to-face
26.	viz.	r.	namely

(From p.113) Exercise: Change these negative statements to positive statements. Note that most positive statements are shorter than the negative version.

1. Employers often give employees year-end bonuses. (14 to 7 words or 50% fewer)
2. I am comfortable with those dealings. (11 to 6 words or 45% fewer)
3. The Court upheld a state law allowing the investment tax credit.
4. Speak up.
5. The operator must remove the red safety tag from the disk drive to boot up the system and continue software installation.
6. The General Partners are liable for non-performance if the Limited partners prove that the General Partners acted in bad faith.
7. We rejected your bid because we accepted a less costly bid for the services.
8. Although you justify the need for a company car, we lack the necessary funding.
9. I intend to appear reasonable.
10. Her response was logical, but it lacked key information
11. You shipment will arrive on time.
12. You reported my comments out of context, violating journalistic ethics.
13. The two situations are similar.
14. Turn off the oven, especially when leaving the house.

(From p.115) Exercise: Think of a suitable synonym.

1. businessman   professional
2. craftsmanship   skill
3. foreman   supervisor
4. middleman   broker
5. sportsmanship   fair play
6. stewardess   flight attendant
7. fatherland   homeland
8. gentlemen's agreement   informal agreement
9. salesman   sales representative
10. waitress   server

(From p.115) Exercise: Edit these sentences to avoid gender bias.

1. Experienced ~~waiters~~ servers make dining more pleasant.
2. The average American drives ~~his~~ a car every day.
3. A ~~man~~ person who wants to get ahead works hard.
4. If ~~a man~~ you plan ahead, ~~he~~ you can retire at age 60.
5. Each senator selects his or her staff.
6. Be sure to bring your ~~husband~~ spouse to the D.C. Armory Flower Show.
7. President Reagan, Premier Gorbachev, and ~~Mrs.~~ Prime Minister Thatcher dominated politics in the 1980s.
8. The ~~fireman~~ firefighter and ~~policeman~~ police officer controlled the crowd.
9. ~~A~~ Homeowners can deduct interest expenses from ~~his~~ their taxes.
10. ~~The user~~ You can make only three attempts to enter ~~his~~ your password before the machine locks ~~him~~ you out.

(From p.117) Exercise: Make these sentences parallel.

1. You can select either the condensed version or the full-text version.

2. The choice between an optimum system design or a less desirable one is affected by our R&D budget and by how we use commercially available software.

3. Management assesses your job performance by the following criteria: Are you neat and well-groomed, do you get your assignments done on time, are you flexible, and are you willing to learn?
    Or Management assesses your job performance by the following criteria: grooming, punctuality, flexibility, and willingness to learn.

4. Our latest magazine issue lost money because we did not fill the advertising space, we needed 2,000 extra copies for promotion, and we paid too much for paper.

5. Based on their requirements, we will recommend either the zoning board approve the plan outright or the review committee request more information.

6. When you make the list, arrange the items in order of importance, write them in parallel form, and number all the items.

7. We propose the following agenda for the meeting:
    a. Call the meeting to order.
    b. Set date for next meeting.
    c. Take the roll call.
    d. Elect new officers.

8. The tax committee voted to
    a. review the materials being purchased for the tax library
    b. submit a report on new billing rates
    c. develop client programs
    d. plan annual tax department party

9. When you build your database, use either dBase IV for Windows or Altbase for OS/9.

10. The new accounting software package fails to meet our requirements for several reasons:
    1. It is too slow.
    2. The menus are too complicated.
    3. It loses all my data if power fails.
    4. The ledger does not balance if you enter a future date.

(From p.119) Exercise: Correct misplaced modifiers. We note modifiers in italics.

1. Our department receives *only* a limited amount of money to spend on office equipment.

2. We designed our mixing bowl *with a round bottom for efficient beating* to please any cook.

3. We want to hire a man *that does not smoke or drink* to take care of our prize cow.

4. The Fish and Game Club announced tuna *off the west coast* are biting.

5. Fred needs to consider all the client's competing requirements, *although extremely difficult to understand.*
    Or Fred needs to consider all the client's competing and *difficult-to-understand* requirements.

6. *The President's scientific advisor* released a recent White House report claiming that acid rain is linked to methane emissions. (Eliminating passive voice fixes the misplaced modifier *by the President's scientific advisor.*)

7. I have enclosed our company's financial statements *for your information.*

8. Senior managers will meet *in the boardroom* with the Chairman about the competition.
    Or Senior managers will meet with the Chairman *in the boardroom* about the competition.

9. We watched the space shuttle *soaring high above the clouds* fly into space.
    Or We watched the space shuttle *soar high above the clouds* into space.

A-37

10. You need to turn in your time sheet *only* at the end of the month.
    Or Turn in your time sheet at the end of the month. (If you cut the modifier altogether, you don't have to worry about misplacing it.)

11. Patients can now *in their homes* take a simple test to detect hearing loss.
    Or Now, patients *in their homes* can take a simple test to detect hearing loss.

12. Please mark April 5 *on your calendars* for the annual tax meeting.

13. Prescribe Simutex for pregnant women *only* when the risk to the fetus is considered.
    Or Doctors, do not prescribe Simutex for a pregnant woman unless both you and the woman consider the risk to the fetus.

14. *Park rangers* found two campers shot to death. (Eliminating passive voice fixes the misplaced modifier *by the park rangers*.)

15. I met a man named Smith *with a wooden leg.* — from the movie *Mary Poppins*

(From p.119) Exercise: Correct the dangling modifiers. We note the formerly dangling modifiers in italics.

1. *Operating at 400 Megahertz*, our system can process your largest files quickly.

2. *To determine the final costs*, we must total the labor-hours multiplied by the hourly rate.

3. The photographers took pictures of the Titanic, which *lay on the bottom of the Atlantic Ocean for 70 years*.

4. *Having studied the client's requirements*, we conclude that the technical approach must include icon-driven menus.

5. *To be a successful manager*, you need good writing skills.

6. *Based on 100 interviews with veterinarians*, we confirmed that cats are cleaner than dogs.

7. *Using the same concept*, we suggest defining defaults for each program.

8. *Confident of our success*, we sent the proposal to the client.

9. *After processing the records*, you print the results.

10. *Because of the rain*, we moved the reception indoors.

11. You must give the *dangling* modifier something to modify.

12. You must put the *misplaced* modifier in the right place.

(From p.120) Final exercise: Edit for clarity to improve the following passage. Find and fix the vague terms, passive voice, shifting tenses, ambiguous pronouns, Latin phrases, negative statements, gender bias, unparallel vertical list, and misplaced modifiers.

Virginia Department of Historical Preservation
111 Broad Street, Richmond, VA 25432

August 20, 2001

Mr. Smith
P. O. Box 2456
Arlington, VA 22145

Dear Ms. Smith:

We reject your request to register your barn as a historical building for four reasons:

1. Although an alleged descendent of Lord Fairfax built the barn built in 1927, the Historical Society places the barn's effective date much later, approximately 1954, when you made improvements to accommodate dairy cows.

2. The barn requires extensive repairs that the owner and the Society can't afford.

3. If the owner repairs the barn, the owner still must pay for insurance.

4. The barn is already condemned to allow construction of a two-lane roadway.

Therefore, you cannot register your old cow barn as a historical site and impede construction of the new Route 230. Frankly, if we had not condemned the barn for road construction, your county intended to condemn your barn as a structural hazard. In that case, you — not the state — pay for razing your barn. Also, the state paid you 150 percent of the assessed value of the condemned land.

If you believe you have other edifices of historical interest, such as a sheep pen or birdhouse, please submit the proper surveys through your county land management office.

Best regards,

William Fairfax
Commissioner

Note how you use the eight editing techniques for clear words and sentences:

1. Use concrete and specific words: *several reasons* becomes *four reasons.*

2. Make verbs active voice and present tense: *have caused the Historical Society to place* becomes *the Historical Society places.*

3. Identify and replace ambiguous pronouns: *if it had not been condemned* becomes *if we had not condemned the barn.* We fixed the passive voice as well.

4. Use standard English words. The Latin *ergo* becomes *In that case.* The Latin abbreviation *ca.* becomes *approximately.* We cut the *i.e.* completely because it referred to shifting terms. We changed the *e.g.* to *such as.*

5. Be positive. *We are not able to approve* becomes *We reject.*

6. Remove gender bias: *his own insurance* becomes *for insurance.*

7. Make sentences parallel. *Neither the owner can afford, nor the Society* becomes *the owner and the Society can't afford.*

8. Test modifiers: *pay for razing the barn instead of the state* (implies you may tear down the whole state) becomes *you — not the state — pay for razing the barn.*

Step 10. Edit for Economy

(From p.123) Exercise: Cut empty verbs. We note the number of words in the original and shorter versions.

1. Please let me spend ten dollars for paper clips. 17 - 9

2. The clients prefer that we meet at their site. 17 - 9

3. This letter notifies you of our intent to adjust our bill. 16 - 11

4. You failed to satisfy our criteria. 9 - 6

5. Having inspected your factory, we conclude that your smokestacks violate the Clean Air Act. 22 - 14

6. We commit to complete your printing job on time. 13 - 9

7. The vice president signs this contract. 10 - 6

8. The cost to enhance the system depends on whether you require duplicate efforts. 24 - 13

9. Your brakes do not stop your car instantly. 20 - 8

10. Please verify which payment applies to the January invoice. 14 - 9

11. We repaired your motorcycle. 11 - 4

12. The board of directors decided to notify employees about this year's pay raises. 17 - 13

13. The auditors determine that BAPCO complies with generally accepted accounting principles. 17 - 11

14. This letter refers to our May 5 visit when we investigated your factory's safety. You violate state and federal law. In our report we suggest you must provide training to comply. When you train, remember that safety benefits your workers as well as satisfies the law. 76 - 46

(From p.125) Exercise: Write alternatives to these prepositional phrases.

1. Call at about 5 o'clock.
    Call at 5 o'clock.

2. In accordance with company policy . . .
    Following company policy . . .

3. He wrote with the purpose of . . .
    He wrote to . . .

4. Submit your plan for the purpose of . . .
    Submit your plan for . . .

5. Put the phone on top of the desk.
    Put the phone on the desk.

6. She is in the midst of a big job.
    She's in a big job.

7. In spite of the fact that . . .
    Although . . .

8. He is an expert in the area of finance.
    He is a finance expert.

9. . . . on a daily basis
    . . . daily

10. In the event of . . .
    If . . . or When . . .

11. Go in back of the shed.
    Go behind the shed.

12. We are in receipt of . . .
    We have . . .

13. He worked over and above . . .
    He worked beyond . . .

14. In the interest of safety . . .
    For safety . . .

15. With regard to your promotion . . .
    Regarding your promotion . . .

16. Indicate as to whether or not . . .
    Indicate if . . .

17. Because of the fact that . . .
    Because . . .

18. Because of this reason . . .
    Therefore . . .

19. At this point in time . . .
    Now . . .

20. In a similar fashion . . .
    Like . . .

(From p.125) Exercise: Cut unnecessary prepositions from the following sentences.

1. To meet test objectives, XYZ, Inc. uses the La Jolla Laboratory staff's expertise. 32 - 13

2. Dr. Roger's review of the committee's draft report awaits DOD's review. 23 - 11

3. To qualify for the local business tax exemption, lecture series ticket sales must match these requirements. 33 - 16

4. The project ensures that the Navy receives maximum return on data documentation. 22 - 12

5. Write the meeting notes, then pass them to the committee members. 17 - 11

6. If these steps fail to restart the motor, take your lawnmower to your dealer. 17 - 14

(From p.125) Exercise: Remove prepositions to shorten this 103-word paragraph.

Third quarter lumber revenues fell five percent although board feet sales rose fifteen percent. Canadian suppliers increased price competition. A further lumber revenue fall risks the stockholder dividend. To improve stockholder relations, the third quarter report needs to highlight company efforts to control costs and maintain profits. (47 words)

(From p.127) Exercise: Cut who, which, and that (plus "to be" verbs) from these sentences.

1. We received resumes from 11 people ~~who are~~ qualified to fill the job. (fixes passive voice)

2. Ann Jones, ~~who is~~ the leader in our contract negotiations, wants to meet you on the six o'clock air shuttle, ~~which is~~ the first flight of the day.

3. Please select a desk ~~that is~~ more suitable to your work.

4. Work continues on the Vega Project, ~~which is~~ scheduled for completion next summer.

5. He added *the same* requirement ~~that was the same~~ as ours.

6. The policy committee, ~~which is~~ composed of local elected officials from Clark County, chose not to include a request for more road salt in their final budget ~~that was~~ submitted on September 10. (fixes two passive voice)

7. Remove the red safety tag~~, which you will find~~ next to the oil drain plug.

8. Your letter discusses many questions ~~that have been~~ bothering me as well.

9. Access the data ~~that will have~~ already ~~been~~ loaded onto your hard drive.

10. If the customer requests statement copies ~~that are~~ older than six months, you must look in the microfilm library.

11. Employees must report any plant accident resulting in lost labor time to the shift supervisor, ~~who is~~ responsible for safety.

12. Employees ~~who are~~ assigned to the new Jupiter Project must submit a form W-2 ~~that can be~~ found in the introduction packet ~~that was~~ issued during last month's orientation.

(From p.129) Exercise: Cut the repetition.

1. He added a requirement.

2. QuickDraw provides a complete set of line-drawing tools for your personal computer, such as
    - free-hand tools as well as common shapes
    - full palette of 256 colors
    - scaling
    - shape and text rotation
    - support for most popular file formats such as GIF, TIP, and Acrobat

3. Each stock item record contains a stocking conversion factor, the number of end-use units contained in one stocking unit.

4. This regulation is more important than others.

5. The road surface must meet state construction standards and be in good condition.

(From p.129) Exercise: Cut unnecessary repetition from this passage.

Training Conferences
We plan three training conferences for government employees. The first occurs approximately 45 days after the contract award. We start with a working meeting and review of initial planning documents and requirements documents for training. The second training conference happens at day 90 to coincide with our first deliverable, the draft AIS training and technical manuals. We review customer comments of the manuals as well as the skills analysis report, plan of instruction, and course outlines. We also resolve concerns before we design and develop the training courses. The third conference happens about 225 days after contract award for reviewing and commenting on training materials and schedules, and for addressing other concerns. (Cut from 137 to 112 words or 19 percent.)

(From p.131) Exercise: Cut redundant words and phrases.

1. The Duraflex tank is 10 feet ~~in volume~~ and stands 2 feet high ~~from bottom to top~~.

2. First ~~and foremost~~, I am sorry ~~and apologize to each and every employee~~ for attempting a little ~~levity and~~ humor ~~now and then~~.

3. BAMCorp's ~~singularly~~ unique personnel and technical package ~~will completely and professionally fulfill, as well as~~ satisfies, ~~all~~ your complex ~~and challenging~~ requirements. By partnering, ~~together with your professional staff and personnel~~, our teams ~~can~~ become interdependent ~~upon each other~~. ~~In other words, BAMCorp can solve all your problems.~~ (Cut from 48 to 19 words, or 60 percent.)

4. Please read ~~and understand~~ this ~~quick and~~ easy guide ~~of instructions~~.

5. Doubling can ~~detract from and~~ confuse the message ~~or idea~~.

6. The company ~~especially wishes to~~ recognizes ~~and compliment~~ Mr. Smith for five years of ~~unselfish and~~ generous ~~aid and~~ support to Little League Baseball in Falls Church.

7. The clients asked these ~~following~~ questions ~~in their request for information~~.

8. Please make sure your tray-tables are ~~fastened and~~ secured ~~in an~~ upright ~~position~~ for landing.

9. Remain securely ~~fastened and~~ buckled ~~in your seat~~ until the plane ~~has come to a full, complete, and final~~ stops.

10. Please make sure your carry-on ~~luggage is of the type and size that~~ can be stored ~~above~~ in the overhead bin ~~compartment~~ or ~~below~~ under ~~the seat space beneath~~ the seat in front of you.

11. Customers can access their account information by modem~~, that is, go online~~.

12. Brokers ~~first~~ introduced junk bonds to the ~~general~~ public in the ~~decade of the~~ 1970s.

13. I spent ~~all the years of~~ my youth ~~studying and~~ learning systems engineering.

14. I choose words ~~and vocabulary~~ to sound more ~~educated,~~ sophisticated~~, and erudite~~.

(From p.133) Exercise: Cut implied phrases.

1. ~~As you may already know (you idiot),~~ Lockheed and Martin Marietta merged to become the world's largest defense company.

2. ~~It should be noted that~~ These new theories mark a radical change in the way scientists view the universe.

3. ~~All things considered (despite his debilitating drinking problem),~~ Our new office manager shows promise.

4. ~~It is suggested that you~~ Send an invoice within 30 days of completing work.

5. ~~Please feel free to (I don't care if you feel anxious)~~ Call me if you have any questions. (We're being a bit aggressive here. You can keep little courtesies in the introduction and the close of your letters.)

6. ~~When you find time (you lazy bum),~~ Please ~~give me your~~ decide ~~sion about whether or not~~ if you want me to work late. Better: Please tell me if you want me to work late.

7. ~~Most experienced experts claim that~~ Children need to eat a well-balanced breakfast before going to school.

8. ~~Before we begin our discussion (Better than remembering after the discussion),~~ Remember, ~~that~~ these remarks are strictly off the record.

9. ~~At this time,~~ we at BAP Industries ~~wish to take this opportunity (but we can't bring ourselves) to~~ thank all our vendors for their support ~~in our on-going activities~~.

10. ~~You may~~ Establish another category ~~for the purpose of~~ to recording, adjusting, and liquidate ~~ing~~ other ~~properly chargeable to the~~ AIS contract *obligations*.

11. On ~~the~~ form ~~in question, called~~ FX-10, please write your claim number ~~in the blank space provided~~ on line 5.

12. ~~It has come to our attention that~~ you *want* ~~may be in the market~~ to buy a new car. ~~We invite you to~~ Test drive the new Hugo Millennium.

(From p.135) Exercise: Cut unnecessary and vague modifiers.

1. I ~~usually~~ write my ~~first~~ drafts ~~very~~ quickly.

2. Please use ~~extreme~~ caution when removing ~~carry-on~~ luggage from the overhead bins.

3. The client asked the following ~~specific~~ questions about our *current* work ~~that is currently in progress~~.

4. Please provide a copy of the ~~original~~ receipt so we can close ~~down~~ your account.

5. BAP Industries offers a ~~most~~ unique solution to your ~~complete~~ personal computer needs.

6. Are you ~~absolutely~~ sure you unplugged the coffeepot? I'm *sure* ~~almost positive~~ I didn't.

7. Management remains ~~fairly~~ optimistic that we can meet our ~~relatively~~ high sales quotas.

8. Martin's analysis was ~~completely~~ accurate, but his conclusion was ~~totally~~ wrong. The ~~end~~ result was confusion.

9. Sally ~~first~~ debuted her ~~new~~ innovation ~~to the public~~ last month.

10. At last, the market survey was completed ~~in its entirety~~. The Market Committee reached a consensus ~~of opinion~~. They decided to ~~stick to the basic essentials of~~ franchise ~~ing~~ new retail stores. ~~In concert~~ With the Products Committee, they decided to ~~exactly~~ replicate store layout and merchandise.

11. If you two ~~will both~~ cooperate ~~with each other~~, we can ~~all~~ achieve our ~~intended~~ goals.

12. Pam and John ~~found it mutually~~ agreed ~~able to join together in the bonds of~~ *to* marry ~~iage~~.

13. When we ~~finally~~ found the car, the battery was ~~completely~~ dead. She left ~~both~~ the headlights ~~turned~~ on, which ~~totally~~ drained the battery ~~of all its power~~.

14. Employees need to be ~~thoroughly~~ convinced that the ~~mutual~~ goals they share with ~~our~~ management ~~team can form the basis for a~~ *create* ~~lasting long-term~~ job security.
    Better: Management must convince employees that shared goals create job security.

(From p.136) Final exercise: Cut 25-50 percent of the 228 words in the letter.

Charles Wiggins
12345 Kings Park
Fairfax, VA 22030

February 20, 2002

Julia Wright
BAPCO, Inc.
Personnel Department
Arlington, VA 22201

Dear Julia Wright:

~~In the interest of~~ exploring ~~employment opportunities with your organization,~~ I ~~am~~ submitt~~ing a copy of~~ my resume for your ~~review and~~ consideration.

~~As you may know by now,~~ I have ~~a variety of~~ work experience~~, which includes providing valuable insight into grasping a combination of~~ in relational database development ~~products~~, front-end development, ~~and analysis of~~ microcomputer graphical user interface (GUI) software ~~applications, as well as analytical and technical support of~~ full life-cycle software ~~development~~ projects.

~~Through my previous experience,~~ I ~~have~~ worked in ~~a myriad of different environments ranging from~~ major corporations to small, start-up companies, holding progressively more responsible positions, ~~which has given me the ability to easily adapt to any situation that might come along.~~ I ~~will~~ work well independently, ~~taking a self-starter, hands-on, and self-reliant approach~~, yet I know the advantages ~~of interdependence and the importance~~ of teamwork.

I am interested in ~~learning more about~~ your company, BAPCO, Inc.~~, and I am confident that we can find a mutually beneficial employment opportunity for both of us~~. In short~~, I am confident that~~ I can be an asset ~~as well as a resource~~ to your company. My salary requirements ~~are subject to~~ negotiation.

~~Perhaps we can~~ arrange ~~a mutually convenient~~ time for an interview ~~so you can meet me and I can meet you to discuss my future with BAPCO~~. Thank you ~~for your time and consideration~~.

Sincerely,

Charles Wiggins

After you remove the deadwood, you get this cleaner version of the letter with 82 words, a reduction of 65 percent. This cleaner version is more likely to get the interview.

I submit my resume for your consideration.

I have work experience in relational databases, front-end development, microcomputer graphical user interface (GUI) software, and full life-cycle software projects.

I worked in major corporations and small, start-up companies, holding progressively more responsible positions. I work well independently, yet I know the advantages of teamwork.

I am interested in your company, BAPCO, Inc. I can be an asset to your company. My salary requirements are negotiable.

I will call to arrange an interview. Thank you.

You can easily change a few sentences to avoid beginning each with the pronoun *I*. For example, *Please consider my attached resume. Your company, BAPCO, Inc. interests me.*

Step 11. Edit for Readability

(From p.139) Exercise: Measure readability by calculating the Gunning Fog Index for each passage. Do not burden yourself with false precision. If your answer is within 10% of ours, consider your answer correct.

> Managing Proposal Commitments
> Total words 185; 6 sentences; 66 long words
> Average Sentence Length = 31 # Long words per 100 = 36
> Fog Index = (31 + 36) * .4 = 26.8
>
> How to Manage Proposal Promises
> Total words 118; 9 sentences; 9 hard words
> Average Sentence Length = 13 # Long Words per 100 = 8
> Fog Index = (13 + 8) * .4 = 8.4

The second passage, which provides the same information as the first, is much easier to read.

(From p.141) Exercise: Replace these long words with short, one-syllable words.

1.	accurate	right	31.	magnitude	size
2.	actuate	start	32.	magnanimous	grand, great
3.	additional	more	33.	methodology	way
4.	allocate	put, place, mark	34.	minimum	least
5.	aggregate	group, sum	35.	modification	change
6.	apparent	clear, plain	36.	necessitate	need, force
7.	ascertain	learn	37.	negative	bad, poor
8.	assimilate	merge	38.	objective	goal
9.	assistance	help	39.	operate	use, run
10.	capability	skill	40.	optimum	best
11.	circular	round	41.	preliminary	first
12.	commensurate	same	42.	prioritize	rank
13.	consistency	feel, blend	43.	probability	chance
14.	demonstrate	show	44.	quantity	size
15.	denominate	name	45.	remuneration	pay
16.	designate	name	46.	represents	shows, is
17.	determination	point, guess	47.	self-conscious	shy
18.	disseminate	spread	48.	sensible	wise, sane, smart
19.	eliminate	cut	49.	stratagem	plan
20.	enumerate	count	50.	substantiate	prove
21.	establish	start, make, place	51.	suitable	right, good
22.	expeditious	fast, quick	52.	supposition	guess
23.	expertise	skill	53.	terminate	end, kill
24.	facilitate	help, ease	54.	uncompromising	firm, stiff, hard
25.	functionality	use	55.	underutilize	waste
26.	generate	cause, make	56.	utilize	use
27.	hesitate	stall, balk	57.	variance	change
28.	identical	same	58.	verification	proof
29.	initiate	start	59.	voluminous	big, large, huge
30.	legitimate	right, good, firm	60.	wonderful	great

(From p.143) Exercise: Break these long sentences to improve readability. Use short sentences for emphasis, vertical lists to group related items, and long sentences to express complex relationships. We cut some deadwood as well.

1. The client ~~had~~ told us that the tanker was purchased in December 1986. After fulfilling an ~~existing~~ obligation to act as a storage facility for fuel in the Caribbean, the tanker proceeded to Portugal in May 1987. There, the tanker was dry-docked for barnacle scraping, painting, and repairs.

2. ~~Because~~ The multi-state Rentacar discount is the only discount plan that ~~would~~ requires these types of functionality. ~~and~~ No other discount plans ~~have been~~ proposed ~~that might~~ require this functionality. Consequently, the multiple levels or alternate level credits ~~will~~ are not addressed in any other functional specifications.

3. ~~To meet~~ The Air Force Controller needs a new financial system ~~that would~~ to provide a single, consolidated repository of a budget execution, general ledger, and external reporting for Air Force-wide financial management purposes. We developed

    *   MegaCount software modifications
    *   custom interface programs to provide the MegaCount application software with data from external Air Force budget execution and reporting applications
    *   conversion programs to convert existing Air Force data to MegaCount formats and data files
    *   additional custom reports, including external reports for submission to Treasury and GAO

4. ~~The purpose of~~ The Uniformed Securities Act ~~is to~~ protects investors from fraudulent securities transactions for ~~which the administrating agency requires~~ securities ~~to be~~ registered with the state. ~~and~~ Unless a security is specifically exempt from registration, or the transaction is ~~considered~~ exempt, the security must be registered before it can be ~~sold or~~ offered for sale within the state.

5. Using the car jack is safe if you follow these four steps:
    1. Don't panic.
    2. Ensure the car is on a level surface that can support the weight of the car on a jack.
    3. Retrieve the spare tire and tools from the trunk before raising the car.
    4. Place the jack at one of the designated phalanges located behind a front wheel.

(From p.144) Final exercise: Reduce the Fog Index to 12 or lower. Cut deadwood, replace long words with short words, and break long sentences. Use vertical lists if you wish. Recalculate the Fog Index.

First, we cut the deadwood.

Uninterruptible Power Supply (UPS)
and Personal Computer Preventive Maintenance

~~Obviously, the corporation's configuration manager has an obligation~~ to provide ~~his or her~~ corporation an electronically secure environment ~~for the corporation's~~ personal computers, ~~and this advertisement will demonstrate an essential preventive maintenance application that provides~~ reduction ~~in the~~ estimated mean time to failure ~~rate for computer processing units,~~ improvements ~~in~~ hard disk performance, and increased ~~reliability of input/output~~ peripheral devices. ~~The pre-eminent~~ prerequisite ~~for establishing a secure preventive maintenance environment is an unparalleled technology known as the~~ uninterruptible power supply (UPS), and we recommend ~~that you consider~~ purchasing the Microman Standby System with its internal EMI/RFI filters and surge protection ~~capability, which provides the most~~ economical protection for your equipment ~~and your data from all serious electrical power interruptions.~~ Microman's ~~marvelous uninterruptible power supplies (UPS) feature technologically~~ superior power transference rates, a comprehensive ~~set of~~ diagnostic and LED status indicators, intelligent communication interfaces, ~~audible~~ alarms, and attractive casings, ~~virtually~~ eliminating power-related risk ~~to sensitive electronics.~~

After you cut the deadwood, you can break sentences, add a list, and change some long words.

UPS Saves Computers

Protect your company's computers. Reduce mean time to failure for CPUs. Improve hard disk speed. Increase the life of input/output devices. To protect your machines, you need an uninterruptible power supply (UPS). We suggest the Microman Standby System. Its internal EMI/RFI filters and surge protection protect your machines and data from power failures. These UPSs feature

1. great power transfer rates
2. complete diagnostics
3. LED status panel
4. smart interfaces
5. alarms
6. handsome casings

End power-related risk.

Total 79 words with 8 sentences and 9 long words, extrapolated to 11 per 100.
Fog Index = (9 + 11) * .4 = 8.

Notes:

1. To help cut empty verbs, unnecessary modifiers, unnecessary prepositions, and implied phrases, change (or cut) the general and abstract words. For example, what is a *pre-eminent prerequisite*? or a *technologically superior power transfer rate*? a *secure preventive maintenance environment*?

2. Eliminate unnecessary modifiers like *obviously, excellent, essential, serious, pre-eminent, marvelous, virtually*, and many others.

3. Change verbs to active voice, present tense, and imperative mood. The imperative mood cuts all the bulky references to configuration manager.

4. Cut redundancies. For example, *Input/output devices* are *peripherals*.

5. Cut implied phrases. *Alarms* are *audible*.

6. Replace three-or-more syllable words with one-or-two syllable words. For example, *performance* becomes *speed*. Power *interruptions* becomes power *failures*. *Eliminating* becomes *end*.

7. Break compound sentences.

8. Use a vertical list for the series of features.

Step 12. Check for Correctness

(From p.147) Exercise: Match the commonly confused words with the definitions. Some words may have more than one definition.

Confused words	Definitions
1. adapt	to adjust to the situation
adept	highly skilled
adopt	to take as one's own
2. addition	increase
addition	attachment
edition	publication
3. advice	a noun meaning counsel given
advise	a verb meaning to recommend
4. alter	change
altar	religious table
5. awhile	a short time (adverb)
a while	a period of time
6. basis	a reason, or a foundation
bases	reasons, or foundations, plural of basis
bases	facilities
7. biennial	every two years
biannual	twice a year
8. capital	seat of government
capital	money owned
capitol	the building where legislators meet
9. cite	to use as proof
cite	to summon to appear in court
sight	act of seeing
sight	that which is seen
site	place or location
10. compliment	a flattering comment
complement	that which completes
11. compose	create or make up the whole
comprise	include
12. continuous	without interruption
continual	repeatedly and regularly
13. counsel	advice (noun)
counsel	advise (verb)
council	a group of people
14. devise	plan
device	equipment
15. disapprove	have an unfavorable opinion
disprove	show to be false
16. discrete	separate or distinct
discreet	tactful
17. effect	a result (noun) *Effect* is usually a noun.
effect	to result in (verb)
affect	to influence — *Affect* is always a verb.

18. elicit   ask for
    illicit   illegal

19. eminent   prominent
    immanent   inherent
    imminent   about to happen

20. envelop   surround
    envelope   container for a letter

21. ensure   to make sure
    assure   to promise someone
    insure   to protect against loss, indemnify

22. everyone   every person of a group
    every one   every person, emphasizing the individual

Both expressions are singular and require the singular form of the verb and possessive pronouns; therefore, you cannot write *Everyone* has *their* own opinion. Instead, *Everyone* has *his or her* own opinion, or *Everyone* has *an* opinion.

23. except   aside from
    accept   to receive with favor

24. expend   pay out
    expand   increase

25. farther   space or distance
    further   to a greater degree

26. formally   according to custom
    formerly   in the past

27. forward   at the front
    foreword   preface

28. illegible   unreadable
    eligible   qualified

29. implicit   not directly expressed
    explicit   expressed directly with clarity

30. it's   contraction of it is
    its   a possessive pronoun

31. lie   to recline
    lay   to place

32. lone   isolated
    loan   the act of lending (verb)
    loan   that which is lent (noun)
    alone   by oneself

33. lose   to part with
    loose   not fastened or confined

34. maybe   adverb meaning perhaps
    may be   verb conditionally possible

35. past   at a former time (adjective)
    past   former time (noun)
    passed   moved on (verb)

36. parameter   variable or constant
    perimeter   boundary

37. people   a large anonymous group
    persons   individuals

38. personal   private
    personnel   employees

39.	physical	of material things
	fiscal	financial
40.	presently	soon
	at present	now, currently
41.	principal	leader, money (noun)
	principal	first or highest (adjective)
	principle	rule
42.	proprietary	exclusively owned
	propriety	appropriateness
	preparatory	introductory
43.	proscribe	condemn or prohibit
	prescribe	set down as a rule
44.	respectively	considered singly
	respectfully	showing respect
45.	stationary	standing still
	stationery	writing paper
46.	statue	carved figure
	statute	rule or law
	stature	height or level
47.	supplement	add to
	augment	increase or magnify
48.	than	in comparison with
	then	at that time
49.	their	possessive pronoun
	there	at that place
	they're	contraction of "they are"
50.	to	toward
	too	in addition
	two	one more than one

(From p.149) Exercise: In each of the following pairs, identify the word that implies *time* and the other that implies *logic*.

	Time	**Logic**
1.	While	Although
2.	Since	Because
3.	Then	Than
4.	After	Once
5.	Hence	Therefore
6.	When	If
7.	Subsequently	Consequently

(From p.151) Exercise: Circle the subject(s) and underline the verb(s) of each sentence. (Subjects are in boldface; verbs are in italics.)

1. **Thunder** *is* loud, but **lightning** *does* all the work.

2. The **customer** *does* not *know* what **we** *can do* for her company.

3. **Fred** and **Barney** *took* Wilma and Betty dancing.

4. Your **contribution** to the project *deserves* our praise.

5. **Sticks** and **stones** *may break* my bones, but **words** *will* never *hurt* me.

6. **You** *can't win* if **you** *don't play.*

(From p.151) Exercise: Identify each word group below as a correct sentence (C), incomplete thought (IT), run-on (RO), or comma splice (CS).

1. IT   Considering that the competition has reacted strongly to our effort to grab more market share.

2. IT   Can type 25 words per minute.

3. IT   Mr. Johnson, unable to attend the afternoon meeting or evening dinner.

4. C   Beverly Timmons, project leader for database development, made three unsuccessful requests for government assistance.

5. C   Whose responsibility is it to clean up the oil spill?

6. IT   Until we found out that Good Food, Inc. had raised its price to cater a cocktail party and the Sheraton Inn had almost doubled the price to rent the ballroom.

7. IT   Now that Sandra has finished her Associate Degree in Accounting.

8. IT   Tax increases choking off economic growth again.

9. C   The office manager interviews all candidates for staff positions.

10. IT   Friendly, courteous, and always available to answer your questions about our software products.

11. C   The favor of reply is requested.

12. CS   We have a scheduling conflict for the conference room, Mr. Smith scheduled a news conference at four and the facility engineer planned to recarpet the floor, please advise.

13. RO   The climb to the top is hard remember that staying at the top is harder.

14. CS   Concentration is the key to economic success, it's also the key to success in life.

(From p.153) Exercise: Circle the correct pronoun. (Correct answer is in boldface.)

1. The two winners were Jane Swanson and (**I,** me).

2. Please send Mr. Jenkins and (I, **me**) to the seminar.

3. Both you and (**he**, him) should apply for the new position.

4. The telephone technician (who, **whom**) you sent for has helped us before.

5. Rebecca is taller than (**I**, me).

6. No one wants to win the AIMS job more than Alice Cairnes and (me, **I**).

7. The company must monitor (**its**, their) sick leave policy carefully. (The word *company* has no gender.)

8. BAP Industries, Inc. has (**its**, their) headquarters in Virginia.

9. The team won (**its**, it's, their) first game of the season. (The team acted as a unit.)

10. (Its, **It's**) not (**I**, me) (whose, **who's**, who am) responsible for losing the key!

11. (Their, **They're**) talking about (**your**, you're) book.

12. (Whose, **Who's**) in charge of marketing?

13. The committee can't agree what (**its**, it's, their) responsibilities are (if the sense is the committee's collective responsibilities). The committee can't agree what (its, it's, **their**) responsibilities are (if the sense is the committee members' individual responsibilities).

14. That's (**he**, him) standing in the lobby.

15. Jerry writes better than (**they**, them), so (**their**, they're, there) supervisor asked (he, **him**) to edit the company newsletter.

16. Everyone cheered for (their, **his or her**) favorite team.

(From p.155) Exercise: Circle the subject. (Answers are in bold.) Write the verb in the form that agrees with the subject. (Changes are in italics.) Some sentences are correct.

1. **Each** of the four divisions in the company is responsible for submitting an annual budget.

2. Neither the **Army** nor the **Air Force** wants to pull troops out of Europe.

3. The senior **scientist and engineer** in this company *want* to work on the space-station contract. (If one person holds the title senior scientist and engineer, then you use the singular form *wants*.)

4. Difficult **decisions** like the one we must make today *take* time.

5. A **collection** of paintings by three local artists is on display in the lobby.

6. A four-member **crew** cleans and maintains each UPS truck.

7. Where *do* the **desk, chair, sofa, and filing cabinet** *go*?

8. **Shoes, belt, and a tie** add a lot to a man's wardrobe.

9. The **board** of directors *agrees* with management.

10. The **carton** of typewriter ribbons *is* sitting on the desk.

11. The **duties** of the police officer *require* courage and self-sacrifice.

12. **Attention** to details *ensures* fewer errors.

13. **Both** have the authority to write checks up to $1,000.

14. **George Burns**, with his companion Gracie Allen, needs no introduction.

15. Here *are* the new **copy machine and its instruction manual**.

16. **Half** a load of bricks *does* not satisfy our order.

17. **I** wish **I** *were* your boss instead of your assistant. (Use subjunctive form of "to be" = were. However, you can avoid the subjunctive mood by writing, *I want to be your boss instead of your assistant.*)

18. If **wishes** were horses, then poor **men** would ride.

19. If **I** *were* a full time employee, **I** would get a salary with benefits, but **I** would lose my overtime. (You can avoid subjunctive mood by writing, *If I become a full-time employee, I get a salary and benefits but lose overtime.*)

20. **ACME Theaters** is a large national chain.

(From p.157) Exercise: Write *a* or *an* before each word.

1. **a** ten percent raise
2. **an** action
3. **an** example
4. **a** European
5. **an** hour
6. **a** hostess
7. **an** MBA
8. **an** order
9. **an** uncle
10. **an** 11 percent drop
11. **a** balancing act
12. **a** donor
13. **an** FBI investigation
14. **a** history book
15. **an** icon
16. **a** one-time write off
17. **an** SOS
18. **a** uniform

(From p.157) Exercise: Write a or an in each blank.

1. <u>A</u> one-month night shift is followed by <u>an</u> 18-day paid leave.
2. Dr. Peters, <u>a</u> history professor, taught <u>a</u> unit about the Civil War.
3. <u>An</u> ambassador from <u>a</u> European country made <u>an</u> unusual request at <u>a</u> UN meeting.
4. His clock has <u>an</u> electrical dial, not <u>an</u> hour, <u>a</u> minute, or <u>a</u> second hand.
5. <u>An</u> aspirin is not always enough for <u>an</u> aching head.
6. Jane earned <u>an</u> MBA with <u>an</u> emphasis on marketing.
7. We need 100 days to complete <u>an</u> order, but we have <u>an</u> 83-day deadline.
8. The doctor told me to start <u>an</u> aerobic activity, which was not <u>an</u> answer I wanted to hear.

(From p.157) Exercise: Correct the double negatives in these sentences.

1. James couldn't find ~~hardly~~ anyone to invest in his gourmet doughnut shop.
2. Nobody ~~doesn't~~ wants to miss the staff meeting.
3. Peter doesn't know *anything* about the value of a dollar.
4. If you don't have a positive attitude, you won't succeed. — OK
    Even better, You need a positive attitude to succeed.
5. She couldn't ~~scarcely~~ hope to get a promotion after one week on the job.
6. Wouldn't Jim rather ~~not~~ go? or Would~~n't~~ Jim rather not go?
7. Let's ~~not~~ give no more thought to the unfortunate incident.
8. Phyllis never ~~hardly~~ saw ~~no~~ records to justify Bill's tax deductions.
9. Roger never met *anybody* that didn't ~~not~~ like his mom's tollhouse cookies.
10. The safety inspector told us that we must not store ~~none of~~ the nitro next to the glycerin.

(From p.159) Exercise: Write the singular possessive and the plural possessive.

1.	clerk's clerks'	2.	Jones's Joneses'	3.	day's days'	4.	business' businesses'	5.	man's men's
6.	facility's facilities'	7.	area's areas'	8.	boss's bosses'	9.	knife's knives'	10.	advisor's advisors'
11.	fence's fences'	12.	city's cities'	13.	guest's guests'	14.	line of credit's lines of credit's	15.	loss's losses'
16.	waitress' waitresses'	17.	year's years'	18.	lunch's lunches'	19.	brother-in-law's brothers-in-law's	20.	friend's friends'

(From p.159) Exercise: Insert an apostrophe and an *s* to show a possessive noun. Make other nouns plural if necessary. (Changes are in italics.)

1. The *employees* attend lectures where they learn techniques to improve their *plant's* efficiency.

2. We investigated *Bill's* complaint.

3. All of the *questions* were answered in turn.

4. The *Treasurer's* recommendation is that we cut overhead *costs*.

5. If we build a *men's* locker room, we'd better build a *women's* locker room, too.

6. We hired several new *employees* for the Jason project.

7. *Fred's* office will need two *coats* of paint.

8. It's the office *manager's* responsibility to make sure the *lights* work in the conference room.

9. The toxic waste response team must respond in a *minute's* notice.

10. Please evaluate *Avis'* proposal to discount our *company's* large car rental fees.

(From p.161) Exercise: Insert commas where needed.

1. The Smith Foundry Tool and Die Company was started by Thomas Smith, an inventor and entrepreneur.

2. I want to see last quarter's income statement, balance sheet, and cash flow statement.

3. Margery, Elizabeth, Susan, and I can just barely fit in her new sedan.

4. IBM, Compaq, Apple, and a host of other personal computer manufacturers are struggling to define their marketing strategies.

5. Employee benefits include paid vacation, holidays, sick leave, bereavement leave, and unpaid maternity leave.

6. The new copy machine is faster, cleaner, more reliable, and more versatile.

7. We can buy industrial grade, fire retardant carpet in either beige, dark blue, green, gray, or burnt orange.

8. Our lounge always keeps pots of regular and decaffeinated coffee, with cream and sugar.

9. Your flight has stops in Atlanta, Denver, Los Angeles, and Melbourne.

10. Because the air conditioner broke down, we're releasing the workers at 2:00 p.m.

11. After I just got a $2 million construction loan, you've got a lot of nerve telling me you underestimated the job.

12. Although they finished paving the parking lot, they have not painted the lines yet.

13. Gigamega, the most powerful computer ever built, has been programmed to invent video games.

14. Our new vice-president for engineering, Dr. Potts, will lead the discussion on cryogenics.

15. William's plan, even though it made no sense to us, won high praise from the Navy.

16. If I had to learn a second language, all things being equal, I would study FORTRAN.

17. Patriots Day, a paid holiday in Massachusetts, does not merit a day off in Virginia.

18. *Slick* magazine, boasting a circulation of five million paid subscribers, charges $1,600 for a quarter-page ad.

19. In the past, success came easily for George.

20. In conclusion, we use commas to separate parenthetical expressions from the main idea of the sentence.

21. Before a conversion starts, the system downloads the source data into three files.

22. Send the blue, yellow, and pink copies of the purchase order to accounting.

(From p.163) Exercise: Insert semicolons where needed.

1. The receptionist area needs new carpet; however, we'll wait until we remodel the entire floor.

2. Although the receptionist area needs new carpet, we'll wait until we remodel the entire floor. — no change.

3. Dr. Latrobe, a propulsion expert, designed a rocket motor that runs on normal jet fuel; nonetheless, liquid hydrogen remains our preferred fuel, because it has a better thrust to weight ratio.

4. Francis will meet us at O'Hare Airport, however, 30 minutes later than expected. — no change.

5. Luck is where preparation meets opportunity; so keep your eyes open and be prepared.

6. We won the contract; now we have to do the work.

7. Karen Kelly brought us some of our most profitable accounts; for example, she landed both the Hechinger and the Safeway accounts.

8. We've added four new sales districts, which are Atlanta, Georgia; Mobile, Alabama; New Orleans, Louisiana; and Houston, Texas.

9. Our company has but one mission, that is, to provide our clients the best value in video home entertainment. — no change.

10. Megatech bid the highest price; nevertheless, they won the contract on technical merit.

11. Conglomerator, Inc.'s most recent acquisitions were Catfish Farms, Ltd. on April 10, 1999; and Carlisle Cosmetics, Inc. on December 2, 2001.

12. Although Mr. Derickson is younger than the other applicants, he deserves to get the job because of his superior performance record. — no change.

13. Our company's policy is to promote from within; for instance, Mr. Jacobs started as a clerk and rose to be chief executive officer.

14. Because John Heath just came to us from the Department of Transportation, where he was a special assistant to the Secretary, we mustn't bid him on the Highway Study Project. — no change.

15. As long as sales continue to increase at the present rate, we can absorb the rising cost of labor without raising our prices. — no change.

(From p.165) Exercise: Insert colons where needed. Check capitalization.

1. Next time, give that pushy salesman an evasive answer: Tell him to take a long walk off a short pier!

2. Note well: The company would have posted a substantial loss in 2000 except for the one-time sale of the Occoquan property.

3. Our company has but one mission: to provide our clients the best value in video home entertainment.

4. Conglomerator, Inc. made two acquisitions: Catfish Farms, Ltd. on April 10, 1999; and Carlisle Cosmetics, Inc. on December 2, 2001.

5. You must add one procedure to lower your worker's compensation insurance: You must aggressively prosecute fraud.

6. Eric made a significant breakthrough in his research: He discovered a new graphite compound.

7. Doc Watson put a sign on his briefcase: Moon or Bust!

8. The odor from the paper mill smoke smells bad, but it's harmless. — no change

9. Managing inter-personal conflict is like the law of thermal dynamics: You can't win, you can't break even, and you can't get out of the game.

10. The employee lounge has three simple rules for everyone's mutual enjoyment: no smoking, no alcoholic beverages, no radio-players without earphones.

(From p.167) Exercise: Insert dashes, parentheses, commas, or colons. Some sentences can be punctuated several ways.

1. The invoice for $215.00 (not $21.50) needs your prompt attention.

2. Writing and editing ability — that's what we want in our senior technical staff.

3. The partnership usually pays a portion of the net profits: for example, $670 per limited partner in 2000 to help cover the limited partners' tax liability.

4. Jeff must fix the rear projector in the conference room today — tomorrow is too late.

5. The Penultimate II cordless phone — you won't find a better value — offers the following features: speed dialing, auto call back, conference calling, and much more.

6. The offices on the sixth floor (Treasury, Marketing, and Human Resources) will be moved to the new building in May.

7. Dorothy had it all: a dog, ruby slippers, and Kansas.

8. Rebecca requested a four-week vacation: she won a cruise, and she has no choice as to dates.

9. Sales rose (see figure 4, page 32) to a record high — however, return on sales fell slightly.

10. A high school diploma, three years' experience, good references — these are the minimum requirements.

(From p.169) Exercise: Punctuate compound adjectives with hyphens.

1. We graduate a hundred-odd students each year.

2. John sent a carefully worded letter to IRS to explain his highly irregular filings for 1998 and 1999. — no change.

3. Send an up-to-date roster of security clearances to Lt. Avery.

4. The security inspector, Lt. Avery, said our security clearance roster was not up to date. — no change

5. We received a well-written proposal to build an off-site data-entry system.

6. He wished his off-the-record remarks had stayed off the record.

7. Alice made a reasonably good attempt to send the package before five o'clock. — no change.

8. John and Martha sublet a one-bedroom apartment in a not-so-nice part of town.

9. Thelma told the interior decorator she wanted eggshell-white paint in the dining facility, but when the paint dried, she swore the color was coffee-stain brown.

10. Mrs. Stern won't tolerate a gum-chewing receptionist.

11. Please follow the simple step-by-step instructions.

12. Be sure to follow the instructions step by step. — no change.

(From p.171) Exercise: Correct the punctuation in these lists.

1. We need to address two conversion issues for Design Release 2.2, including
    1) conversion of information from the VAX to IBM environment
    2) initialization and maintenance of the operator's manual

2. Avoid ambiguity with three techniques:
    1) Choose words carefully.
    2) Place modifiers close to words they modify.
    3) Use active voice.

3. Before you turn off the LAN host computer, you must
    1. close any open files and exit any active programs
    2. run the backup to tape procedure
    3. run the LAN check to warn users of system shutdown
    4. input a valid LAN operator ID#, then end the LAN program

4. The strengths of the Shazbot system include
    a. error trapping prevents faulty data entry
    b. online help functions decrease training time

5. The flag's three colors are
    1. red
    2. green
    3. gold

6. The flag has three colors:
    1. Top field is red.
    2. Bottom field is green.
    3. Star in the center is gold.

(From p.173) Exercise: Improve the mechanics of these sentences.

1. At our 9:00 a.m. meeting, we reviewed the four-month extension through September, 2001. We learned yesterday that Department of Defense (DOD) will request another two-month extension. We decided to submit the extension to DOD for two months with two one-month options.

2. Beginning March 19, 2002, Ben Brown will handle any material or supplies request through the MS/Plus computer system.

3. The mayor introduced former president Bush at the local Veteran's Day celebration in Alexandria, Virginia.

4. Enter your user-ID in the IBM; then transmit your Lotus files from the PC's hard disk to your own floppy disk.

5. Two hundred and fifty people attended the Air Force convention in Palm Springs, California.

6. Mr. Smith called this morning. (He left his telephone and fax numbers.)

7. The order was for twelve 6-inch pipes; we shipped them to Joe's Hardware, Inc. yesterday at 5 p.m.

8. See figure 4 on page 9.

9. My favorite book is *How to Repair Your Volkswagen: A Step-by-Step Manual for the Complete Idiot.*

10. This occurrence only strengthens our commitment to proceed with BAP Industries' expansion into nickel mining.

(From p.174) Final exercise 1: Circle the correct word. (Answers are in bold.)

1. We are (adapt, **adept**) at software design.

2. Please indicate your (ascent, **assent**) by signing the contract.

3. The improved lighting has had a good (affect, **effect**) on productivity.

4. Careful pre-writing (assures, **ensures**, insures) effective writing.

5. Dewey, Cheetham, and Howe serves as (council, **counsel**) to the city (**council,** counsel).

6. The salad makes a fine (compliment, **complement**) to the broiled fish.

7. It helps to break the problem into (discreet, **discrete**) topics.

8. (**Everyone**, Every one) must attend the safety briefing.

9. We cannot discount our hourly rates any (farther, **further**).

10. Can we (forego, **forgo**) the interview process?

11. Mr. Smith was (formally, **formerly**) self-employed.

12. The operator must get (**past**, passed) the shut-off valve before seeing the display.

13. We will not allow an employee administrative leave unless we believe there is a serious (personnel, **personal**) problem.

14. The key to persuasive writing is seeing the reader's (**perspective**, prospective).

15. The students felt sure of success because they had a (principal, **principle**) at stake.

16. Please examine each cost item (respectfully, **respectively**).

17. Please (sit, **set**) yourself a place at the table.

18. What harm is a couple of beers (between, **among**) friends?

19. The Fairfax County Symphony gave a (credible, **creditable**) performance.

20. Doctors recommend we eat a (healthy, **healthful**) breakfast.

21. There are (less, **fewer**) than six days left to complete the work.

22. We moved our offices to the suburbs (since, **because**, due to) the lease expired and (since, **because of**, due to) the high prices in the city.

23. As the company's founder, Mr. Adam Smith raised the company to a (**respectable**, respectful) position in the steel industry.

24. Refer to the letter, (that, **which**) I sent last Tuesday. — Note the comma after *letter*.

25. The lawyer had no (**further**, farther) questions for the witness.

(From p.175) Final exercise 2: Punctuate these sentences correctly.

1. If ever you've nothing to do, and plenty of time to do it in, why don't you come up and see me. — Mae West in the movie *My Little Chickadee*.

2. In his best selling book *Wabbit Hunting*, the author Elmer Fudd discusses a hundred ways to trap, snare, or shoot cwazy wabbits.

3. Our bookkeeper, Teresa, impressed the auditors with her accurate files.

4. The temporary services agency Temps & Co. will give us eight hours of temp services at no charge, just so we can evaluate their company.

5. Erica, the company expert on time management, suggests that we conduct all staff meetings standing up.

6. We billed four hours at the principal rate of $180 per hour, and eight hours at the staff rate of $42 per hour.

7. Lorna Ewald, Ph.D. in computer sciences, started her own company in 1985, but she sold her interest to Logicon, Inc., and then she came to work for us.

8. Population growth in the United States, according to the latest census data, has fallen if you take out immigration.

9. The qualities we seek include good people skills, willingness to learn, and willingness to travel.

10. Sam's motto — cash is king — made a lot of sense in the 90s, when so many companies struggled with debt.

11. Steel, oil, and railroads — the great monopolies of the 19th Century — changed the face of capitalism forever.

12. Dr. Nathan, our only nuclear engineer, decided that the company's research into cold fusion is a poor investment.

13. A typical engine-overhaul is a one-day job.

14. Red, white, and blue will wrap our Fourth of July Sale in the flag.

15. The telecommunications van must be able to operate in the tropics; therefore, we added a dehumidifier to its on-board equipment.

16. Dr. Harold Brown, chairman of the Loudon Board of Trade, met with the Loudon County Zoning Commission to attempt a compromise between local environmentalists and developers.

17. AMTRAK's Metroliner runs between Washington, D.C. and New York in 2 hours and 52 minutes, with stops in New Carrolton, Maryland; Baltimore, Maryland; Wilmington, Delaware; and Philadelphia, Pennsylvania.

18. Any member of our cross-trained staff (that include me) can help you solve your most difficult files management problems.

(From p.176) Final exercise 3: Find and correct the word choice, grammar, punctuation, and mechanics errors in this excerpt.

Implementation of B-2 Module

This plan outlines the requirements for the successful B-2 Module implementation in an MBE application. This document describes the high-level requirements, according to agreed standards within BAPCO's marketing department. The B-2 Module supports two users: VP of Marketing, Mr. John, and his supervisor, Treasurer, Mr. Bynum.

The B-2 Module serves three purposes:

1. management of assignment for sales representatives
2. appraisal of success rate for each sales representative
3. determination of commission level for each sales representative

However, we must first set up a one-time event report. Although the report lists the prospects respectively by sales representatives, Mr. Bynum also wants to see all prospects — even those not retrieved by the B-2 Module. Therefore, we must create a report to show the relevant information of those prospects as a baseline. This change presupposes Mr. Bynum's agreement to this plan.

Relevant prospects have the following three prospect criteria:

1. Lead (prospestat_id="LEAD")
2. Hot (prospestat_id="HOT")
3. Inactive (prospestat_id="INACT")

Everyone of the sales representatives works in three countries: Canada, Mexico, and the United States. Retrieved prospects have a site located in a city that corresponds to *ZIPcode* ranging from 00000 to 99999 such as $4000 < prospect.zip\_code < 7900$. A valid prospect has a *site type* designated *commercial,* such as *prospect.sitetype_id="COM."*

Because the report also shows the contact person's first and last name, the queries need to access the *prospect* table, the *contact_link,* and *contact* tables. The keys to success are *prospect_no* and the *contact_no.* Each has links from the *prospect_link* to prospect tables and from the *contact_link* to the contact tables.

Word Choice changes include *while — although*; *firstly — first*; *cite* and *sight — site*; *respectfully — respectively*; *since — because.* Use the plural *criteria* instead of singular *criterion.*

Grammar changes include *which — that*; several subject-verb disagreements such as *Mr. Bynum want, everyone . . . work,* and *each have*; sentence fragment: *Presupposes . . . .*

Punctuation changes include remove parentheses *(high level), (Canada . . .),* and *(400> . . .).* Add hyphen for *high-level* and *one-time.* Use colon instead of comma after *two users:* Use dash to offset — *even those . . . .* Remove both colons in last paragraph, and use apostrophe to make *person's* possessive. Add commas to separate items in series *Mexico, and . . .* and to offset titles. Both vertical lists' punctuation are incorrect. Delete second period after *dept..* or spell *department.*

Mechanics changes include spelling of *department, two, three,* and *United States.* Indent lists. Remove italics from *prospect criteria.* All other italics denote variables. Make *B-2 Module* consistent.

Step 13. Proofread

(From p.179) Exercise: Even professionals make mistakes. Find and fix the errors.

"Welcome to the Writing Center! This unique area is designed to help you improve the style, presentation, and **effectiveness** of your writing. Whether **you're** writing reports for work, term papers for school, or **you're** working on that first novel, you'll discover amazingly useful information **on every** aspect of writing well." — Prodigy Writing Center, 1997.

"When you turn on **Grammar**-As-You-Go, Spell-As-You-Go is turned on as well." — Corel WordPerfect Documentation, 1977.

"Go To Class — **It's** a Blast!!!" — Washington, DC School Board's advertisement to combat truancy, 2001.

(From p. 179) Exercise: Proofread the following letter. Identify errors as word choice, grammar, punctuation, mechanics, typing, or accuracy.

12 June 2002

Graphics Leasing Corporation
Attn: Accounts Receivable Manager
VGS Park Dept A
5701 9th Ave., NW
Washington, DC 20005

Dear Accounts Receivable Manager:

Below is a list of Alcor Corporation check numbers, invoice dates, and amounts in payment of the lease and maintenance agreement on our POS-320 camera. We obtained this information through our disbursement summary report for fiscal year 1998.

Because these items are old, we can find neither cancelled checks nor duplicate copies for your review. I suggest that you check your deposit records for the time in question to verify the amounts.

Check Number	Invoice Date	Amount paid
037614	04/25/98	932.04
043569	04/25/98	804.12
012847	04/28/98	804.04
019383	05/14/98	425.12
036001	07/03/98	445.12
036002	08/15/98	388.24
037455	09/11/98	432.17
045672	11/22/98	464.25
Total Paid		$ 4,695.10

These problems occurred because of your inaccurate files. The discrepancy is three and one half years old. Therefore, we are not responsible for proving any further payment of these items. I consider this matter closed with this letter.

Sincerely,

Jane Walters
Accounting Supervisor

Some errors include missing commas, inconsistencies such as *number vs #,* misaligned columns, impossible check numbers, transposed numbers and inconsistent date format, comma instead of decimal *425,12,* comma after *I suggest,* repeated line *019383. . . ,* addition error, missing *s* on *problem,* repeated words *and one half,* missing name from signature block, misspelled words such as *summary, discrepancy, verify,* and *occurred.*

(From p.181) Exercise: Check live copy against the dead copy. What errors were corrected? What errors remain? Did new errors creep in?

Line	Error
3.	remains, change "your" to "you"
15.	new error, "men" to "menues" instead of "menus"
16.	corrected, "user's" to "users"
21.	corrected, delete period end of list
25.	new error, deleted comma but also closed space
32.	remains, change the double "you you" to "you"

(From p.182) Final exercise: Proofread this memorandum. We note the changes in bold.

INTEROFFICE CORRESPONDENCE

To: Distribution
From: Mary Poole
Date: **September 2, 2000**
Re: Briefing for Training Facilitators

You have been assigned training responsibilities in conjunction with next year**'s** MGR training effort. The two short tapes **that** will be used for the 2001 training **will be** "Timekeeping" and "Harassment.**"** The tapes are already in production and will **be shipped to** you approximately October 1, 2000.

A briefing session will be held at 11 **a.m.** on **October** 28, 2000**,** at headquarters to review the content of the tapes, identify expected discussion topics, and provide some direction for leading the discussion periods. I look forward to seeing **you** at the meeting. Although we may extend into the noon hour, you may **expect** that we will be finished by 2 p.**m.**

Please move forward with scheduling training sessions at your employees' locations**, with** the goal of completing all training **by the** end of **August.**

Distribution:
President
Comptroller's Office
All Senior Technical Staff

Letters, Memos, and Email

This appendix shows you how to apply the writing system to short documents such as letters, memos, and email. You also learn accepted formats and mechanics used in these short documents.

Letters, memos, and email — three action-oriented documents — differ in how they deliver your message:

1. Letters are the most formal of the three short documents. In letters, format can be as important as the content.

2. Memos provide a more flexible medium and consequently follow less rigorous guidelines.

3. Email is a new, still-evolving, and often misunderstood medium used instead of phone calls, letters, or memos.

Email is often more efficient than phone calls, although less personable. Email can also serve as a brochure or flyer, a form of direct-mail advertising.

When writing these short documents, you need to get to the point quickly without being abrupt. Follow the techniques you learned in *The Writing System.* Consider what the audience needs to know to ensure that you provide enough information. Begin your message with a sound purpose statement to get to the main point. Use outlining techniques. Write down the subpoints you want to make in your short document.

Write the draft body to those subpoints. Next, conclude with *what happens next*, usually a call to action tied to the purpose statement. Finally, draft the introduction, using the purpose statement and adding background, if necessary.

Use the editing techniques in this book to ensure that your short documents are clear, concise, and easy to read.

Discussion

Master the short letter, memo, and email, and become a valuable asset to your organization. Set a professional tone by opening with a purpose statement and following with a well-organized discussion. Avoid pomposity by using active voice and personal pronouns:
> *Applications must be received by January 10*, becomes *We must receive your application by January 10*, or *Please send your application before January 10*.

Achieve a more natural, modern tone by cutting cliches and by using shorter words and sentences:
> *It has been brought to our attention . . .* becomes *We notice . . .*
> *To maximize successful implementation of software capabilities, users must first assimilate operating procedures* becomes *For best results, read the user guide before using the system.*

Stress the action-oriented nature of your letter, memo, or email by closing with *what happens next*.

Letters present our personal and corporate face to the public. Our letters can make a lasting good or bad impression. Consequently, many organizations establish letter standards to ensure consistent quality. Learn what, if any, standards your organization follows.

Use these guidelines to format four categories of letters:

1. **Cover or transmittal letters**: Restate the purpose statement of the attachment, then highlight any information that may be particularly useful to the audience. End with *what happens next*.

   The attached bid describes the cost and schedule for upgrading your web site. Note in the cost section that you get an additional 50 megabytes of storage at no additional charge. We can compress the schedule if necessary.
   After you return your signed copy, we can begin work immediately.

2. **Acknowledgement letters**: The purpose is self-evident. Your audience just needs to know that you received whatever they sent and *what happens next*.

   Thank you for sending us your resume. I forwarded it to Mr. Green, who will call you to arrange your interviews.

3. **Application, complaint, inquiries, requests, responses and most other letters**: Follow the writing system:

   Introduction — Begin with the purpose statement; follow with background, references, and any pleasantries.

   Body — Limit to what your audience needs to know, without extraneous pleasantries.

   Conclusion — Tell *what happens next* with specifics; add pleasantries, if appropriate.

4. **Bad news letters**: If your audience can reasonably anticipate bad news, treat the letter as a typical response. If the bad news is also a surprise, use the following strategy:

   Introduction — Begin with a statement of compatibility and follow immediately with the purpose statement.

   Body — Detail the specific bad news and follow with positive news if any.

   Conclusion — Offer assistance and end with a courteous, never a sarcastic, close.

   The past year has been particularly difficult for all the Dot.Coms, and we are no exception. This letter informs you that we can no longer afford to keep you on staff. Also, we want to help you find employment.

   Your last day on salary is this Friday. Fortunately we have enough cash to pay you a lump sum for your salary and any accrued vacation.

   In addition to your contractual one-week's severance, we shall provide you a second week's severance. We brought in career counselors to help you. We wish you the best.

Preview Press
P. O. Box 2116, Fairfax VA 22031
(703) 978-0122 pp@thewritingsystem.com
(allow 2 blank lines)

September 1, 2002

(Allow 4 to 10 blank lines, depending on the length of the letter.)

Mr. Pat Jones
123 Maple Ave.
Vienna, VA 22030

(Allow 1 blank line.)

Dear Pat Jones:

(Allow 1 blank line.)

This letter shows our preferred letter format so you have a model for your own letters. Begin your letter with a purpose statement, then follow with the plan of your letter and any background.

(Allow 1 blank line between paragraphs.)

We recommend the full-block format for your business correspondence. The full-block format is easier to type and widely recognized as a standard. Set your page margins to 1 inch: left, right, top and bottom. Keep your paragraphs left justified. Use an 11 or 12-point type. We recommend you use a serif font, such as Times Roman.

You can add or remove blank lines to keep your letter centered on the page or to keep the letter from running onto a second page. Allow up to 5 or as few as 2 blank lines before the typed signature. Add or delete blank lines before closing details. Also, you can shrink your margins to ¾ or ½ inch.

(Allow 1 blank line before the complimentary close.)

Best regards,

(Allow three blank lines before typed name and title as space for signature.)

Daniel Graham
Editor

(Allow 1 blank line before additional closing details.)

Enclosures:

Organizations use memos for all kinds of purposes and topics: report findings, record actions, announce policies, disseminate information, provide analysis, make recommendations, and record decisions. Some organizations assign reference numbers to memos to facilitate electronic retrieval, and they may even require that routine documents like time sheets conform to the numbered memo. Therefore, memos vary in content, length, and format.

Follow these four guidelines to improve the quality of your memos:

1. **Use the writing system analytical steps to ensure you know the purpose of your memo.** Begin your memo with a purpose statement. When appropriate, identify the content: *This report, this announcement, this policy* . . . instead of automatically writing *This memo*. Memos usually get wider distribution than letters; therefore, in your purpose statement, identify the intended audience, what they need to know, and what they do with the information in the memo. The purpose statement forces you to get to the point and, at the same time, keeps your memo from being too abrupt.

2. **Use the writing system to organize the body of your memo.** Ensure that paragraphs begin with simple points, then follow with supporting facts. If the writing task is repetitive, you may find that your memo conforms to a predetermined format or template.

3. **Use coherence devices such as subheads, lists, and tables.** For long memos, you may even need to partition the content into sections for a multiple audience. For example, in a memo on student aid, the memo might partition the memo accordingly: first, determine if you qualify; second, learn how to apply.

4. **Write meaningful subject lines.** Too many memos have cryptic subject lines. Use the key words in your purpose statements to write a meaningful subject line. Concentrate on what your audience does with the information and therefore what they need to know.

Your subject line allows you 50 or more characters, plenty of space to write a meaningful subject line. Contrast these subject lines:

Poor subject lines	Subject lines giving the topic and outcome of a purpose statement
Sales Meeting	Highlights from the 6/3 sales meeting so you can stay current
Backlog	List of backlogged orders so you can notify your affected customers
X-33 Turbo Card	Features and benefits of X-33 Turbo Card you can explain to customers
Advertisements	Proposed copy of next month's print ads for your review and comments
Regional Quotas	Changes in Northeast Corridor quotas and territories so you can make plans
Sick Leave	For your amusement: Letterman's ten best reasons to take sick leave

Acme, Inc. Human Resources Department (HRD)
Memo

(allow 1 blank line)

To: Field Offices
From: Irma Gold, VP HRD
Date: April 8, 2001 10:22 a.m.
Subject: Changes in HRD advisory services to field offices

(allow 1 blank line)

This bulletin announces changes in corporate headquarter HRD advisory services that you in the field offices must incorporate into your local policies. We have recently streamlined our operations.

Corporate HRD functional areas have changed. We eliminated the Workforce Management Branch and Recruitment and Training offices. We transferred those functions to the Employee and Labor Relations Office (ELRO), under the direction of Ms. Barbara McCarthy.

The consolidation of functions under ELRO has a downside. With fewer caseworkers, we can not handle walk-ins as efficiently. Please encourage field office employees to make an appointment whenever possible with the appropriate functional manager to discuss their HRD issues. If you have doubts with whom to schedule an appointment, call or email Barbara McCarthy directly. Our doors are always open, but the appointments increase our ability to provide more focused and complete advisory services.

Recruitment bonus procedures have changed. To avoid regulatory violations, HRD at headquarters must authorize any recruitment bonuses recommended by a field office. Submit your recruitment bonus requests to ELRO to the attention of Mr. Carl Martinez.

Effective immediately, please send your Personnel Data Requests (PDRs) and your Monthly Training Summaries (MTSs) to ELRO, to the attention of Ms. Ann Covington.

The following are the functional managers in ELRO listed by function:

Function	Name	Email	(202) 123-3456
Director	Barbara McCarthy	bc@hrd.acme.com	ext. 451
Recruitment	Carl Martinez	cm@hrd.acme.com	ext. 452
Health Services	Joanna Ahmed	ja@hrd.acme.com	ext. 491
Training/Career Development	Ann Covington	ac@hrd.acme.com	ext. 444
EEO-Union Relations	Stu Hindert	sh@hrd.acme.com	ext. 445
Payroll/Tax, Pension, Leave	Julie Tzu	jt@hrd.acme.com	ext. 446

By helping us implement these few changes, you can ensure that we continue to offer the same high level of support our employees expect.

(allow 1 blank line)

cc: Barbara McCarthy, Carl Martinez, Joanna Ahmed, Ann Covington, Stu Hindert, Julie Tzu

Email is just a medium, however versatile. Email can take the place of telephone calls, as well as written correspondence, principally memos. Often email acts as the transmittal memo to which you append larger documents. Follow these six guidelines to produce better email:

1. **Decide whether your email is a pseudotelephone call or written correspondence.** We disagree with the prevailing notion that email formality is *somewhere between telephone conversation and a memo.* No, your email is *either* a pseudotelephone call *or* a memo. Choose, then apply standards of etiquette and formality accordingly.

   If your message is a pseudotelephone call, use phone etiquette. Depending on your familiarity with the recipient, you can use informal courtesies such as *Hiya!* instead of *Dear Mr. Smith.* However, when in doubt, keep the more formal, professional format of the letter or memo.

   If your email takes the place of written correspondence, use letter or memo formats. Begin the email with a purpose statement and organize your thoughts before you write.

   Treat your email as a letter or memo if sent to multiple addressees. Model your email as a letter or memo, instead of a private, more intimate telephone call.

2. **Write meaningful subject lines,** just as you do for a memo. Adequate subject lines help the recipient prioritize email without opening and reading each.

3. **Do not write something that you don't want to hear read back to you in court.** Email provides a record of the communication and is easy to save and forward. Whereas some things are better left unsaid, many more are better left unwritten.

4. **For most short email, edit for clarity.** You can skimp on the other edits. The more formal the situation, the more you must check for correctness: word choice, grammar, punctuation, and mechanics. Most email software provides basic spellchecking.

5. **Avoid appending your message to incoming email.** You do not want your business correspondence to look like a transcript of an Internet chat room. Often those appended emails go through a dozen back-and-forth iterations. We must piece together a coherent message from all the bits and pieces. *Reply with History* email is either a pseudotelephone call or a poor attempt at written communication. These back-and-forth *Reply with History* emails try to clarify the initial email. Reduce much of the back and forth by taking greater care with the purpose statement and body of the initial email. If you choose to *Reply with History*, append your message at the beginning.

6. **Send email sparingly.** Always consider the trade-off of keeping everyone informed and over transmitting. Make your criterion *Will the receiver appreciate being interrupted to get this information?* If you have doubts, ask the receiver if he or she wants copies of all your emails, or if he or she prefers that you use your judgment to send only those emails you think pertinent.

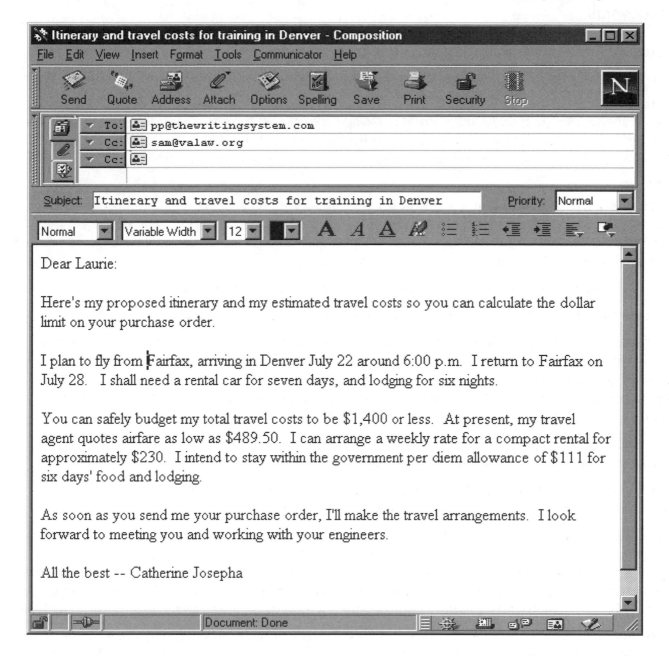

If you use a preprogrammed signature block, separate the signature block from the text with three blank lines plus a visual device, such as a ruling line made of underlines (_) or equal signs (=).

=========================
Catherine Josepha, Ph.D.
Preview Press
P. O. Box 2116, Fairfax VA 22031
Ph: (703) 555-5555 Fax (703) 555-4321
http://www.thewritingsystem.com

Letters follow established mechanics for dates and salutations.

Civilians in the United States use the date format: April 2, 2001. The date is not 2nd, not 02. The year is not '01. The U.S. military and Europeans use the date format: 2 April 2001.

Avoid salutations such as *To Whom It May Concern*, or *Dear Sir or Madame*. Address the letter to the job title or organization if you cannot identify the person: *Dear Accounts Payable* or *Dear Customer*. If you have no clue to whom you are writing, you can open with the generic *Good Morning*.

Put a colon after the salutation for business letters and a comma after the salutation for personal letters. Use accepted abbreviations of titles: Mr., Mrs., Ms., Dr., Atty., Hon., and Ph.D. Do not double the title: *Dr.* William Smith, *Ph.D.* Drop gender-specific titles and use the full given name if you are unsure of the person's sex. Do not abbreviate a person's name.

The Gregg Reference Manual is a reliable guide for letter writing format and mechanics.

Memos follow varied mechanics for dates, salutations, and subject lines.

Most memos conform to the 8½"x11" page. The organization's name appears at the top with the word Memorandum or Memo. Most have a *To, From, Date*, and *Subject* line. The *To* line can identify an individual name, multiple names, an audience such as *All employees*, or *Distribution*, where the names appear at the end of the memo. The sender typically initials the *From* line for authentication, because the memo has no signature block. The *Date* line can show the date of the writing or the date (time) of transmission.

Email mechanics affect the tone of the communication.

Use proper capitalization, spelling, punctuation, and mechanics. An email in all lower case says, *i care so little about you, i can't be bothered to hit the shift key.*

Keep the mechanics simple. Because many email programs lack full word-processing capabilities, many email writers use capital letters or asterisks *for emphasis* and intermittent underlining for citations: _The Writing System_. These work-arounds are distracting. Also, email does a mediocre job of transmitting tables and graphs. If your message is complicated enough to need different fonts, tables, or graphs, write your document with a wordprocessor and attach to a transmittal email.

In business email, do not use the trendy chat-room abbreviations and *emoticons,* sideways faces made with punctuation marks such as :-) = ☺.

Appendix C
English as a Second Language

This appendix suggests how English as a Second Language (ESL) professionals can take advantage of the writing system. In addition, this appendix provides guidance on nine topics:

1. Linear Logic

2. Sentence Length

3. Tone

4. Articles

5. Verbs: Passive Voice, Tenses, and Moods

6. Word Choice — Finding the Perfect Word

7. Prepositions

8. Possession

9. American and British English

English has become the international language for business and technology. The European community adopted English as the official *second* language for European Union countries. China has more people who speak English than the United States has. In fact, more than half of the people who speak English learned English as a second language.

Although the English language is complex, communication needs to remain simple. Do not try to impress your audience with your mastery of the intricacies of the English language. Instead, impress your audience with your mastery of your subject matter. Write simple sentences using simple words. Do not use synonyms; rather, repeat your key words. Write each sentence to have one interpretation. Cut unnecessary words. By following these guidelines, you make your writing easy to read, and you avoid many grammar and punctuation errors.

Discussion

For a thorough treatment of English as a second language, read *ESL Resource Book for Engineers and Scientists*. Elaine Campbell, Ph.D. John Wiley & Sons: New York, 1995.

Also, author Richard Lederer writes extensively on the English language in books like *The Miracle of Language*. Pocket Books: New York, 1991.

By no means do we suggest that English is *better* than other languages. English has its strengths and weaknesses. In this appendix we help you avoid the weaknesses and capitalize on the strengths of American English used for business and technical documents.

Concentrate on making your point at the beginning of the paragraph. Then use the writing system's line-editing techniques to simplify your prose. If you have a special challenge such as English articles, memorize the rules.

Linear Logic

English, especially American English, uses a linear logic at both the document and paragraph level. Other cultures allow more digressions within the paragraph, and they use more intricate arguments. To other cultures, American writing may seem overly direct — even blunt. However, the simpler linear logic serves your audience well when your subject is complex, as technical subjects often are.

The writing system in this book teaches you how to organize your document in a linear fashion as you partition subject matter and sentence outline. The sentence outline ensures that you begin each paragraph with an assertion or covering generality; then you follow with supporting detail. Limit the body of your paragraph to the supporting details, and avoid digressions such as parenthetical comments or unrelated discussions.

Sentence Length

American English has a "plain style": simple words with fewer syllables and short, simple sentences. The argument for plain style is that one can describe more complex subject matter if one uses simpler language. Complex language plus complex subject matter is more than most people can bear. Therefore, plain style is well-suited for technology.

Plain style isn't an American invention. Shakespeare wrote in plain style, as did the English seventeenth-century metaphysical poets. Early Americans wrote the *Declaration of Independence* in the style of their day — plain style. While writing style changed in England, the Americans clung to plain style. Other cultures, both East and West, have had literary periods characterized as plain style. However, today most other languages prefer the more ornate style of longer, more complex sentences.

Following is an excerpt of the English, French, and Spanish label on a box for a Hewlett-Packard™ toner cartridge for a laser printer:

English	**French**	**Spanish**
All HP toner cartridges are warranted for the life of the cartridge until HP toner is depleted. Further details inside.	Toutes les cartouches de toner HP sont garanties pendant la durée de la cartouche, jusqu'à épuisement du toner HP. Voir les détails à l'intérieur.	Todos los cartuchos de tóner de HP están garantizados durante toda la vida del cartucho, hasta que se acabe el tóner HP. Más detalles en el interior.
20 words, 30 syllables	25 words, 39 syllables	27 words, 50 syllables

By using the techniques in this book, you keep your average sentence length comfortably within American plain-style standards:

1. Sentence outlining ensures that you begin paragraphs with a short sentence.
2. Breaking long series into vertical lists, a coherence device, improves sentence length.
3. Editing for clarity shortens sentences and puts them in simple subject-verb-object form.
4. Editing for economy cuts unnecessary words, often 20 percent or more.
5. If your sentences are still too long, averaging more than 20 words, editing for readability shows you how to break compound and complex sentences into simple sentences.

Tone

The tone in American business correspondence is less formal than in other cultures. Americans write with a "you attitude" that they think is more friendly, yet sometimes gets misconstrued as pushy. In contrast, other cultures prefer a "we approach" that they think is more collegial, but Americans often consider presumptuous. Finally, some cultures prefer an "official attitude" that avoids any mention of *I, you,* or *we.* The "official attitude" is by design impersonal and unemotional, but it sounds bureaucratic and cold to the American audience.

American "you attitude"	You did not win the competitive bid. Your price was not competitive.
"We attitude"	We thank you for submitting a bid. However, we selected another vendor based on price competitiveness.
"Official attitude"	Regrettably, the bid offered by BAP, Inc. must be declined. The issue of price competitiveness affected the decision.

Use the purpose statement to manage tone. First, the purpose statement forces you to adopt the American style "you attitude," because the purpose statement focuses on what *you*, the audience, needs to know, so *you*, the audience, can achieve some outcome.

Second, the verb you choose as the actor for your purpose statement establishes the tone for your document. For example, *This letter notifies* is more authoritative than *This letter informs.*

After you set the tone with your purpose statement, you can relax about matters of tone. The first impression lasts.

When writing instructions, use the imperative mood, active voice, and present tense. This sentence structure reinforces the "you attitude." To some ears, the imperative mood may sound like a set of rude commands. However, most people use the simple imperative mood when giving instructions or making requests to their most intimate friends. You can always preface a set of commands with the universally polite *please.*

Poor: The safety switch should have been put in the off position before the removal of the battery. Better: Put the safety switch in the off position, then remove the battery.

Most romance languages have a formal and familiar form for the second person, complete with verb conjugation. Modern English no longer has a formal and informal form for the second person, *you.* Therefore, do not try to infer tone from the use of the second person.

Articles

Many languages do not use articles. Therefore, many ESL writers can't lean on their native language for help in understanding English articles. To make matters worse, English doesn't provide clean rules for using articles. At best, we can offer some guidelines based on traditional grammar rules and the concept of *count* and *mass.*

Traditional grammar rules for articles

English has three articles — *a, an,* and *the.* Again, to make matters worse, you omit the article in many circumstances. Therefore, you really have four alternatives: *a, an, the,* and *no article.*

Guideline: Definite and indefinite nouns
Use *the* for definite nouns and *a* or *an* for indefinite nouns. A definite noun names something you can point to: *Sit in the chair by my desk.* An indefinite noun names something that you do not point

to: *Bring a chair to my office.* *A* and *an* derive from the word *one* or *any*. Therefore, *Bring a chair to my office* has the same sense as *Bring one* or *Bring any chair to my office*.

Guideline: Plural and singular indefinite nouns
If the indefinite noun — you can't point to the item or items — is singular, use *a* or *an*. If the indefinite noun is plural you use *no article*. *Download a file. Download [no article] files.* In both cases, *any* file or files satisfies the request.

Guideline: Plural and singular definite nouns
Whether the definite noun — you can point to the item or items — is singular or plural, use *the*. *Download the file. Download the files.* Here, you point to specific files.

Guideline: Consonant beginnings of indefinite nouns
When the noun begins with a vowel sound — not necessarily a vowel — use *an: an hour, an orange*. When the noun begins with a consonant sound — not necessarily a consonant — use the article *a: a table, a unit*.

Concept of *count* and *mass*
Unfortunately, English has many examples of words that appear to be indefinite nouns that are singular, yet do not get articles *a* or *an*. In "*Fatigue* makes cowards of us all," *fatigue* appears to be a singular indefinite noun requiring *a* or *an*. In "*Fire* requires *fuel*, *heat*, and *oxygen*," singular indefinite nouns also appear to violate the rule for using *a* or *an*. Finally, one can write "*Canadians* live in *Canada*," which appears to violate the rule for using article *the* with plural proper nouns. Use the following guidelines based on the concept of *count* and *mass* to help you solve most of these exceptions to the previous traditional grammar rules.

Guideline: Count and mass
Most common nouns are *count* nouns. They behave like definite or indefinite nouns. Because the noun is countable, the noun can have a singular or plural form. Also you can point to it (definite) or not point to it (indefinite) as you wish. If you can count the items such as *chair*, *file*, *hour*, *orange*, *table*, or *unit*, apply the traditional grammar rules with confidence. However, do not use an article for plural countable nouns used as complements: The two applicants were *engineers*.

Mass nouns cause the trouble. *Mass* nouns refer to a group, collection, concept, or abstract quality that you wish to identify as a whole or distinguish from parts. *Mass* nouns rarely have a plural form, yet despite their singular form, they do not use articles *a, an* or *the*. Instead, you use the *no article*:
> *Youth* and *skill* are no match for *old age* and *treachery*.
> *Oil* and *gas* are two forms of *energy*.
> We have *time* on our side.
> You need *education* and *experience* before you can find *work*.

Guideline: Words that quantify
If you quantify the *mass*, you change it to a *count* noun and then treat it as a definite or indefinite noun, using the articles *a, an*, or *the*.
> A *barrel of oil* and *the gallon of gas* . . . The *last drop of rain* . . .
> A *moment of time* . . . .   An *ounce of prevention* is worth *a pound of cure*.

Guideline: Proper nouns
A proper noun, always capitalized, names a specific person, place, or thing: for example, *Doctor Brown*, *Yellowstone Park*, and *Thanksgiving*. In general you do not use an article for singular proper nouns:
> *Pinocchio* became a real boy. We live on *Cherry Street*. *Memorial Day* is a holiday.

When the proper noun is an adjective, you add the article:

The *Thanksgiving Day* parade . . . A *Yellowstone Park* vacation . . . A *Kleenex* tissue . . .

When you use proper noun *things*, especially brand names, treat the proper name as if it were an adjective, even if you drop the common noun and use the definite or indefinite article:

He sneezed into a *Kleenex* (tissue).

He wears a *Rolodex* (wristwatch).

I drive a *Volkswagen* (car). I prefer the 1968 *Volkswagen* (car).

Guideline: Context of the sentence

You can often use the article — or *no article* — in different ways depending on the context of the sentence.

Canadians live north of the United States. — *Mass* of people (proper noun)

The Canadians live north of the United States. — Definite group of people separated from other national groups.

As frustrating as English articles appear, they provide useful distinctions.

Rainfall helps crops. *Mass*

The rainfall helped *the* crops. Definitive: I point to *that* rainfall and *those* crops.

A rainfall helped *the* crops. Indefinite rainfall helped definite crops.

Can we arrange *a* time to meet? Indefinite: any time will do.

I do not have *the* time to spare. Definite: I don't have the specific time to spare.

I do not have time to spare. *Mass*: I don't have time — even in the abstract — to spare.

I do not have *a minute of* time to spare. *Mass* changed to *count* by measure word, indefinite.

Industry (*no article—mass*) has *an* economic interest (indefinite singular) in *the* government guidelines (definite) for safety inspections (*no article—*indefinite plural).

Verbs: Passive Voice, Tenses, and Moods

See *Step 9 — Edit for Clarity*. In addition to the techniques and exercises found on those pages, consider these points about verbs.

Passive voice

Passive voice is as big a problem for native English writers as for ESL writers. Passive voice is typical of an academic style with an official attitude. Passive voice also contributes to sentence structure problems such as misplaced modifiers.

Infinitives

In English, the word *to* is sometimes dropped in the infinitive form of the verb, especially when the infinitive is a direct object: for example, Please help the customer *test* the new procedure, and We watched the floodwaters *recede*.

Tenses

As a technical writer, you don't need the full range of nuances provided by English's 12 tenses. Most American writers use the perfect, progressive, and future tenses more from habit than careful purpose.

Try to write in present tense as much as possible. Often you can change the perfect tenses into either present or past tense. Often you can change the progressive and future tenses into present tense. You need the future tense much less than you think.

Don't rearrange sentences to change verbs. When you try to change your future, perfect, or progressive tenses to present or past, remember: either make the change *easily*, or leave the tense alone. If you have difficulty changing the tense, the chances are good that you need the future, perfect, or progressive tense in your sentence.

When you simplify your tenses, you get additional benefits. You eliminate most of the problems associated with shifting tenses. For example, most problems with parallelism occur because of shifting tense. Also, by simplifying your tenses, you greatly reduce the challenge of conjugating irregular English verbs.

Subjunctive mood

Many ESL writers learn to use the words *would, should,* and *could* in conversational English to be polite. Unfortunately, those words cause ambiguity, especially in written communication. Use *Step 9 — Edit for Clarity* techniques to cut *would, should,* and *could.*

Word Choice: Finding the Perfect Word

Don't struggle to find the *perfect* word. Be content with a *good* word. English has many synonyms, and often the *perfect* word is just a matter of opinion.

English has between 615,000 and 1.2 million root words depending on your reference. With the addition of new technical terms, English bulges to two million words. The next largest language is German with about 185,000 root words. French has fewer than 100,000 root words.

English grew through the assimilation of other cultures' words. In addition to its Anglo-Saxon, French, Latin, and Greek roots, English borrows from every language, from the Finnish *sauna,* to the Haitian *canoe,* to the Malaysian *ketchup.* In fact, fewer than 20 percent of English words come from the original Anglo-Saxon.

In addition to borrowing words, we invent new words. Shakespeare invented — or was the first to write — more than 1,700 new words, words you use every day such as *lonely, bump, hurry, road, useless, critic,* and *apostrophe.* We invent words to describe new technology at such a pace that dictionaries can't keep up.

English is less disciplined, but more adaptable than other languages. Most languages have an academy of scholars to maintain standards. English relies on a consensus of (sometimes contradictory) style guides and dictionaries that often adapt to the culture of "accepted usage."

Fortunately, you don't need to know a million English words. Shakespeare, for example, wrote with only 20,138 different words, including his own inventions.

Here are a few tips to help you build your vocabulary. Use a good dictionary that gives examples of usage. We recommend the *American Heritage Dictionary,* because it gives more examples of usage. When you look up a word, mark a dot in the margin next to the word. When you find four or more dots, memorize the word and its definitions.

Try to limit your use of a word to its first few definitions. For example, the seemingly simple verb *raise* has 22 definitions, many of which have 2 or 3 sub-definitions.

Repeat your key words. See *Step 8 — Edit for Coherence.* English writers have a bad habit of using synonyms that confuse. Cutting deadwood eliminates many word choice problems. See *Step 10 — Edit for Economy.* The ESL professional struggles with word choice in the sentence, *We want to (take, make, have) a decision (on, upon, about, to) this issue.* By cutting the deadwood, the sentence becomes *We want to decide this issue.* Questions concerning word choice vanish as you cut deadwood.

Prepositions

English has 72 prepositions, far more than other languages. Most languages have fewer than 20 prepositions. Many English prepositions are synonyms such as *below, beneath, under*, and *underneath.*

Languages with fewer prepositions have more precise rules to govern use of prepositions. Therefore, most ESL writers naturally expect that English, too, has precise rules regarding prepositions. The ESL writer has difficulty picking the "right" preposition with so many to choose from. For example, the ESL writer wonders which preposition is correct: minutes *of* the meeting, minutes *from* the meeting, minutes *about* the meeting, minutes *on* the meeting, minutes *for* the meeting, and so forth. All the options are grammatically correct.

Many preposition uses are idioms, especially when used with verbs, as illustrated below.

abide by (rule)	*comply with*	*exempt from*	*proceed to (begin)*
abide in (place)	*concur in (consensus)*	*expect from (things)*	*proceed with (plan)*
abstain from	*concur with (person)*	*expect of (person)*	*proficient in*
accordance with	*conform to*	*expert in*	*profit by (things)*
according to	*consist of*	*hand out (distribute)*	*profit from (actions)*
account for	*convenient for (action)*	*identical with, to*	*prohibit from*
adapt from (source)	*convenient to (place)*	*identical with, to*	*qualify as (person)*
adapt to (situation)	*deal with*	*impose on*	*qualify by (experience)*
adept in	*depend on*	*improve on*	*qualify for (position)*
adhere to	*deprive of*	*inconsistent with*	*rely on*
agree to (plan)	*devoid of*	*increase by (action)*	*responsibility for, of*
agree with (person)	*devoted to*	*increase in (amount)*	*reward for (action)*
approve of	*differ about (issue)*	*independent of*	*reward with (prize)*
acquaint with	*differ from (thing)*	*infer from*	*rise (fall) in (amount)*
argue for, against	*differ on (terms)*	*inferior to*	*similar to*
aware of	*differ with (person)*	*interfere with*	*superior to*
based on/upon	*different from*	*mediate between*	*surround by (person)*
blame for (action)	*disagree with (person)*	*necessary for (action)*	*surround with (things)*
blame on (person)	*disappointed in*	*necessary to (be)*	*talk to (group)*
capable of	*disagree on (issue)*	*occupied by (things)*	*talk with (person)*
charge for (cost)	*divide between, among*	*occupied with (tasks)*	*wait at (place)*
close down (forever)	*divide into (parts)*	*part from (person)*	*wait for (person)*
compare to (similar)	*engage in*	*part with (possession)*	*wait on (to serve)*
compare with (alike)	*exclude from*	*prior to*	*yield to*

A few idioms are more standard than others. English employs a convention when using prepositions referring to time: *at* refers to the clock, *on* refers to date, and *in* refers to month and year — *We met at 9:00 a.m. on Tuesday. He was born in March 1964.* On the other hand, many idioms simply reflect regional preferences. In New York, you hear people *standing on line*, while two hundred miles away people are *standing in line*.

Do not obsess over idioms. If your sentences are simple and clear, your audience can manage minor idiomatic flaws. For example, correct idioms used with the verb *compare* include

> We *compare* apples *to* oranges. (similar in that both are fruit, but not the same kind)
> We *compare* Red Delicious apples *with* Macintosh apples. (alike, the same kind of fruit)

However, if you write, *We compare apples with oranges*, most people understand.

To make matters worse, many English verbs have, what the dictionary calls, the phrasal verb form, where the verb plus a preposition has a specific meaning. For example, in the sentence *Look up the tree*, the word *up* is a preposition. However, in the sentence *Look up my address*, the word up is part of the phrasal verb. Many verbs have phrasal forms, and phrasal verbs are idiomatic.

The best defense against idiomatic phrasal verbs is to use specific verbs instead. Here are just a few examples:

Phrasal verb	*Specific verb*
We called down the wrath of the client.	We invoked the wrath of the client.
We called up the computer program.	We started the computer program.
We called out your name.	We shouted your name.
We chimed in.	We added our opinion.
We looked up your address	We found your address.
We look up to our boss.	We admire our boss.
We took out an insurance policy.	We bought an insurance policy.

You can also avoid phrasal verbs by finding and using buried verbs. See *Step 10—Edit for Economy: cut empty verbs; cut unnecessary prepositions.*

Phrasal verb	*Specific verb*
We worked out a settlement.	We settled the case.
We sent out an invitation to the stockholders.	We invited the stockholders.
We set up a conference with our lawyers.	We conferred with our lawyers.
We took out an insurance policy.	We insured ourselves.

The best remedy is to eliminate as many prepositions as possible. Instead of anxiously writing *minutes of the meeting*, confidently write *meeting minutes*. By eliminating prepositions, you also avoid the problem of redundant prepositions: *back behind the cabinet* becomes *behind the cabinet*. Cutting prepositions also limits idioms — *We met 9:00 a.m. to 10:30 a.m., March 15, 2001.* Likewise, *We compare apples and oranges* avoids the controversy. If you can't cut the preposition, and if you have a phrasal verb, use a specific verb instead.

Possession

English has three ways to show possession:

1. possessive case	apostrophe 's	*the company's computer*
	possessive pronoun	*her accomplishment*
2. preposition	of	*design of the computer*
	for	*computer for the company*
	by	*accomplishment by Joan*

3. adjective   *the computer hard drive*
                                      computer design

The challenge for the ESL writer is choosing which way to show possession for different situations. For example, why does English use the adjective form of possession to say *airplane wing* instead of using the possessive case, *airplane's wing*?

A few generations ago, the rule was that only animate objects or inanimate objects that merit a proper name, like a ship, might use the possessive case: *Jane's hat*. Other inanimate objects possessed by means of prepositions: *The brim of the hat*. Therefore in the old days, one wrote *the wing of the airplane*.

The rule relaxed over time to allow possessive case when the inanimate object had a proper name. For example, because your project has a proper name, the Saturn IV Project, you can use the possessive case to write about the *project's* budget.

The rule relaxed further and now modern usage allows *the hat's brim*. Also, one may now write *the airplane's wing*. Some people still find the possessive case awkward when applied to inanimate objects.

You can avoid the controversy of possessive case of inanimate objects by using the adjective form for possession. For example, *design of the system* or *system's design*, becomes *system design*. *Wing of the airplane* or *airplane's wing* becomes *airplane wing*. *Brim of the hat* or *hat's brim* becomes *hat brim*.

American and British English

Many ESL professionals learn English in the British mode. Know the differences for word choice, grammar, punctuation, and spelling. Use your wordprocessor to help. Select your dictionary: English (United States). You can also set the grammar checker to use the American preference for punctuation.

Word choice

Most of the differences between British and American word choice are charming, if not amusing. However, in business and technical documents, the misunderstandings can be more consequential. A few examples follow:

British	American
invitation to tender	request for proposal
billion	thousand billion or 1,000,000,000,000
milliard	billion or 1,000,000,000
subway	underpass
underground	subway
aerial	antenna
accumulator	battery
rates	taxes
docket	calendar
overleaf	next page
intcrwork	work with

Grammar

American and British grammar are almost identical. One difference is collective nouns. Americans treat collective nouns as singular unless the collective noun refers to discrete actions of the members. The British treat all collective nouns as plural.

American collective noun

The jury gives its verdict. Jury acts as a unit. Therefore, jury is singular with the singular form of the verb.

The jury retire to their hotel rooms. Jury acts as individuals. The plural individuals require the plural form of the verb and the plural possessive pronoun.

British collective noun

The jury give their verdict. The jury retire to their hotel rooms. In both cases, the British treat the collective noun as plural and require agreement with the plural form of verbs and pronouns.

Spelling

Most word processors let you select either an American or a British dictionary for your spellchecker. The easiest remedy is to use the appropriate spellchecker dictionary. British spelling often reflects French influence. American spelling is usually more phonetic. Some common differences in spelling follow:

	British	**American**
-or to -our	colour	color
-re to -er	centre	center
-s- to -z-	analyse	analyze
-mme to -m	programme	program
past tense	burnt	burned
-ce to -se	defence	defense

American punctuation

In a series, European writers omit the last comma before the word *and*.

> The French flag is red, white and blue.

In contrast, American and British writers put the comma before the *and*. The Oxford University Press style guide and most American style guides agree on this punctuation.

> The Union Jack is red, white, and blue.

The British-American rule for commas adds a bit more precision. Also, by delimiting each item in the series, one can better delimit pairs.

Another controversy is the placement of periods and commas with ending quotation marks. Americans put commas and periods inside ending quotation marks. The British and Europeans put them outside.

American: We sang "Take Me Out to the Ball Game," then Harry said, "Hot dog, please."
British: We sang "Take me Out to the Rugby Scrum", then Harry said "Banger, please".

Colons and semi-colons go outside the ending quotation marks. The placement of question marks depends on whether the entire question resides within the quotation mark.

> He asked, "Do you want a hotdog?"
> Must we sing "Take Me Out to the Ball Game"?

Long Documents

This appendix expands upon *Step 5 — Write Sentence Outline* and *Step 8 — Edit for Coherence* techniques to help you write longer, more complex technical documents.

The kinds of writing projects that we discuss in this appendix include proposals, requirements documents, functional descriptions, general and detailed designs, and manuals. This appendix also helps authors of hypertext management language (HTML) and multi-media applications.

This appendix begins by showing you what a modular layout looks like. Then you overview the techniques needed to master the modular layout. You learn to add the *storyboard* techniques to your sentence outlining techniques. Storyboards help you organize massive subjects into discrete topics. Also, you learn new coherence techniques to use the modular layout to display discrete topics.

As we show you techniques for writing long documents, we discuss, when appropriate, separate tips for the long proposal document. Proposals are more difficult to write than most long documents, because you need to superimpose *themes* — your competitive advantage. Also, you need to frame your discussions in terms of *benefits*, when often the client merely states the request in terms of *features* they want.

Large writing projects overwhelm many writing teams. Your team may find itself confronted with a 400-page deliverable that must address hundreds of complex topics. The team must know where to begin and how to manage time and resources. The techniques in this appendix help you break the large writing project into manageable tasks.

As a pre-requisite to using these advanced techniques, you need to understand the fundamentals of the writing system in Steps 1 though 13. Throughout this appendix, we refer to the other writing system techniques.

Discussion

Modular layout helps you re-use documents by making topics easy to identify. Topics gracefully fall into other documents that use modular layout. You re-use modular documents in much the same way systems engineers re-use modular software. In systems engineering, we often take modules from one system that we modify to meet the client's specific needs. Similarly, we rarely re-use a whole document; rather, we re-use topics.

Present each topic in a two-page, left right module: modular layout.

Modular layout differs radically from conventional layout. Conventional layout is a continuous flow from topic to topic like a novel. Topic lengths vary, and the shifts occur anywhere on the page. In a modular layout, each topic occupies two pages (one page each in some cases), and all the topic shifts occur at the top-left corner of the page.

The Writing System is an example of modular layout. Turn to page 8 and note that the topic is a two-page, left-right presentation. When you turn the page, you notice that you are on a new topic. In fact, every topic begins at the top of the left page and ends at the bottom of the right page. Using this book as a template, you have a typical modular layout where each section has

Pg 1	Right	Introduce section
Pg 2-pg 3	Left-Right	Topic One
Pg 4-pg 5	Left-Right	Topic Two
Pg 6-pg 7	Left-Right	Topic Three
Pg x pg y	Left-Right	Topic n . . .
Pg z	Left	Conclude section

A typical left-right presentation accommodates 960 words, less whatever space you allocate for a figure. Any unused space becomes white space. The modular layout is flexible.

In *The Writing System* we use the left page for instructions and right page for exercises. At the top left, the reader sees the subhead that defines the topic. The first sentence that follows is the main assertion or covering generality. Thereafter, the document uses the ordinary coherence devices, such as subheads, paragraphs, and vertical lists, to provide subpoints and supporting details. Typically, the graphic, if needed, appears on the right page. Every graphic has a caption that briefly describes what the graphic does.

The two-page, 960-word limit per topic may seem restrictive, but the limit actually conforms nicely to a typical topic's length. Studies of topic length in conventional documents show that topics vary from 250 to 1,100 words, with a mean around 700 words.

Modular layout in business and technical documents uses about the same amount of white space as does conventional layout.

Discussion:

For a good discussion of why the modular approach works and for a good history of storyboarding, read *Sequential Thematic Organization of Publications*: *STOP.* Hughes Aircraft Company: Fullerton, California, 1965.

These business and technical documents lend themselves naturally to modular layout:

1. proposals
2. requirements
3. functional descriptions
4. detailed designs
5. specifications
6. test plans
7. user manuals
8. procedures and policy documents

Any subject matter that you can break down into discrete topics is a candidate for modular layout. For example, manuals and planning documents naturally break into steps or processes, which you can gracefully display in modular layout. Modular layout was originally developed for writing proposals.

Below are examples of modular layouts.

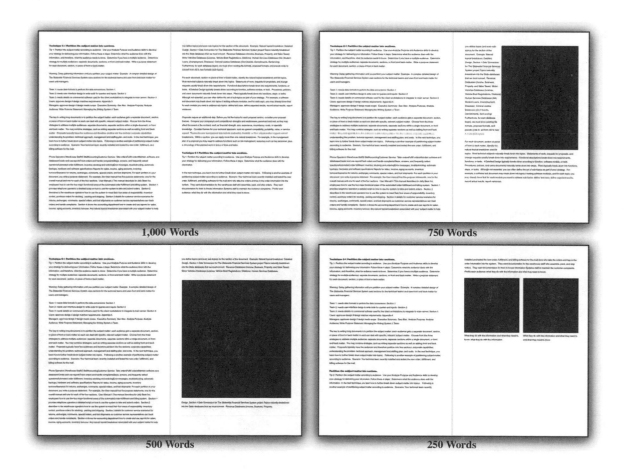

1,000 Words   750 Words

500 Words   250 Words

Overview how to make a modular layout document.

This overview introduces six techniques to make a modular layout document. A detailed explanation of each technique follows this overview.

1. Partition subject matter into sections:
Use purpose and audience techniques.
Identify sections according to audience needs.

Phone Operators	Warehouse Staff	IS Staff	Accounting	Customer Service
Take orders	Fulfill orders	Maintain software and databases	Create and use reports	Track orders and handle complaints
Steps, screens, and frequently asked questions	Automated order fulfillment; inventory stocking and ordering	Error messages, troubleshooting, automatic backups, hardware and software specifications	Reports for sales, income, aging accounts, inventory turnover	Scenarios for returns, exchanges, comments, special orders, and lost shipments

Write purpose statement for each section.

Section 3 describes how the finance and accounting department creates reports.

2. Break down sections into discrete topics:
Consider what the audience needs to know.
Consult predecessor documents.

Users Manual for Jelly Bean Inc.			
Section 1 Telephone Orders	**Section 2 Warehouse Operations**	**Section 3 Customer Service**	**Section 4 Accounting Reports**
Ordinal	Functional	Examples; Steps	Topical
Workstation setup	Taking inventory	Tracking shipments	Daily inventory
Call initiation	Ordering EOQ	Refunds	Inventory turnover
Get customer ID	Receiving orders	Price guarantee rebate	Invoices
Build customer record	Packaging & labeling	Item availability	Aging accounts
Take order	Bundling shipments	Quantity discounts	Cashflow
Methods of payment	Special orders	Complaints to refer	
Total charges	Returns		
Shipping instructions	Safety		
Submit order			

3. Fill in a storyboard for each topic:
Identify topic title.
Make main assertion.
Add supporting assertions.
Add supporting detail.
Sketch graphics.

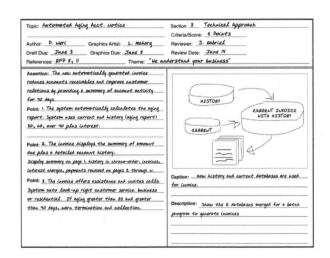

4. Revise and review storyboards:
Check topic titles.
Use content and organization tests.
Check assertions.
Check supporting detail.
Break or combine topics if necessary.

5. Write drafts and produce graphics for
Topics (the body)
Conclusions (each section)
Introductions (each section)

6. Edit the drafts:
Achieve one voice.
Cut deadwood to fit two-page limit.

Technique D-1   Partition subject matter into sections.

Tip   Partition the subject matter according to audience. Use your analyze purpose and audience skills to develop your strategy for delivering your information. Follow these four steps:

1. Determine what the audience does with the information, and therefore, what the audience needs to know.
2. Determine if you have a multiple audience.
3. Determine strategy for multiple audiences: separate documents, sections, or front and back matter.
4. Write a purpose statement for each document, section, or piece of front or back matter.

Warning   Delay gathering information until you partition your subject matter.

Example   A complex detailed design of the Statewide Financial Services System uses sections for the technical teams and uses front and back matter for users and managers.

Team 1:   needs data formats to perform the data conversions: Section 1

Team 2:   needs user interface design to write code for queries and inputs: Section 2

Team 3:   needs details on commercial software used for the client workstations to integrate to main server: Section 3

Users: approve design if design matches requirements: Appendix A

Managers: approve design if design meets scope: Executive Summary

See also   Analyze purpose; analyze audience; purpose statement.

Discussion:

The key to writing long documents is to partition the subject matter. Each audience gets a separate document, section, or piece of front or back matter, so each can deal with specific, relevant subject matter.

Choose from the three strategies to address multiple audiences: separate documents, separate sections within a single document, or front and back matter. You may combine strategies, such as writing separate sections as well as adding front and back matter.

Proposals typically have five audiences and therefore partition into five sections: corporate capabilities, understanding the problem, technical approach, management and staffing plan, and costs.

In the next technique, you learn how to further break down subject matter into topics.

Example: Following is another example of partitioning subject matter according to audience.

Scenario: Your technical team recently installed and tested the new order, fulfillment, and billing software for the mail order department of Jelly Bean, Inc. Now the company wants you to document the system. Specifically, they want a guide for the telephone operators who take the orders and key the order information into the system. They want a procedural manual for the warehouse staff who assemble, pack, and ship orders. They want a maintenance manual for their in-house Information Systems (IS) staff to maintain the software and databases. Management wants an explanation of the report-generating module of the software, primarily for the accounting department. Lastly, the client wants you to document the new process for customer service to help them track shipments and handle customer complaints.

Profile each audience: what they do with the information and what they need to know.

Phone Operators	Warehouse Staff	IS Staff	Accounting	Customer Service
Take orders	Fulfill orders	Maintain software and databases	Create and use reports	Track orders and handle complaints
Steps, screens, and frequently asked questions	Automated order fulfillment; inventory stocking and ordering	Error messages, troubleshooting, automatic backups, hardware and software specifications	Reports for sales, income, aging accounts, inventory turnover	Scenarios for returns, exchanges, comments, special orders, and lost shipments

After partitioning the subject matter, you develop a strategy to partition your document. You partition the subject matter into two documents, each with sections or back matter.

User manual
Section 1 Telephone Order-taking
Section 2 Warehouse Operations
Section 3 Customer Service
Section 4 Accounting Reports

Maintenance manual
Section 1 Software Maintenance
Section 2 Database Maintenance
Appendix A Software Specifications
Appendix B Hardware Specifications

For each partition in your document, you write a purpose statement. For example, the user manual has five purpose statements, one for the overall manual and one for each of the four sections.

User manual — This manual describes for Jelly Bean, Inc. employees how to use the four major functional areas of the automated order-fulfillment and billing system.

Section 1 provides telephone operators a detailed script on how to use the system to take and submit orders.

Section 2 describes to the warehouse operators how to use the system to meet their four areas of responsibility: inventory controls, purchase orders for stocking, packing, and shipping.

Section 3 details for customer service scenarios for returns, exchanges, comments, special orders, and lost shipments so customer service representatives can track orders and handle complaints.

Section 4 shows the accounting department how to create and use reports for sales, income, aging accounts, and inventory turnover.

Technique D-2   Break down each section into discrete topics.

Tip 1   Consider what topics the audience needs to know about in the section.

Use any topical breakdown associated with your subject matter to help you break down topics for the section.

Warning   Do not gather information about the topics yet. Do not worry about putting the topics in order yet.

Example   Topical breakdown: Detailed design, Section 1 — *Data conversion for the Statewide Financial Services System project*

Topics break down into the state databases that we must convert. Furthermore, for each database (topic), we must show existing file formats, proposed formats, and logic to convert from old to new formats (sub-topics).

Database — topic	File format — sub–topics
Revenue Databases	income, business, property, and sales taxes
Motor Vehicles Databases	license, vehicle-boat registrations, citations
Human Services Databases	aid, student loans, unemployment, diseases
Criminal Justice Databases	civil awards, garnishments, sentencing, fines

See also   Audience; sentence outline.

Discussion:

For each document, section, or piece of front or back matter, identify the topical breakdown and list topics.

Most technical subjects break down into topics. Statements of work, requests for proposals, and change requests usually break down into requirements. Functional descriptions break down into requirements, functions, or tasks. A detailed design typically breaks down according to function, software module, or task. Procedures, policies, and user documents break down into steps. Plans typically break down into functions, steps, or tasks.

Although not essential, you can often define the set of sub-topics as part of your strategy. For example, a software test document may break down into topics — testing software modules. For each topic, you may already know that for each module you need to address sub-topics: define test case, define expected results, record results, report variances.

Proposals require an additional step. Before you list the topics for each proposal section, consider your proposal themes. Compare your company's and competition's strengths and weaknesses, perceived and real, as they may affect the award of the contract, such as financial strength, size, experience, incumbency, costs, or specialty knowledge. Consider themes for your technical approach, such as upward compatibility, portability, value, or service support. Themes for your management may include partnership, flexibility, or risk mitigation. Devise a list of themes for your proposal, themes that emphasize your strengths and compensate for any perceived weaknesses. Your themes need to answer the question: *why hire us?* Make sure your topics can address your themes.

Example: Subject matter suggests topic breakdowns. Although you can get useful clues from standard formats, make sure your topical breakdown reflects subject matter. For example, make sure today's proposal discusses all the topics the audiences need to know rather than simply retelling or updating the topics in the format of last year's proposal. The following are some typical long documents and suggested topical breakdowns:

Typical documents with sections	**Topical breakdowns**
Detailed design	
Section 1 Data conversion	databases, step by step
Section 2 Processes	functions
Section 3 Workstations	hardware, software, modifications
User manual	
Section 1 Telephone order taking	step by step
Section 2 Warehouse operations	function
Section 3 Customer service	situations (topical)
Section 4 Accounting reports	reports with examples
Maintenance manual	
Section 1 Software maintenance	modules
Section 2 Database maintenance	functions
Appendix A Software specifications	modules
Appendix B Hardware specification	devices
Proposal	
Section 1: Corporate capabilities	attributes
Section 2: Understanding the client problem	requirements — general to specific
Section 3: Technical approach	process, examples
Section 4: Management plan	functions, resources, time, task
Section 5: Cost	category, time

Often the Request for Proposal (RFP) dictates the sections and even the topics for your proposal. Otherwise, use your themes to help you determine your topical breakdown. Suppose, for example, a major theme is that your company has experience integrating commercial software packages on workstations to large data servers. Your *Section 3 — Technical approach* needs to show examples of your success to illustrate your approach. On the other hand, you want to stress the theme that you understand the client's *unique* requirements. Your *Section 2 — Understanding the client problem* needs to examine the requirements, citing first the *general* industry standard requirements, then focusing on the client's *specific* — perhaps *unique* from their point of view — needs.

Tip 2   Use predecessor documents to determine what your audience needs to know.

If the predecessor document uses a modular layout, you merely extract the discrete topics that need further discussion in your new document. For example, you extract the topics from a *requirements document* to help you determine what your audience needs to know for a *functional description*.

If the predecessor document uses a continuous flow layout, you must deconstruct the document to extract topics. If the document is well organized, extracting topics is as easy as finding the logical breaks as they fall randomly on the page. If the document is poorly organized, you must examine each paragraph to find the point, then regroup those points into topics. (See *Step 7 — Revise Content and Organization.*)

Use *Step 9 — Edit for Clarity* techniques to identify ambiguity in your predecessor documents. Resolve questions before you gather information.

Warning   Do not assume that predecessor documents provide the standard for your document.

See also   Sentence outline; clarity.

Discussion:

In technical writing, a document often has a predecessor. For example, a Request for Proposal (RFP) begets the proposal. A functional description begets a detailed design that begets the test plan, system documentation, and the user manual. One major benefit of using the modular layout is that each successor document becomes easier to write when the predecessor documents already present discrete topics.

For proposal writing, you typically work from an RFP that includes instructions to the offerors, evaluation criteria, contract data requirements list, statement of work, or work breakdown structure. One way or the other, the predecessor document describes the deliverables or services required. Extract from the predecessors a list of compliance criteria and list them in a matrix, referencing the RFP Page and paragraph, plus a short description of the criteria. The compliance criteria require some response, and therefore they suggest topics.

So, for proposal writing, you create a detailed list of compliance criteria that become your topics. You already have a list of themes. Post these two lists in your proposal room.

With your list of topics, you can estimate the length of your document. Each section needs an introduction page (right), a series of topics (left-right), and a conclusion page (left). Therefore, you estimate the number of pages as the (# topics plus 1) times 2. This page-length estimate is a valuable input when estimating the time required to write a document. A rough estimate is six labor hours per page of technical documentation.

Example: The following passage from a functional description is in a continuous flow layout and poorly organized at the paragraph level. You can't easily extract topics.

The state requires that the system be able to sort by account number, tax number, date, and account balances. The account balance sorts must include logic that allows the sort by amount of overpayment or underpayment, plus length of time past due. Interest on past due accounts is automatically calculated and compounded daily. Therefore, any past due accounts, must be automatically sorted each day; the new interest and penalty calculations made and the new due amount recoded in the database.

The State Internal Revenue (SIR) system has three databases operating on a Cybase system: Income Tax Revenue, Business Tax, and Property Tax. The State Sales Tax database operates on a standalone relational database system tied directly to the U.S. Department of the Treasury. The state can track both federal and state revenue from the taxes on gasoline.

The databases operating on the Cybase system have the following five fields in common: payer tax number, last name, address, phone number, account balance. In addition the different databases have between 32 and 89 additional fields. The following four fields, although not named identically, are in fact the same.

We may treat them as fields in common upon changing the names to a common name in the SIR:

Income	Property	Business	SIR
FY	Fiscal Year	Acct Year	Fiscal Year
Credit	Overpaid	Refund Due	Credit
Center	Filing Center	Agency	Center

Aside from the commonality stated above, each of the databases has its unique fields. Some of those fields need to be changed to allow easy sorting. For example, the Business Tax database has a name for both the business (sole proprietorship, partnership, or corporation) and the name of the tax payer, which can be a number of entities— an S Corporation passes the tax liability to the shareholders.

The income tax database is by far the largest database with the most relational links to other state and federal agencies. The SIR format uses the Income Tax Database format as much as possible, although all fields must change to plain language instead of acronyms. The fields relate to three general areas: Personal Information, Account History, and Account status. We discuss the fields of each area in turn.

46

47

Note the ease in extracting topics from this modular layout of the same subject matter.

Income Tax Database Layout

The Income tax database layout is the closest to the proposed State Internal Revenue (SIR) layout. Therefore the SIR uses the Income Tax Database format as much as possible, which is by far the largest database with the most relational links to other state and federal agencies.

Commonality

The databases operating on the Cybase system have the following five fields in common: payer tax number, last name, address, phone number, account balance. In addition the Income Tax database has 32 additional fields. We anticipate an increase in the Zipcode field size requirement from 9 to 12 numbers. Some fields need only name changes to plain language instead of acronyms. Therefore, we change field "FY" name only to "Fiscal Year."

Sorting Requirements

The state requires that the SIR sort by account number, tax number, date, and account balances.

The account balance sorts must include logic that allows the SIR to sort by amount of overpayment or under-payment, plus length of time past due. Interest on past due accounts is automatcially calculated and compounded daily. Therefore, the system must automatically sort any past due accounts each day, make the new interest and penalty calculations, and record the new due amount in the Income Tax database.

The following is a table of the 37 fields in the Income Tax Database showing the present version and the SIR version.

46

47

Tip 3   Put the topics in order.

Use natural patterns.

Warning   Do not assume that the topics must flow from one to the next. Many technical documents such as requirements documents and proposals have no chronology or particular ranking. One problem with continuous flow layout is that the flow presupposes a link from topic to topic, when in fact, each topic is independent.

Example   Traditional continuous flow organization purposefully or inadvertently shows subordination of ideas. Although this type of organization is good for essays, the continuous flow organization fails for technical documents that are more topical. In contrast, the modular organization simply lists the major topics. In this example, the continuous flow infers a relationship of ideas that does not really exist and is therefore confusing.

Continuous flow organization

I. Database conversion requirements
A. Introduction
    1. Scope of the changes
    2. Two methods for conversions
        a. Rename fields and copy
        b. Conversion programs
B. Common fields
    1. Income tax revenue database
    2. Other tax revenue databases
        a. Property taxes
            (1) Automobiles
            (2) House and furnishings
        b. Business taxes
    3. Sales taxes

Modular organization

I State revenue database basics
II Conversion of income tax database
III Conversion of property tax databases
IV Conversion of sales tax database

See also   Sentence outline; natural patterns.

Discussion

When you write your topics, use descriptive language. Instead using of just a noun, add a verb or prepositional phrase to convey meaning.

For example
Poor topic: Income tax database
Better: Conversion of income tax database

Continuous flow organizations tend to be vertical and hard to follow. Modular or topical organization is more horizontal and easier to follow.

Example: Continue with the Jelly Bean, Inc. scenario. You already partitioned the subject matter into two documents with sections plus front and back matter. Now you break down each partition into discrete topics. The charts below also indicate the natural pattern employed.

User Manual for Jelly Bean, Inc.			
Section 1 Telephone orders	**Section 2 Warehouse operations**	**Section 3 Customer service**	**Section 4 Accounting reports**
Ordinal	*Functional*	*Examples; Steps*	*Topical*
Workstation setup	Taking inventory	Tracking shipments	Daily inventory
Call initiation	Ordering EOQ	Refunds	Inventory turnover
Getting customer ID	Receiving orders	Price guarantee rebate	Invoices
Building customer record	Packaging & labeling	Item availability	Aging accounts
Taking order	Bundling shipments	Quantity discounts	Cashflow
Methods of payment	Special orders	Complaints, referrals	
Total charges	Returns		
Shipping instructions	Safety		
Submitting order			

Maintenance Manual for Jelly Bean, Inc.			
Section 1 Software maintenance	**Section 2 Database maintenance**	**Appendix A Software specifications**	**Appendix B Hardware specifications**
Topical; cause effect	*Ordinal*	*Functional*	*Spatial, topical*
Change management process	Daily string search	GUI Software	Parallel processor server
Communications security tests	Data contamination tests	Zybert dBase	ISD communications suite
Nightly error log	Nightly backup	YYServer com	Workstation – customer service
	Weekly merge-purge	Processes	Workstation –warehouse
	Weekly "fire" copy	Lotus Notes™ with modifications	LAN server
	Monthly archival		

Technique D-3 Fill in a Storyboard for each topic.

Tip 1   Design your storyboard form.

Fill in the overhead, beginning with a specific and concrete title for your topic.

Warning   Do not add overhead to the storyboard sheet unless you know you need the information.

Example   Design the overhead for a proposal storyboard to keep track of assignments, deadlines, compliance criteria, scoring, references, and themes.

Topic: *Automated Aging Acct. Notice*	Section *3* *Technical Approach*
	Criteria/Score: *5 Points*
Author: *P. Neri* Graphics Artist: *L. Maharg*	Reviewer: *S. Gabriel*
Draft Due: *June 3* Graphics Due: *June 8*	Review Date: *June 14*
References: *RFP 8, 11*	Theme: *"We understand your business"*

See also   Sentence outline.

Discussion

Design your own storyboard blank sheets on 8½"x11" or 11"x17" paper. You can adapt from the formats pictured in this appendix, but build a format to suit your writing project. Limit the overhead items to those you need.

Typical overhead items include
    1. topic title
    2. responsibilities such as author, graphics artist, reviewer, editor
    3. due dates for pink team review, draft, graphics, final copy, production
    4. predecessor documents such as specific items on the deliverables and criteria list
    5. key links to other sections

Proposals typically need more overhead. Add themes, compliance criteria, and scoring to the overhead. Often, an RFP tells you how the reviewers intend to score the different compliance criteria, and you want to alert authors and reviewers to distinguish between big and little issues.

Under the overhead, the storyboard blank needs space for

Left side Topic	**Right Side** Sketch of graphic
Main assertion	Caption
Subordinate points	Word description of graphic

After you develop the whole set of storyboards, you can review and revise the topic headings, assertions, and supporting details.

If office space allows, put your storyboards on a wall where everyone on the team can see them.

Example: Following is a storyboard with the overhead filled in. This storyboard is for the topic *automated aging account notice,* part of section 3, Technical Approach of a proposal. Predecessor document is the RFP, pages 8 and 11.

Topic: *Automated Aging Acct. Notice*   Section *3*   *Technical Approach*

Criteria/Score: *5 Points*

Author: *P. Neri*   Graphics Artist: *L. Maharg*   Reviewer: *S. Gabriel*

Draft Due: *June 3*   Graphics Due: *June 8*   Review Date: *June 14*

References: *RFP 8, 11*   Theme: *"We understand your business"*

Assertion: _____

Point: _____

Point: _____

Point: _____

Point: _____

Caption: _____

Description: _____

If you can make 11″ x 17″ storyboards, and if your storyboard room can display that much paper, the large size helps keep your work from getting cramped.

Tip 2   Write points as assertions or covering generalities for each topic.

Write two to five minor points that support your main point.

Warning   Do not simply repeat the assertions from a predecessor document.

Example   The RFP states, "BAPCO requires that the new fulfillment system operate 500 percent faster than the current system, and the system must be up-gradable to operate on larger machines so we can handle larger databases in the future without loss of speed."

Too often, the proposal writer merely repeats the words used in the RFP, coming up with weak assertions:

- We propose to build a system that operates at least 500 percent faster than current system.
- Our proposed architecture allows you to upgrade to faster machines to handle larger databases.

The clever proposal writer makes inferences. In the example above, the client wants the speed to increase throughput per employee to achieve a higher return on sales. The client wants to upgrade the system, anticipating growth. Therefore, the stronger assertions are

- We propose to increase your return on sales by giving your sales force a 500 percent faster fulfillment system.
- We shall build a system that grows with your business.

See also   Sentence outline.

Discussion

Technical documents such as requirements, functional descriptions, detailed designs, and manuals use mostly covering generalities. Make your generalities *results oriented*. Instead of "Begin with these three steps," write "Log into your personal mailbox by following these three steps."

Proposals use more assertions. When writing assertions for proposals, take your list of compliance criteria and infer a benefit for each criterion. Then write your assertions based on the inferred benefits — do not simply repeat the criteria or requirements. A typical RFP stated: *"Simply rephrasing or restating the Government's requirements is insufficient and will result in the proposal being considered non-responsive."* — *DTFA01-89-R-00215*. To write winning assertions, you must infer the benefits that the client seeks.

Also, for proposals, consult your list of themes as you craft winning assertions. Your themes often speak to the benefits of hiring your firm. For example: *As the incumbent vendor who helped you analyze your business processes, we are uniquely suited to build your automated order-fulfillment system.*

Example: In the following storyboard for a proposal, we take the *feature* requested in an RFP and evolve it into a *benefit* that we express as an *assertion*.

Feature: The billing system must print invoices that provide a summary of account activity for the past 90 days.

Benefit: The account summary helps collections by casually reminding the customers of past due accounts, and by helping the customer and the service representative quickly resolve any disputed charges.

Assertion: The new automatically generated invoice reduces accounts receivables and improves customer relations by providing a summary of account activity for 90 days.

Write your assertion plus minor points on your storyboard:

Topic: Automated Aging Acct. Notice Section **3** Technical Approach
Criteria/Score: **5 Points**
Author: **P. Neri** Graphics Artist: **L. Maharg** Reviewer: **S. Gabriel**
Draft Due: **June 3** Graphics Due: **June 8** Review Date: **June 14**
References: **RFP 8, 11** Theme: "We understand your business"

Assertion: The new automatically generated invoice reduces accounts receivables and improve customer relations by providing a summary of account activity for 90 days.

Point: 1. The system automatically calculates the aging report.

Point: 2. The invoice displays the summary of amount due plus a detailed account history.

Point: 3. The invoice offers assistance and invites calls.

Caption: _____

Description: _____

Work at the level of assertion and minor point for all your topics, *before* you add detail or draw sketches to any of your topics.

Tip 3   Add supporting details and sketch the graphic.

Without writing the paragraphs or vertical lists, jot down the key supporting details for your major assertion and minor points.

Sketch the graphic, table or figure in minimal detail. Write the caption for the graphic as specifically as possible. Write a note to the graphic artist describing what you want the graphic to do.

Warning   Do not concern yourself with *how you say it;* rather, focus on *what you say*. Before you write the draft, time spent worrying about word choice, tone, and phrasing is usually wasted.

Example   Detailed design storyboard topic: Conversion of income tax databases.

Assertion: To convert the income tax database into SIR layout, we use Cybase utilities plus our proprietary SIR conversion program.

Minor point 1 Rename four fields with the Cybase utility: RENAME.
Supporting Details: change add_2 to add_b; FY to fiscal year; Zipcode from 9 to 12 numbers; change Zipcode from alpha to numeric; re-sort.

Minor point 2. Use the following field names, field lengths, and other field characteristics to run the SIR conversion program.
Supporting details: Turn off "Check for Duplicate records." See table below for values.

Field Name	Field Length	Number-Character	Logical	Comments
Last_Name	50	Characters	N	Hot key to Business_Name
First_Name	50	Characters	N	None

See also   Sentence outline.

Discussion:

Writing supporting details onto the storyboard departs from our sentence outlining technique. Recall that for normal-sized documents, we add the detail when we write the draft. Then we revise content and organization as the first step of editing. However, for long documents, we add the key details in the storyboard, then we review and revise *before* we write the draft. Storyboard reviewers need to see supporting details.

Group your details under the points they support. If you have important details that do not fall under an assertion or minor point, you either add the point, or you find the supporting point on another storyboard.

After you (and perhaps your colleagues) add supporting details, expect your storyboards to look messy. In fact, another common name for storyboards is *scribble-boards*.

Example: The following storyboard shows the added detail and sketch.

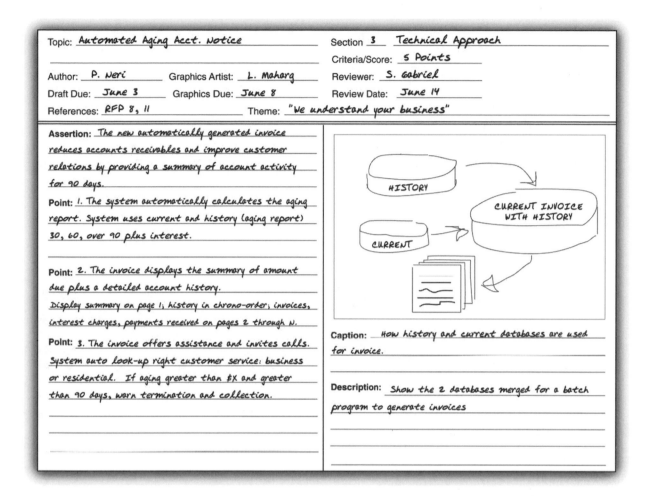

In the storyboard room, you find different colored pens, tape, stick-on notes, staplers, and paper clips — just about anything you can imagine to mark and past information on a wall. In practice, your storyboard may become littered with stick-on notes, excerpts or boilerplate from other documents, even news clippings, meeting notes, and clarifications. Before you review and revise, you need to tidy your storyboards. Display only the details you intend to use. Save the other odds and ends in a folder just in case the review determines that you need one of those bits of information.

Technique D-3   *Review and revise the storyboards.*

Tips   First, check each storyboard as a separate topic.

Apply the content and organization tests for individual storyboards. (See *Step 7 — Revise Content and Organization.*)

Specifically check the following five items:
1. Check topic headings. Make them concrete and specific.
2. Check the major and minor points to make sure they address what the audience needs to know.
3. Check details to ensure that they adequately support the points.
4. Check graphics to ensure value; ensure that caption describes the point made in the graphic.
5. Check for modular layout problems. Split a topic that has grown too large, or combine two topics for which you have little to say.

Second, check the storyboards as they relate to each other:
1. Identify and eliminate redundancy.
2. Identify holes in your document.

Warning   Wait until the team finishes all the storyboards. Part of the process is to ensure that you eliminate redundancy and fill in gaps, which you cannot do until you see the whole document in storyboard form.

Do not bother with tone, word choice, grammar, punctuation, or mechanics — or any other editing concerns.

See also   Content and organization tests.

Discussion

Invite your graphics professionals to the review. They can suggest better graphics and avoid the waste of trial-and-error graphics production.

If you need to split a long topic, elevate minor points to the level of topic. For example, the following topic fills much more than two pages: *Sending and receiving email by intracompany access to the Internet.* You can break the topics into two topics:
1. *Sending email by intracompany access to the Internet*
2. *Receiving email by intracompany access to the Internet*

Using reverse logic, you combine two or more short topics into one.
1. *Benefits of using graphite fiber in fuel cells* barely fills one page.
2. *Risks of using graphite fiber in fuel cells* barely exceeds one page.

Combined, *Benefits of using graphite fibers in fuel cells outweigh the risks* makes a two-page topic.

In addition to combining and splitting topics, you can occasionally cheat. For example, in this book we expanded an exercise from one to three pages, turning our typical two-page topic into a rare four-page topic.

The proposal team, plus other company experts, review and revise the storyboards. Often called the *Pink Team*, they critique the content to make sure

- proposal addresses all the selection criteria in the RFP

- topics address competitive themes

- assertions are relevant and address benefits instead of features

- supporting details and graphics are relevant and true

In addition, the Pink Team

- ensures that topics can fit the left-right layout (or must be split or combined)

- removes topic heading vagueness

- identifies gaps or redundancies

When you perform the Pink Team for a deliverable, such as a functional description or a user manual, invite the client to participate. You thereby virtually guarantee that your client will accept the document.

Technique D-4   Write the draft.

Tips   Write a two-page draft for each topic in the section. Write up to 50 percent more words than you think you need. If you think you need 700 words to cover all the material in a topic, write up to 1,050 words. Feel confident that you can edit those words down to your 700-word limit.

Write the one-page conclusion for each section, usually *what happens next*.

Write the one-page introduction for the section.

Warning   Do not interrupt your writing by editing.

See also   Writing phase.

Discussion

Transcribe the information from the storyboards into your wordprocessor, but leave the storyboards on the wall as a reference tool for the team.

Because you review and revise the storyboards before you write your draft, you minimize surprises. Nevertheless, if you get a new idea or you have a question, make a note and stick it to the appropriate storyboard when you take a break.

Storyboards and modular layout let you break large writing jobs into manageable tasks. As you write, concentrate on one topic — do not divert your attention to other topics.

Do not worry if you see white space. Studies show that conventional continuous flow documents and modular layout documents have similar amounts of white space.

Compare your final drafts to the storyboards to ensure that the topics, assertions, minor points, supporting details, graphics and captions convey the message. If you are writing a proposal, make a special pass to ensure that the draft addresses your list of themes, and addresses each point in the evaluations criteria list.

Example: Continuing the example of the proposal, the author writes more draft than two pages can hold.

Automated Aging Account Notice

The new automatically generated invoice reduces accounts receivables and improves customer relations by providing them a summary of account activity for 90 days.

Jelly Bean sends invoices on a monthly or bi-weekly billing cycle to different classes of customer: mostly business or residential. The system already has a record of each transaction.

The system automatically calculates the aging report. At the monthly billing cycle, the system automatically sorts the current billing history, then compares that history to the historical record to identify any customers with an outstanding balance due. If the customer has a balance due, the system queries the historical record to extract the information required for the aging report: all invoices more than 30, 60, or 90 days older than the current billing due date. The system calculates interest to charge for each past invoice.

The invoice displays the summary of amount due plus a detailed account history. On page 1, we add a line for past due charges, which is the summary of past due and interest calculated above. If the invoice has a value for

46

past due greater than zero, the printing routine creates as many pages as necessary to display the account history – usually just a second page. The account

Fig. 2 Scheme to add aging report

history shows a table, in chronological order, all invoices, interest charges, and payments with a running balance in a right column.

We propose to add a second table to anticipate customer questions and help customer service answer billing questions. The system automatically presents a second table with all the customer purchases not yet paid in full. Each purchase has the item code, short description, date, quantity, amount, tax, shipping, and employee code of the Fig.2 Scheme to add aging report order taker.

The machine time to generate the table is negligible; the table requires an additional sheet of paper only .01% of the time, so printing and mailing costs are likewise negligible. Meanwhile, your clients get more complete information, are less likely to call your 1-800 number and expend time and money asking questions.

47

Finally, the aging report on the invoice offers assistance and invites calls. The system automatically looks up the appropriate customer service representative name and phone number from a tag in the client's current record that directs a quick look-up in the Jelly Bean corporate directory. The invoice printing module prints the suggestion that the customer call his or her service representative with questions. Consequently, your customers – especially your bigger business accounts – resolve problems quickly with less frustration.

If past due account is greater than $X or older than Y days – you can determine both variables for each customer or set as a policy – the invoice printing module prints a warning that you may terminate the account and submit the past due amount to a collection agency.

This draft is about 20 percent too long, but we can shrink the graphic and cut some deadwood to make the text fit.

Technique D-5   Edit the drafts.

Tips   Use *The Writing System* editing techniques to

- give the message one clear meaning
- make topics fit the two-page limit
- provide one voice

Check the entire document — *all sections, front and back matter* — for consistency.

Ensure that the document meets any client-specified standards for word choice, acronyms, symbols, and other conventions.

Warning   Unless you find a glaring deficiency, avoid making changes to the content. Do not let the *perfect* become the enemy of the *good*.

See also   Proofread.

Discussion

Authors edit their own drafts for clarity and economy. Technical editors, if available, typically add the most value when editing for coherence and readability. Authors and editors correct word choice, grammar, punctuation, and mechanics, then proofread for quality assurance.

A coherence device that works well with modular layout is to **bold** the assertions and minor points.

Before you split a topic, try using deadwood cutting techniques (see *Step 10 — Edit for Clarity*) to fit the topic into the two-page limit.

A systematic edit of the document sections gives the whole document one voice, *even if your team of writers come from different cultures and professional backgrounds.* In the end, all the document paragraphs begin with a point — a short sentence. During the edit for clarity, everybody cuts passive voice, subjunctive mood, and ambiguous pronouns. The edit for economy eliminates many of the clichés found as prepositions, idioms, and implied phrases, and thereby rids the document of regional dialect. Finally, the edit for readability makes everybody's prose read at approximately the same grade level.

Example: The following is a picture of the draft after the editing. Deadwood cutting alone reduced the draft enough to fit the text within the two-page limit.

Automated Aging Account Notice

The new automatically generated invoice reduces accounts receivables and improves customer relations by providing a summary of account activity for 90 days.

Jelly Bean sends invoices monthly or bi-weekly to different classes of customer: mostly business or residential. The system already has a record of each transaction.

The system automatically calculates the aging report. At the monthly billing cycle, the system sorts current billing history, then compares that history to the historical record to identify customers with a balance due. Then the system extracts information required for the aging report: invoices older than 30 days. Then the system calculates interest charges.

The invoice displays a summary plus a detailed history. On page 1, we add past due charges including interest. If the past due amount exceeds zero, the printing routine creates pages to display account history. An account history shows the order of all invoices, interest charges, and payments with a running balance.

We add a second table to anticipate customer questions and help customer service answer billing questions. The

system presents a second table with unpaid purchases. Each purchase has the item code, short description, date, quantity, amount, tax, shipping, and employee code.

Fig. 2 Scheme to add aging report

The time to generate the table is negligible. Likewise printing and mailing costs are negligible. Meanwhile, your clients get more complete information, are less likely to call your 1-800 number and spend time asking questions. Finally, the aging report on the invoice offers help. The system looks up the client's service representative name and phone number from a tag in the client's records and Jelly Bean corporate directory.

The invoice printing module prints the suggestion that the customer call his or her service representative with questions. Consequently, your customers – especially your bigger business accounts – resolve problems quickly with less frustration. If past due account is greater than $X or older than Y days – you set the variables X and Y for each customer – the invoice printing module prints a warning that you may terminate the account and submit the past due amount to a collection agency.

46

47

Compare advantages of the modular layout and storyboarding.

Modular layout and storyboarding offer many advantages over the conventional continuous flow.

Modular Layout and Storyboarding	Conventional Continuous Flow
Writing modular documents is easier to manage. Partitioning subjects down to two-page topics scopes your effort. You can more accurately budget and manage time — essential for projects with tight deadlines.	Without a way to scope the size of the document, you have difficulty budgeting and managing time for large document efforts.
Boundaries for each topic ensure that you give appropriate weight to each topic; they keep the author from over-reaching with unnecessary detail. Modular layout helps you write documents with a page limit, because you allocate your allotted pages to topics.	Lack of boundaries lets the author skimp on hard topics and over-write familiar topics. In proposals, this lack of discipline causes you to unwittingly highlight your weaknesses or uncertainties.
Strengthened coherence helps your audience skim the document, follow the logic, and refer back to topics. A modular layout document is easier for your in-house experts to critique and easier for your clients to use. Figures always accompany text.	Continuous flow often implies relationships among topics that don't really exist, thus confusing the reader. The major assertion or covering generality is not prominent, if it exists. Figures do not always accompany text, and thus are difficult to find.
Modular layout reduces production problems: pagination, figures, widows and orphans. Indexing is easier. Modular layout helps when writing "living documents," such as software designs or policy documents that change. The topical left-right presentation lets you "pull out and plug in" material.	Changes tend to have a *ripple effect* throughout your document.
Modular layout helps you re-use documents, because topics are easy to identify: they begin at the top of the left page and end at the bottom of the right page. Because the modular layout organizes your documents into discrete topics, you can easily find and extract those topics you wish to re-use in other documents.	In continuous flow documents, topics begin and end randomly on the pages throughout the document and are therefore difficult to identify.

Appendix E

Quick Reference Guide

This Quick Reference Guide summarizes the writing system and general document formats so you can refresh your memory at a glance.

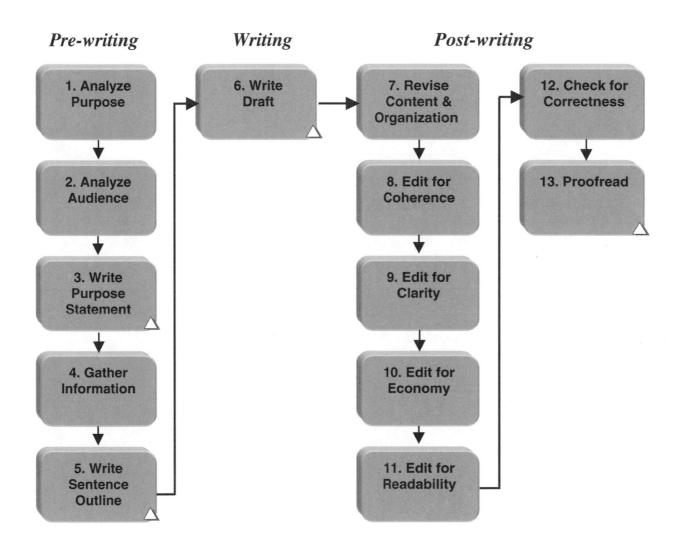

Pre-writing Phase — Analytical Skills

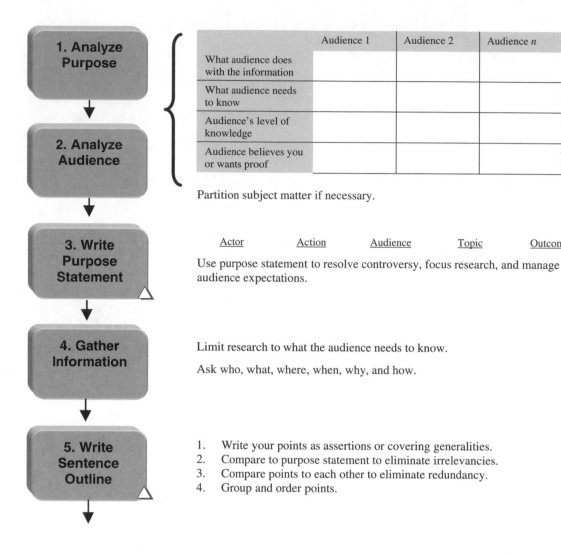

1. Analyze Purpose

2. Analyze Audience

	Audience 1	Audience 2	Audience *n*
What audience does with the information			
What audience needs to know			
Audience's level of knowledge			
Audience believes you or wants proof			

Partition subject matter if necessary.

3. Write Purpose Statement

Actor   Action   Audience   Topic   Outcome

Use purpose statement to resolve controversy, focus research, and manage audience expectations.

4. Gather Information

Limit research to what the audience needs to know.

Ask who, what, where, when, why, and how.

5. Write Sentence Outline

1. Write your points as assertions or covering generalities.
2. Compare to purpose statement to eliminate irrelevancies.
3. Compare points to each other to eliminate redundancy.
4. Group and order points.

Writing Phase — Composition Skills

6. Write Draft

DO NOT WRITE DRAFT UNTIL YOU FINISH ANAYLSIS.

1. Transcribe purpose statement and sentence outline into your wordprocessor.
2. Write in order the body, conclusion, and introduction.

DO NOT EDIT WHILE YOU WRITE THE DRAFT.

Post-writing Phase — Editing Skills

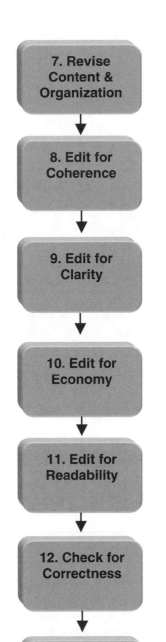

	Content test		Organization test
1.	Is the topic focused?	1.	Data dump?
2.	So what?	2.	Story?
3.	Adequately supported?	3.	I, me, and mine?

8. Edit for Coherence

Repeat key terms. Begin paragraphs with the point and follow with data. Use transition words. Present the logic of your lists, tables, and graphics explicitly. Practice restraint when using visual devices.

9. Edit for Clarity

Keep words concrete and specific. Make verbs active; simplify tense, and eliminate subjective mood. Eliminate ambiguous pronouns.

Use standard English, make sentences parallel, and keep modifiers next to the word modified.

10. Edit for Economy

Cut the following unnecessary words: buried verbs, prepositions, who-which-that, repetition, redundancy, implied phrases, and modifiers.

11. Edit for Readability

Calculate readability.

If necessary, break long sentences and replace big words.

12. Check for Correctness

In order, check word choice, grammar, punctuation, and mechanics.

13. Proofread

Do not edit while you proofread!
Use a series of readings. Check live copy against dead copy.

Tip 1   Short documents that have only one audience require three parts:

1. introduction with a purpose statement
2. body telling what your audience needs to know
3. conclusion telling what happens next

Example   **A short letter**

Introduction

> This mock letter illustrates how you write a short business or technical document using an introduction, body, and conclusion.

Body

> Introductions begin with a purpose statement. If the purpose statement does not imply a plan for the document, add a sentence to show the plan. The introduction may include other information about the background, audience, methods, key terms, and limitations. The introduction can be as simple as a one-sentence purpose statement.

> At the paragraph level, always make your point first. Then follow with supporting facts. Sentence outlining ensures that your paragraphs conform to this important rule.

> Always conclude your document by telling your audience *what happens next*. Rarely do you provide a summary at the end of a business or technical document.

Conclusion

> By using this simple format, you write short documents — such as email, letters, and memos — that always get to the point.

Tip 2   Longer and more complex documents typically use different formats to accommodate different audiences. The only essential parts of a document are the introduction, body, and conclusion. All other parts are optional depending on your audience.

Example   The following are parts that one can find in a complex document. The parts are in order.

Part	Required	Comments
Transmittal or cover letter, memo, email	No	Refer to core document in the purpose statement.
Executive summary	No	Include a purpose statement, recommendation, key findings, and *what happens next*.
Abstract	No	Include topic, significance, methods, findings, and conclusion. Don't use abstract if you have an executive summary.
Title	No	
Table of Contents	No	
Introduction	**Yes**	**Include purpose statement,** plan of document, background, audience, sources and methods, key terms, and limitations.
Body	**Yes**	If you partition the body into sections, give each section an introduction, body, and conclusion.
Conclusion	**Yes**	Include *what happens next*, not a summary.
Appendices	No	
Attachments or exhibits	No	
Glossary	No	
Notes	No	Use footnotes, shadowboxes, or backmatter notes.
Index	No	

Here are the front and back of a 3x5 note card with the essence of *The Writing System*. One side outlines the system. The second side shows the parts of a document. You may copy this 3x5 note card.

The Writing System	Techniques
1. Analyze purpose	Determine what the audience does with the information.
2. Analyze audience	Determine: what the audience needs to know audience has high or low knowledge of subject audience believes or wants proof Partition document if necessary to accommodate multiple audiences.
3. Write purpose statement	Include actor, action, audience, topic, and outcome.
4. Gather information	Ask who, what, where, when, why, and how.
5. Write sentence outline	1. Write points. 2. Remove irrelevancy. 3. Remove redundancy. 4. Group and order points.
6. Write draft	In order, write body, conclusion, introduction, then front and back matter. *Do not edit!*
7. Revise content & organization	Apply content test: topic focused? so what? adequately supported? Apply organization test: data dump? story? I, me, and mine?
8. Edit for coherence	Repeat key terms. Begin paragraphs with point. Define series in list.
9. Edit for clarity	Begin at word level: be concrete and specific. Use active voice. Simplify tense. Avoid subjunctive mood. Replace pronouns.
10. Edit for economy	Cut buried verbs, prepositions, implied phrases and others.
11. Edit for readability	Calculate. To lower, break sentences; replace long words.
12. Check for correctness	Check word choice, grammar, punctuation, mechanics.
13. Proofread	Only after edits!

Document Part	Required	Comments
Transmittal memo, letter, or message	No	Refer to core document in the purpose statement.
Executive summary	No	Include a purpose statement, recommendation, key findings, and *what happens next*.
Abstract	No	Include topic, significance, methods, findings, and conclusion. Don't use abstract if you have an executive summary.
Title	No	
Table of contents	No	
Introduction	**Yes**	**Include purpose statement,** plan of document, background, audience, sources and methods, key terms, and limitations.
Body	**Yes**	If you partition the body into sections, give each section an introduction, body, and conclusion.
Conclusion	**Yes**	Include *what happens next*, not a summary.
Appendices, attachments, exhibits	No	
Glossary	No	
Notes	No	Treat footnotes and shadowboxes like backmatter notes.
Index	No	© Graham Associates 2002 www.thewritingsystem.com

Index

How to Contact Us

We welcome your comments and suggestions about *The Writing System*. Please write, call, or fax your thoughts to

Graham Associates
9117 Saranac Court, Fairfax VA 22032
Telephone: (703) 978-0122   FAX: (703) 978-0525
email dgraham3@cox.rr.com

Visit us at http://www.thewritingsystem.com

Also, if you need more copies of *The Writing System*, or want information about our writing seminars, please call us directly at (703) 978-0122.